THE MATH DETECTIVE

by Ernest Woodward

A Reproducible Teacher's Book

J. Weston Walch, Publisher

ACKNOWLEDGMENTS

The author would like to acknowledge the contributions of his wife, Marilyn, whose assistance in the writing and editing of the manuscript was invaluable. The author is also indebted to Martha Wall, who typed the manuscript and drew the illustrations.

ISBN 0-8251-0344-4

Portland, Maine 04104
Printed in the United States of America

CONTENTS

TO THE TEACHER

The Math Detective was written as a problem-solving supplement for high school and junior high school mathematics classes, although some of the cases are appropriate for younger children.

The book makes math fun and intriguing by making it a mystery. The student must discover a mathematical answer the way a detective would discover "whodunit" – by using clues to narrow down a number of possibilities until only one remains. Along the way, mathematical terms are introduced to give students tools they will need to solve the mystery. And because students must learn these terms to solve the mystery, this learning becomes fun – an inescapable part of some interesting detective work.

For your convenience, we have put *The Math Detective* in this reproducible teacher book form. You can run off on a copying machine those cases that pertain to the lesson you are teaching on any given day. Then sit back and watch your students become top-notch math detectives!

—J. Weston Walch, Publisher

ANSWERS

CHAPTER I

W-1: 6, W-2: 14, W-3: 18, W-4: 23, W-5: 19, W-6: 21 , W-7: 293, W-8: 1012, W-9: 1428, W-10: 8, W-11: 28, W-12: 6, W-13: 33, W-14: 36, W-15: 9, W-16: 22, W-17: 758, W-18: 34, W-19: 27, W-20: 57, W-21: 12, W-22: 26, W-23: 7, W-24: 19, W-25: 23, W-26: 4, W-27: 33, W-28: 765, W-29: 801, W-30: 657, W-31: 639, W-32: 492, W-33: 742, W-34: 29, W-35: 13, W-36: 18, W-37: 24, W-38: 9, W-39: 18, W-40: 18, W-41: 7, W-42: 13, W-43: 24, W-44: 13, W-45: 15, W-46: 6, W-47: 60, W-48: 2, W-49: 9, W-50: 8, W-51: 8, W-52: 18, W-53: 14, W-54: 11, W-55: 10, W-56: 18, W-57: 5, W-58: 12, W-59: 19, W-60: 16, W-61: 464, W-62: 478, W-63: 485, W-64: 371, W-65: 275, W-66: 547, W-67: Zim = 4, Zam = 9, W-68: Zoom = 3, Zum = 9, W-69: 18, W-70: 19, W-71: 1, W-72: 13, W-73: 70, W-74: 10, W-75: Fee = 42, Fi = 21, W-76: Tip = 9, Rip = 30, W-77: Pip = 20, Kip = 40, W-78: 6, W-79: Top = 6, Sop = 3, W-80: 32, W-81: 10, W-82: D, W-83: B, W-84: B, W-85: A, W-86: D, W-87: D.

CHAPTER II

F-1: 11/12, F-2: 7/9, F-3: 8/17, F-4: 12/57, F-5: 2/6, F-6: 2/14, F-7: 5/15, F-8: 11/12, F-9: 2/7, F-10: 5/4, F-11: 11/9, F-12: 4/11, F-13: 7/25, F-14: 3/5, F-15: 1/8, F-16: 2/11, F-17: 3/5, F-18: 7/5, F-19: 5/6, F-20: 1/4, F-21: 5/6, F-22: 2/5, F-23: 1/3, F-24: 1 1/6, F-25: 5 7/9, F-26: 2 5/7, F-27: 1/2, F-28: 3/7, F-29: 2/3, F-30: 1/4, F-31: 1/7, F-32: Bip = 3/6 (or 1/2), Dip = 3/8, F-33: Nop = 1/5, Mop = 2/5, F-34: Kip = 4/3, Rip = 5/3, F-35: 2/3, F-36: 3/5, F-37: 3/10, F-38: 2/5, F-39: 2/7, F-40: 3/4, F-41: 7/3, F-42: 3/8, F-43: 5/6, F-44: 2/5, F-45: A, F-46: B, F-47: C.

CHAPTER III

D-1: 4.93, D-2: 7.62, D-3: 1.02, D-4: 4.7, D-5: 7.6, D-6: 2.49, D-7: 2.71, D-8: 1.36, D-9: 0.72, D-10: 2.61, D-11: 5.96, D-12: 0.46, D-13: 4.98, D-14: 3.8, D-15: 0.616161..., D-16: 0.75, D-17: 0.6, D-18: 0.6666..., D-19: 0.82, D-20: 1.04, D-21: 0.62, D-22: 0.7777..., D-23: 0.434343..., D-24: 5.24, D-25: 7.43, D-26: 3.12, D-27: 11.2, D-28: 3.47, D-29: 0.53, D-30: 0.9, D-31: 0.9, D-32: 2.1, D-33: 0.3, D-34: 0.4, D-35: 0.2, D-36: 2.3, D-37: 2, D-38: 2.1, D-39: 7, D-40: 1.1, D-41: 2.3, D-42: 5.2, D-43: 3.7, D-44: 3.9, D-45: Kae = .5, Fae = 2.5, D-46: Moe = 3.1, Joe = 4.1, D-47: Rob = .3, Bob = 1.5, D-48: Dop = 1.1, Fop = 2.2, D-49: B, D-50: A, D-51: D, D-52: 68%, D-53: 47%, D-54: 43%, D-55: 93%, D-56: 114%, D-57: 73%, D-58: 41%, D-59: 80%, D-60: 40%.

CHAPTER IV

I-1: −2, I-2: −5, I-3: 2, I-4: −1, I-5: 0, I-6: −4, I-7: −6, I-8: −2, I-9: −5, I-10: −3, I-11: −2, I-12: 2, I-13: −8, I-14: 3, I-15: 4, I-16: −5, I-17: 1, I-18: AIP, I-19: APA, I-20: CPM, I-21: CPA, I-22: APM, I-23: 18, I-24: −3, I-25: −10, I-26: 2, I-27: D, I-28: C, I-29: E, I-30: D, I-31: Tam = 6, Sam =-4, I-32: Tock = −3, Rock = 7, I-33: Rick = −2, Nick = 12, I-34: Rae = 1, Mae = −1, I-35: Moe = −1, Joe = 3, I-36: Nip = −3, Pip = −6, I-37: 2, I-38: 1, I-39: −3, I-40: 0, I-41: 5, I-42: −1, I-43: 2.

CHAPTER V

G-1: $\overline{CD}$, G-2: $\overline{GH}$, G-3: $\overline{EF}$, G-4: $\overline{CD}$, G-5: $\overline{EF}$, G-6: $\overline{GH}$, G-7: $\overline{AB}$, G-8: $\overleftrightarrow{CD}$, G-9: $\overleftrightarrow{GH}$, G-10: $\overleftrightarrow{EF}$, G-11: $\angle D$, G-12: $\angle C$, G-13: $\angle E$, G-14: $\angle A$, G-15: ___B, G-16: V, G-17: II, G-18: I, G-19: VI, G-20: IV, G-21: III, G-22: K, G-23: G, G-24: M, G-25: J, G-26: I, G-27: H, G-28: L, G-29: II, G-30: IV, G-31: III, G-32: I, G-33: I, G-34: III, G-35: III, G-36: II, G-37: IV, G-38: I, G-39: V, G-40: IV, G-41: I, G-42: III, G-43: II, G-44: IV, G-45: I, G-46: IV, G-47: III, G-48: II, G-49: $\overline{OH}$, G-50: $\overline{LM}$, G-51: $\overline{JK}$, G-52: IV, G-53: II, G-54: III, G-55: I, G-56: IV, G-57: I, G-58: II, G-59: III, G-60: VI, G-61: VII, G-62: V, G-63: II, G-64: I, G-65: III, G-66: IV, G-67: 70, G-68: 29, G-69: 43, G-70: 84, G-71: 34, G-72: 73, G-73: 137, G-74: V, G-75: II, G-76: III, G-77: I, G-78: IV, G-79: I, G-80: V, G-81: III, G-82: II, G-83: V, G-84: IV, G-85: III, G-86: I, G-87: IV, G-88: III, G-89: I, G-90: V, G-91: II, G-92: VI, G-93: II, G-94: III, G-95: I, G-96: IV, G-97: I, G-98: III, G-99: IV, G-100: V, G-101: V, G-102: IV, G-103: I, G-104: 3, G-105: 10, G-106: 12, G-107: IV, G-108: I, G-109: III, G-110: II.

CHAPTER VI

M-1: General Motors, M-2: Chrysler, M-3: Ford, M-4: Coca Cola, M-5: Dr. Pepper, M-6: Pepsi Cola, M-7: B, M-8: E, M-9: E, M-10: A, M-11: Salt Lake City, M-12: Boston, M-13: Houston, M-14: 11, M-15: 28, M-16: 23, M-17: 19, M-18: Chicago, M-19: Atlanta, M-20: Los Angeles, M-21: Atlanta, M-22: Washington, M-23: Seattle, M-24: 7,3,4,6,8, M-25: 4, M-26: 31, M-27: 188, M-28: 4, M-29: 31, M-30: 83, M-31: 125, M-32: $55, M-33: $84, M-34: $77, M-35: $6, M-36: $10, M-37: One quarter and one penny, M-38: One fifty-cent piece and one dime, M-39: Two nickels and one penny, M-40: 2,4, M-41: 4,3, M-42: 1,5, M-43: 1,4, M-44: A one-dollar bill and a twenty-dollar bill, M-45: 5,2, M-46: $20.10, M-47: $20.45, M-48: $20.85, M-49: $19.28, M-50: $20.00, M-51: 14, M-52: 46, M-53: 74, M-54: 50, M-55: 98, M-56: Blue, M-57: Purple, M-58: White, M-59: Harry, M-60: 97, M-61: 113, M-62: 30, M-63: [a,b,c,d], M-64: Ø or [ ], M-65: [b,d], M-66: [1,3], M-67: [1,3,6], M-68: [1,4,5], M-69: 3, M-70: 6, M-71: 4.

CHAPTER I

WHOLE NUMBERS

This is a book of detective stories. However, these detective stories are probably different from any you have read before. Instead of being about people, these stories are about mathematical things - usually numbers, but sometimes geometric figures. Also, you are to be the detective and are to find the mystery numbers or mystery figures. You will find the mystery numbers or figures by examining the clues that will be given to you. Occasionally you may be given a clue which you don't understand. If that happens, get your teacher to help you with it.

Since this chapter is about whole numbers, the clues in this chapter will be about whole numbers and the mystery numbers will also be whole numbers. The cases in the early part of the chapter have exactly one mystery number as their answer. In these instances you should use the clues to eliminate number suspects until only one whole number is left. For Case W-1 some hints are given concerning how you are to proceed. After that, try to solve the cases by yourself.

Case W-1

NUMBER SUSPECTS: *3, 4, 5, 6, 7, 8, 9*

CLUE 1: The number is an even number. (Cross out 3, 5, 7, and 9 leaving 4, 6, and 8)

CLUE 2: The number is not 4 × 2. (Cross out 8)

CLUE 3: The number is not 12 ÷ 3. (Cross out 4)

The number is ______. (Since all the number suspects except 6 have been eliminated, 6 is the number and you should write 6 in the blank.)

Case W-2

NUMBER SUSPECTS: *7, 11, 13, 14, 16, 24*

CLUE 1: The number is less than 5 × 3.

CLUE 2: The number is an even number.

The number is ______.

Case W-3

NUMBER SUSPECTS: 12, 13, 14, 15, 16, 17, 18

CLUE 1: The number is an even number.

CLUE 2: The number is not 4×3.

CLUE 3: The number is not $8 + 8$.

CLUE 4: The number is not 7×2.

The number is ______.

Case W-4

NUMBER SUSPECTS: 21, 23, 28, 32, 35

CLUE 1: One of the digits of the number is 3 and the other digit is 2.

CLUE 2: The number is less than 25.

The number is ______.

Case W-5

NUMBER SUSPECTS: 19, 22, 24, 26, 28, 31, 33, 36

CLUE 1: The sum of the digits of the number is greater than 6.

CLUE 2: The units digit of the number is not 6.

CLUE 3: The number is not $15 + 13$.

The number is ______.

Case W-6

NUMBER SUSPECTS: 8, 9, 10, 16, 20, 21, 28, 33, 35, 36

CLUE 1: The number is greater than $20 \div 2$.

CLUE 2: The number is less than 8×4.

CLUE 3: The number is an odd number.

The number is ______.

Case W-7

NUMBER SUSPECTS: 27, 84, 156, 293, 511

CLUE 1: The number is a three-digit number.

CLUE 2: The number is not $200 + 311$.

CLUE 3: The number is not $496 - 340$.

The number is ______.

Case W-8

NUMBER SUSPECTS: 49, 143, 781, 942, 1012, 2541

CLUE 1: The number is not a three-digit number.

CLUE 2: The number is not 7×7.

CLUE 3: The number is not $2000 + 500 + 40 + 1$.

The number is ______.

Case W-9

NUMBER SUSPECTS: 471, 582, 651, 1122, 1428

CLUE 1: The number is not a three-digit number.

CLUE 2: The sum of the digits of the number is 15.

The number is ______.

Case W-10

NUMBER SUSPECTS: 2, 3, 5, 7, 8, 9

CLUE 1: The number is a **divisor*** of 24.

CLUE 2: The number is greater than 4.

The number is ______.

Case W-11

NUMBER SUSPECTS: 3, 4, 5, 6, 8, 12, 24, 28

CLUE 1: The number is not a divisor of 12.

CLUE 2: The number is greater than 10.

CLUE 3: The number is not two dozen.

The number is ______.

Case W-12

NUMBER SUSPECTS: 5, 6, 7, 11, 13, 15

CLUE 1: If you add 10 to the number, you get a number which is less than 20.

CLUE 2: If you subtract 5 from the number, you get a number which is not 0.

CLUE 3: The number is not $5 + 2$.

The number is ______.

---

*The **DIVISORS** of a number are the numbers which evenly divide the number. For instance, the divisors of 6 are 1, 2, 3, and 6.

Case W-13

NUMBER SUSPECTS: 11, 15, 18, 22, 27, 29, 33, 35

CLUE 1: The tens digit of the number is not 2.

CLUE 2: The units digit of the number is not 5.

CLUE 3: The number is not 22 ÷ 2.

CLUE 4: The number is not 3 × 6.

The number is ______.

Case W-14

NUMBER SUSPECTS: 8, 11, 14, 21, 25, 36

CLUE 1: The number is a two-digit number.

CLUE 2: The number is divisible by 3.

CLUE 3: The number is not divisible by 7.

The number is ______.

Case W-15

NUMBER SUSPECTS: 1, 5, 9, 14, 25, 28, 36

CLUE 1: The number is a **perfect square.***

CLUE 2: The number is divisible by 3.

CLUE 3: The number is not 4 × 9.

The number is ______.

Case W-16

NUMBER SUSPECTS: 7, 10, 11, 13, 22, 27, 29

CLUE 1: The number is not a **prime*** number.

CLUE 2: The number is not 100 ÷ 10.

CLUE 3: The number is not 3 × 9.

The number is ______.

---

*__PERFECT SQUARES__ are found by **multiplying** a **number** by **itself.** For instance, 4 is a perfect square since 4 = 2 × 2.

*A **PRIME NUMBER** is a number, **greater** than **1**, with exactly **two** divisors, **itself** and **1**. Examples of prime numbers are 13 (divisors of 1 and 13) and 17 (divisors of 1 and 17). Note that 10 is not prime because it has 4 divisors, 1, 2, 5, and 10.

Case W-17

NUMBER SUSPECTS: 758, 923, 1141, 2056

CLUE 1: The number is less than 1,000.

CLUE 2: The number is not $(9 \cdot 100) + (2 \cdot 10) + 3$.

The number is ______.

Case W-18

NUMBER SUSPECTS: 15, 16, 21, 25, 27, 34, 43, 45, 56

CLUE 1: If you subtract 3 from the number, you get an odd number.

CLUE 2: The sum of the digits of the number is 7.

CLUE 3: If you subtract 10 from the number, you get a number which is greater than 10.

The number is ______.

Case W-19

NUMBER SUSPECTS: 7, 9, 14, 20, 24, 27

CLUE 1: The number is a **multiple*** of 3.

CLUE 2: The number is a two-digit number.

CLUE 3: The number is not a multiple of 8.

The number is ______.

Case W-20

NUMBER SUSPECTS: 27, 38, 42, 45, 57

CLUE 1: The number is an odd number.

CLUE 2: The number is represented by the dot in the picture below.

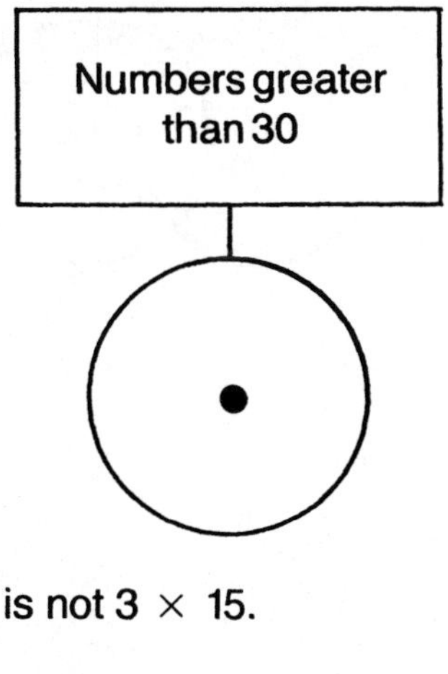

CLUE 3: The number is not 3×15.

The number is ______.

---

*For example, the **MULTIPLES** of 5 are 5, 10, 15, 20, ... , while the multiples of 8 are 8, 16, 24, ...

Case W-21

NUMBER SUSPECTS: 6, 8, 9, 12, 14, 15

CLUE 1: The number is represented by the **dot*** in the picture below.

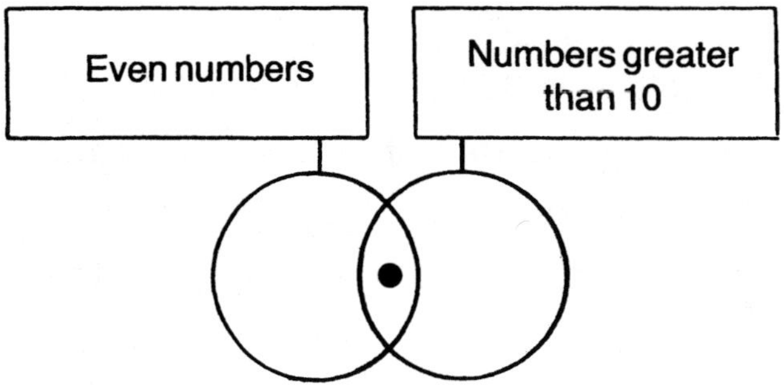

CLUE 2: The number is not 2 × 7.

The number is ______.

Case W-22

NUMBER SUSPECTS: 7, 12, 16, 17, 26, 44

CLUE 1: The number is represented by the dot in the picture below.

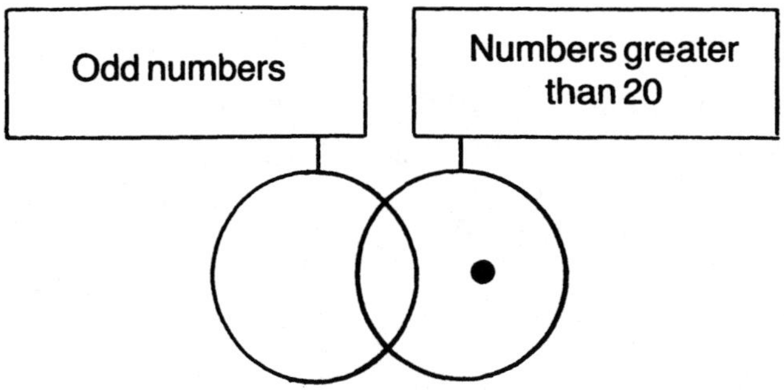

CLUE 2: The number is not 4 × 11.

The number is ______.

---

*Since the dot is in the circle for even numbers, the number is an even number and since the dot is also in the circle for numbers greater than 10, the number is also greater than 10.

Case W-23

NUMBER SUSPECTS: 2, 3, 4, 7, 9, 11, 15, 16

CLUE 1: The number is represented by the dot in the picture below

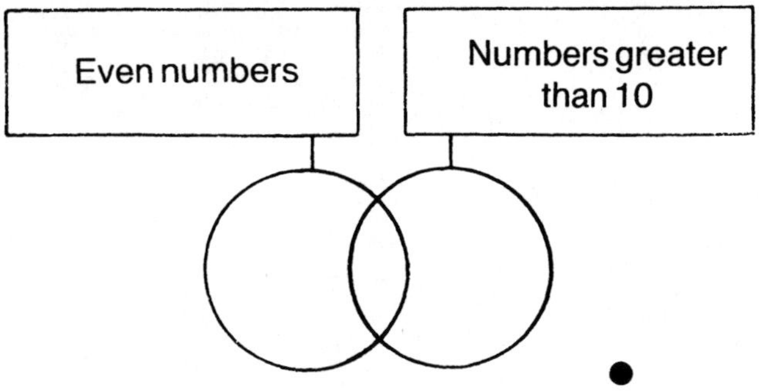

CLUE 2: The number is a prime number.

CLUE 3: The number is not 300 ÷ 100.

The number is ______.

Case W-24

NUMBER SUSPECTS: 3, 4, 6, 11, 17, 19, 21

CLUE 1: The number is represented by the dot in the picture below.

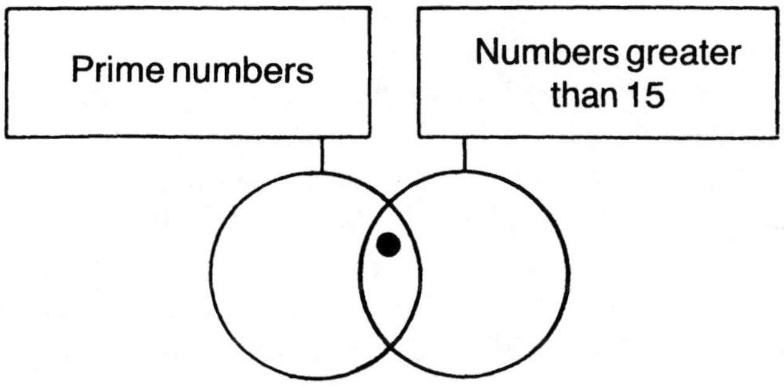

CLUE 2: The number is not 51 ÷ 3.

The number is ______.

For the next three detective stories, in addition to finding the mystery number, you are also to find the number suspects by using Clue 1. Write these number suspects in the blanks provided.

Case W-25

CLUE 1: I am a whole number between 17 and 25.

_____, _____, _____, _____, _____, _____, _____

CLUE 2: I am not an even number.

CLUE 3: I am not 7 × 3.

CLUE 4: I am not 10 + 9.

Who am I? ______

Case W-26

CLUE 1: I am a whole number less than 7.

____, ____, ____, ____, ____, ____, ____

CLUE 2: I am an even number.

CLUE 3: I am greater than 3.

CLUE 4: I am not a multiple of 3.

Who am I? ______

Case W-27

CLUE 1: I am a whole number between 26 and 34.

____, ____, ____, ____, ____, ____, ____

CLUE 2: The sum of my digits is greater than 5.

CLUE 3: 3 is a divisor of me.

CLUE 4: I am not 3×9.

Who am I? ______

The next six detective stories all involve three-digit numbers. In each case the first clue will help you identify one of the digits. The second clue will help you identify another of the digits and the third clue will help you identify the third digit. As you find each digit, write that digit in the appropriate position in the sentence "I am __ __ __." Of course, the blank to the **left** is for the **HUNDRED'S** digit, the **middle** blank is for the **TEN'S** digit, and the blank on the **right** is for the **UNIT'S** (or one's) digit. Several cases have clues concerning identity numbers. Since $x + 0 = x$ and $x \cdot 1 = x$ for every whole number x, **0** is the **IDENTITY NUMBER** for **ADDITION** and **1** is the **IDENTITY NUMBER** for **MULTIPLICATION.**

CASE W-28

CLUE 1: My unit's digit is an odd number between 3 and 7.

CLUE 2: My hundred's digit is two more than my unit's digit.

CLUE 3: My ten's digit is one less than my hundred's digit.

I am __ __ __.

Case W-29

CLUE 1: My ten's digit is the identity number for addition.

CLUE 2: My unit's digit is the identity number for multiplication.

CLUE 3: My hundred's digit is 7 more than my unit's digit.

I am __ __ __.

Case W-30

CLUE 1: My ten's digit is 55 ÷ 11.

CLUE 2: My unit's digit is 3 less than twice the ten's digit.

CLUE 3: My hundred's digit is half the sum of the unit's and ten's digit.

I am __ __ __.

Case W-31

CLUE 1: My unit's digit is 3 × 6 ÷ 2.

CLUE 2: My ten's digit is one third of my unit's digit.

CLUE 3: My hundred's digit is 3 more than my ten's digit.

I am __ __ __.

Case W-32

CLUE 1: My hundred's digit is 44 ÷ 11.

CLUE 2: My ten's digit is 5 more than my hundred's digit.

CLUE 3: My unit's digit is 7 less than my ten's digit.

I am __ __ __.

Case W-33

CLUE 1: My hundred's digit is 83 − 76.

CLUE 2: My unit's digit is 5 less than the hundred's digit.

CLUE 3: My ten's digit is twice my unit's digit.

I am __ __ __.

Case W-34

CLUE 1: I am one of the numbers represented by a **dot*** in the picture below.

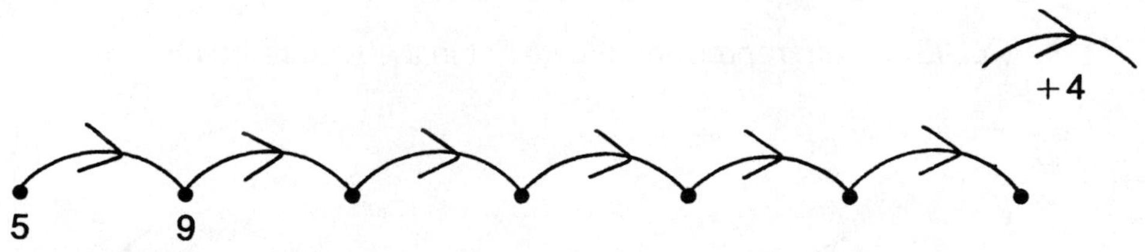

____, ____, ____, ____, ____, ____, ____

CLUE 2: I am a prime number.

CLUE 3: I am greater than 20.

Who am I? ______

---

*Note the **arrow** in the story means "add 4". Since the first dot is for 5, the second dot is for 9. You need to find numbers for the other dots.

Case W-35

CLUE 1: I am a whole number between 8 and 20.

____, ____, ____, ____, ____, ____, ____, ____, ____, ____, ____

CLUE 2: I am a prime number.

CLUE 3: I am represented by one of the dots in the picture below.

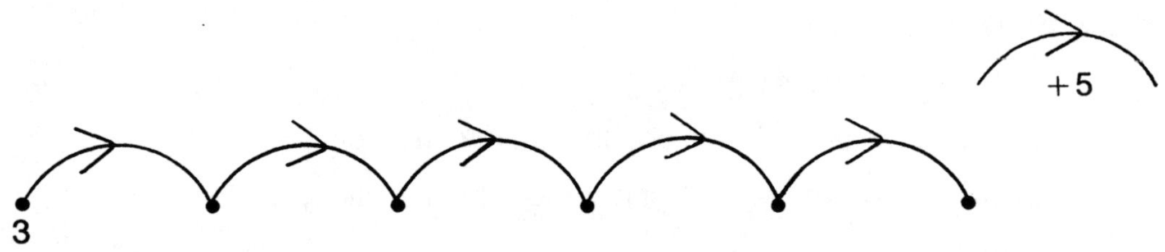

Who am I? ______

Occasionally you will be given a first clue where you will have an **INFINITE NUMBER** of number suspects. For instance, if Clue 1 were

"I am an odd whole number,"

then you would describe these numbers as follows:

1, 3, 5, 7, 9, 11, ... (**numbers continue without end**).

When this happens, you will be given a number of blanks followed by .... Fill in the blanks but remember that you must eventually eliminate numbers which come after the last number in the blanks.

Case W-36

CLUE 1: I am a multiple of 3.

____, ____, ____, ____, ____, ____, ____, ____, ____, ...

CLUE 2: I am represented by a dot in the picture below.

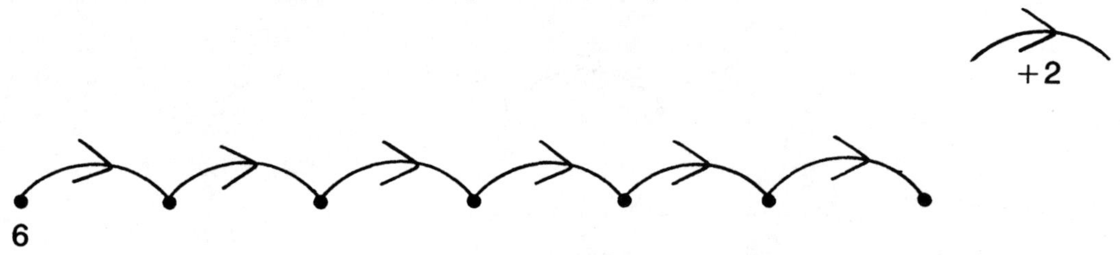

CLUE 3: I am greater than 10.

CLUE 4: I am not a dozen.

Who am I? ______

Case W-37

CLUE 1: I am an even whole number between 6 and 30.

____, ____, ____, ____, ____, ____, ____, ____, ____, ____, ____

CLUE 2: One of my digits is 2 and the other digit is less than 8.

CLUE 3: If you subtract 10 from me you will get a number which is greater than 10.

CLUE 4: I am a multiple of 4.

Who am I? ____

Case W-38

CLUE 1: I am an odd whole number between 5 and 27.

____, ____, ____, ____, ____, ____, ____, ____, ____, ____

CLUE 2: I am a perfect square.

CLUE 3: I am not 100 ÷ 4.

Who am I? ____

Case W-39

CLUE 1: I am a whole number between 5 and 21.

____, ____, ____, ____, ____, ____, ____, ____, ____, ____, ____,
____, ____, ____, ____

CLUE 2: If you subtract 5 from me, your answer will be an odd number.

CLUE 3: If you add 2 to me, your answer will be a multiple of 4.

CLUE 4: If you subtract 6 from me, your answer will be a two-digit number.

Who am I? ____

Case W-40

CLUE 1: I am a multiple of 3.

____, ____, ____, ____, ____, ____, ____, ____, ____,...

CLUE 2: I am represented by the dot in the picture below.

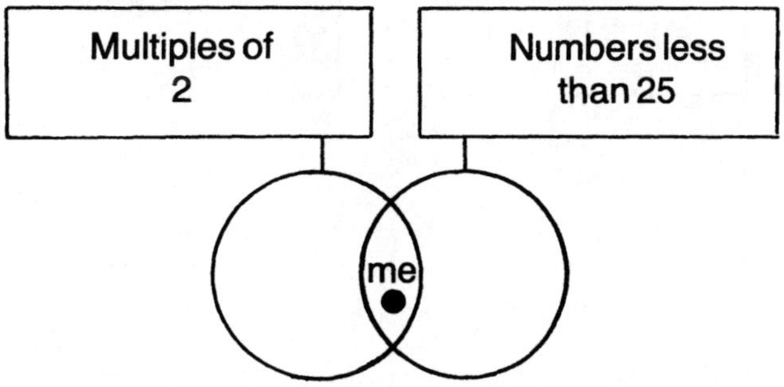

CLUE 3: I am a two-digit number.

CLUE 4: I am not a dozen.

CLUE 5: I am not two dozen.

Who am I? ____

Case W-41

CLUE 1: I am represented by the dot in the picture below.

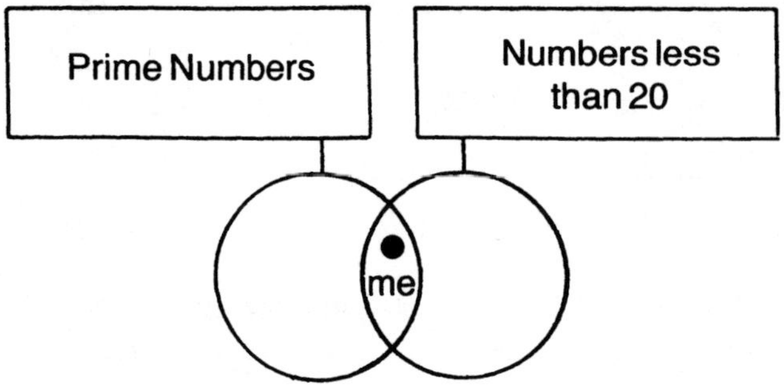

_____, _____, _____, _____, _____, _____, _____, _____

CLUE 2: I am not a two-digit number.

CLUE 3: I am not 105 ÷ 35.

CLUE 4: I am not 5,000 ÷ 1,000.

CLUE 5: I am not an even number.

Who am I? _____

Case W-42

CLUE 1: I am an odd number greater than 11.

_____, _____, _____, _____, _____, _____, _____, _____, _____, _____, ...

CLUE 2: I am represented by the dot in the picture below.

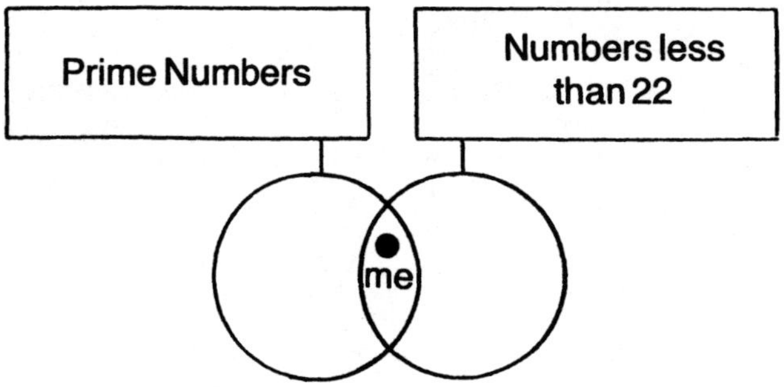

CLUE 3: The sum of my digits is less than 7.

Who am I? _____

Case W-43

CLUE 1: I am an even whole number greater than 8.

_____, _____, _____, _____, _____, _____, _____, _____, _____,
_____, _____

CLUE 2: I am represented by the dot in the picture below.

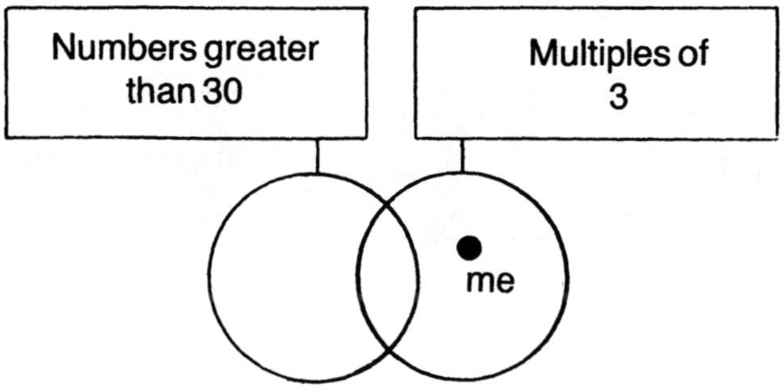

CLUE 3: 12 is one of my divisors.

CLUE 4: I am not 60 ÷ 5.

Who am I? _____

Case W-44

CLUE 1: I am represented by a dot* in the picture below.

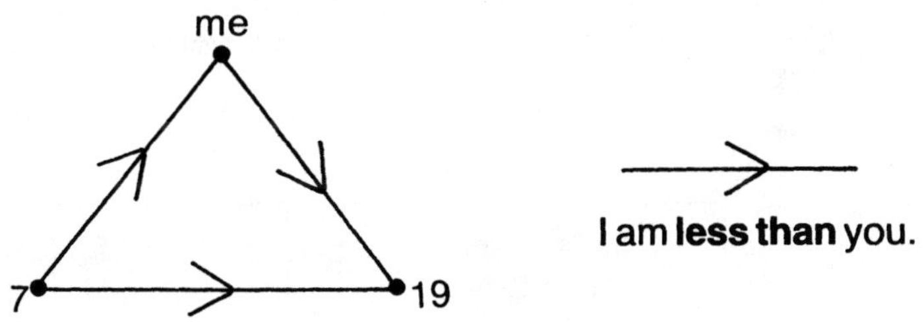

_____, _____, _____, _____, _____, _____,
_____, _____, _____, _____, _____ . . .

CLUE 2: I am a prime number.

CLUE 3: Of the three number suspects left, I am not the greatest of these suspects and I am not the least of these number suspects.

I am _____.

---

*Notice that 8 is one of the number suspects since 7 is **LESS THAN** 8 and 8 is less than 19. Also 9 is a number suspect since 7 is less than 9 and 9 is less than 19.

Case W-45

CLUE 1: I am a whole number which is not a prime number.

____, ____, ____, ____, ____, ____, ____,
____, ____, ____, ____, ____, ____, ____, ...

CLUE 2: I am represented by a dot in the picture below.

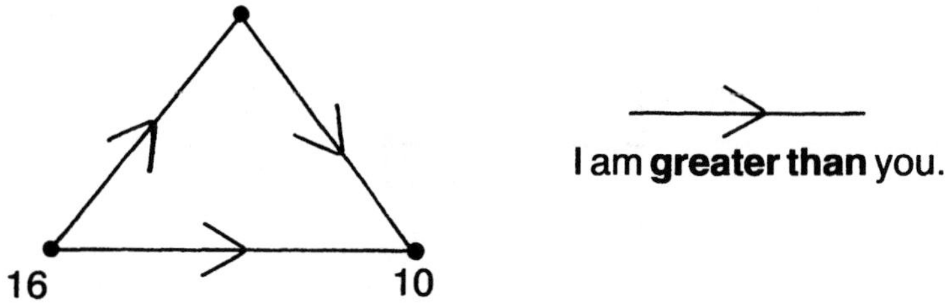

CLUE 3: I am an odd number.

Who am I? ____

Case W-46

CLUE 1: I am a whole number.

____, ____, ____, ____, ____,
____, ____, ____, ____, ____,
____, ____, ____, ____, ____

CLUE 2: If you **square*** me, you will get a number less than 200.

CLUE 3: If you subtract 3 from me, you will get an odd whole number.

CLUE 4: I am represented by the dot in the picture below.

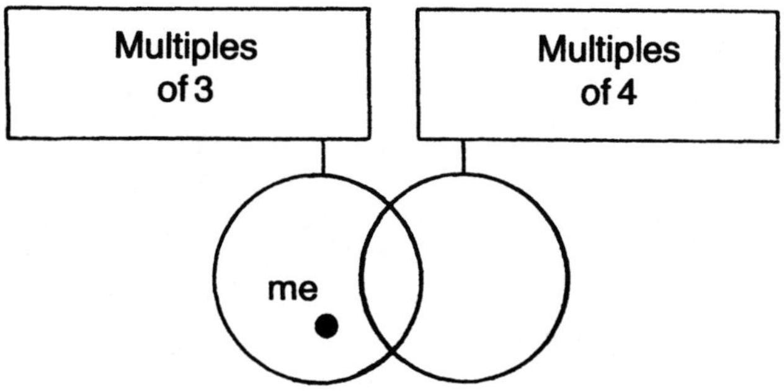

Who am I? ____

*To **SQUARE** a number you **multiply** that **number** by itself. For instance, the square of 5 is 25 because $5 \times 5 = 25$.

Case W-47

CLUE 1: I am in the picture below.

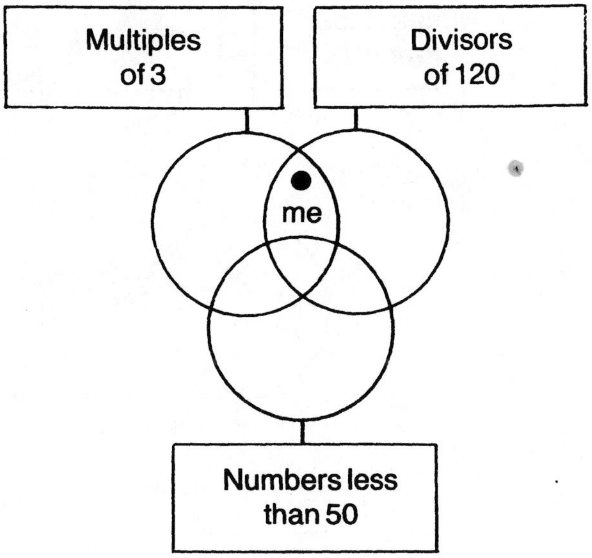

____, ____

CLUE 2: I am less than 100.

Who am I? ______

Case W-48

CLUE 1: I am represented by the dot in the picture below.

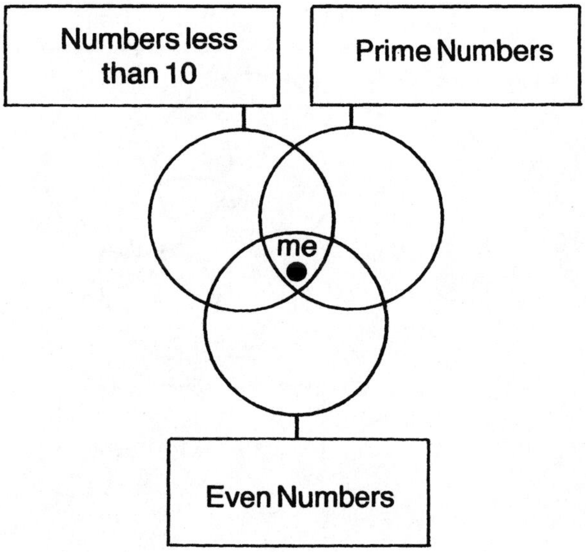

Who am I? ______

Case W-49

CLUE 1: I am represented by the dot in the picture below.

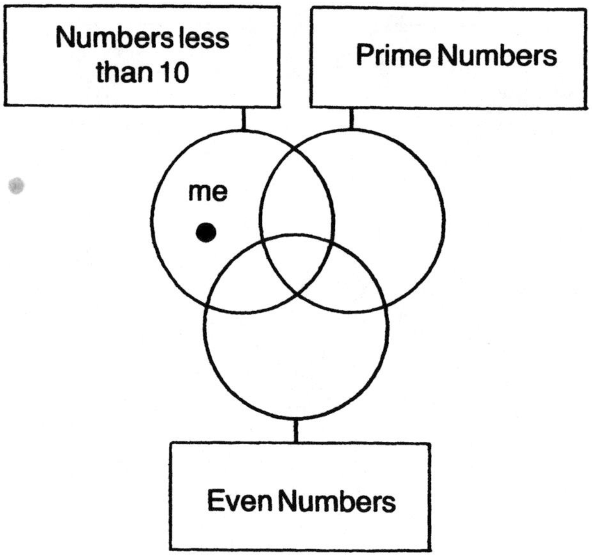

CLUE 2: I am not 462 ÷ 462.

Who am I? ______.

Case W-50

CLUE 1: I am a nonzero number represented by the dot in the picture below.

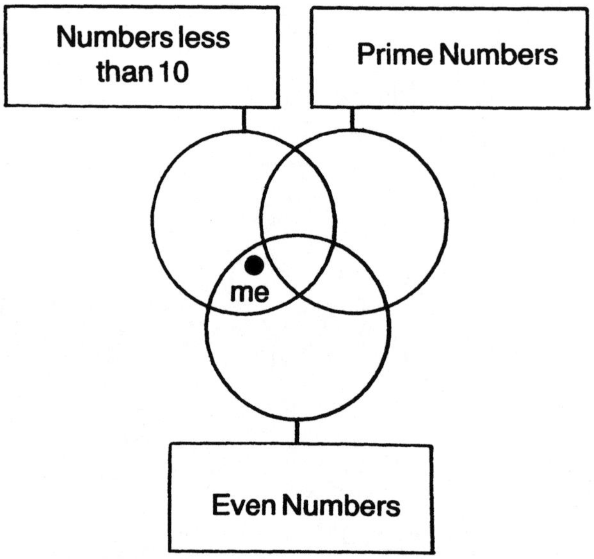

______, ______, ______

CLUE 2: I am not half a dozen.

CLUE 3: I am not a third of a dozen.

Who am I? ______

Case W-51

CLUE 1: I am an even number between 3 and 17.

_____, _____, _____, _____, _____, _____, _____

CLUE 2: I am a divisor of 24.

CLUE 3: I am not the **greatest common divisor*** of 16 and 20.

CLUE 4: I am not a multiple of 3.

Who am I? _____

Case W-52

CLUE 1: I am represented by the dot in the picture below.

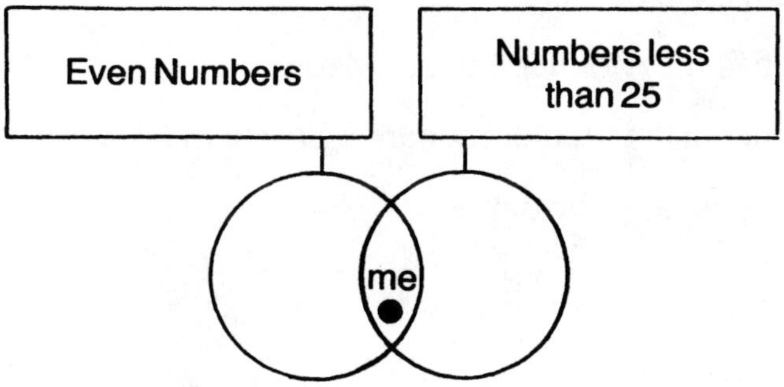

_____, _____, _____, _____, _____, _____, _____,
_____, _____, _____, _____, _____, _____

CLUE 2: I am not a multiple of 8.

CLUE 3: I do not have 5 as a divisor.

CLUE 4: I am greater than 5.

CLUE 5: I am not the **least common multiple*** of 6 and 4.

CLUE 6: I am not the greatest common divisor of 12 and 18.

CLUE 7: I am a multiple of 6.

Who am I? _____

---

*The **GREATEST COMMON DIVISOR** of two numbers is the **largest** number which is a **divisor** of **both** of them.
***The LEAST COMMON MULTIPLE** of two numbers is the **smallest** number which is a **multiple** of **both** of them.

Case W-53

CLUE 1: I am represented by the dot in the picture below.

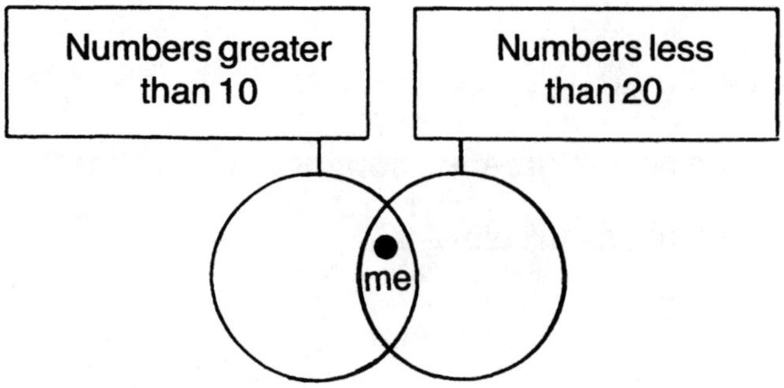

_____, _____, _____, _____, _____, _____, _____, _____, _____

CLUE 2: I am a multiple of 2.

CLUE 3: I have an even number of divisors.

CLUE 4: I am not the greatest common divisor of 24 and 36.

CLUE 5: I am not a multiple of 9.

Who am I? ______

Case W-54

CLUE 1: I am represented by the dot in the picture below.

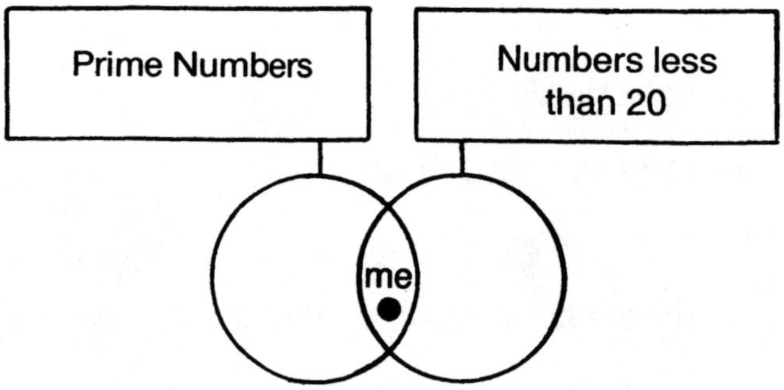

_____, _____, _____, _____, _____, _____, _____, _____

CLUE 2: If you add 4 to me, the answer will be a multiple of 3.

CLUE 3: I am not a divisor of 10.

CLUE 4: The sum of my digits is not 8.

Who am I? ______

Case W-55

CLUE 1: I am represented by the dot in the picture below.

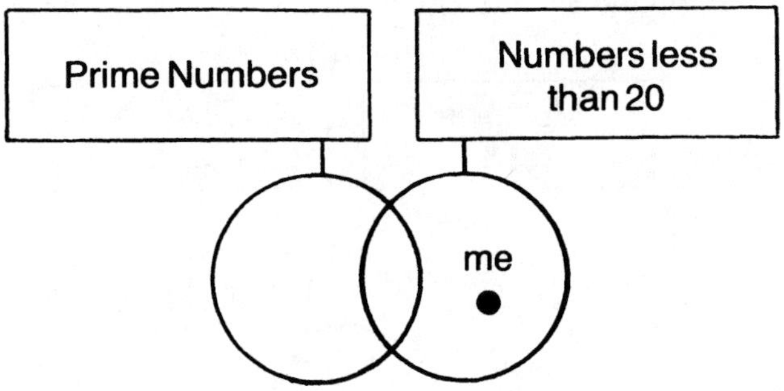

____, ____, ____, ____, ____, ____,
____, ____, ____, ____, ____, ____

CLUE 2: I am not a multiple of 3.

CLUE 3: I am not a multiple of 4.

CLUE 4: I am not the identity number for multiplication.

CLUE 5: I am not $42 \div 3$.

CLUE 6: I am not the identity number for addition.

Who am I? ____

Case W-56

CLUE 1: I am represented by the dot in the picture below.

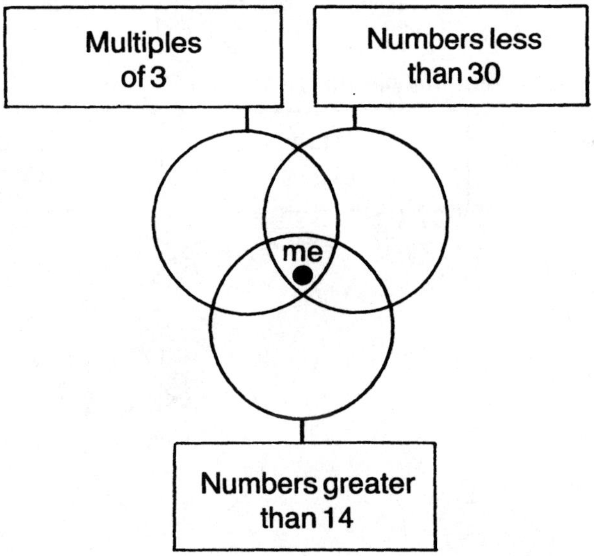

____, ____, ____, ____, ____,

CLUE 2: I am not the least common multiple of 12 and 8.

CLUE 3: I am not the greatest common divisor of 30 and 45.

CLUE 4: I am not 3^3.*

CLUE 5: I am not a multiple of 7.

Who am I? ____

*3^3 means $3 \times 3 \times 3$.

Case W-57

CLUE 1: I am in the picture below.

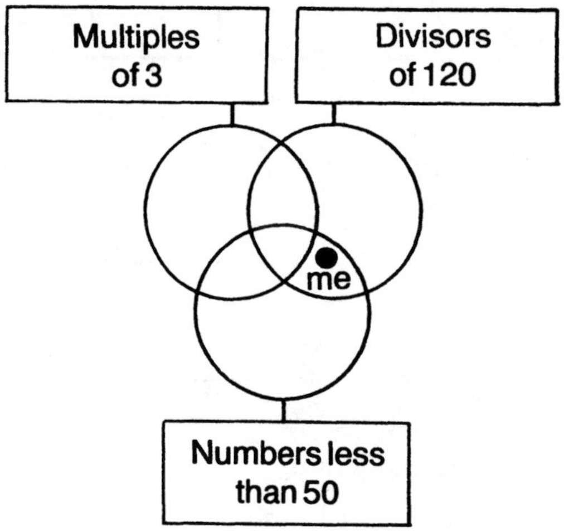

______, ______, ______, ______, ______, ______, ______, ______

CLUE 2: I am an odd number.

CLUE 3: I am not the identity number for multiplication.

Who am I? ______

Case W-58

CLUE 1: I am in the picture below.

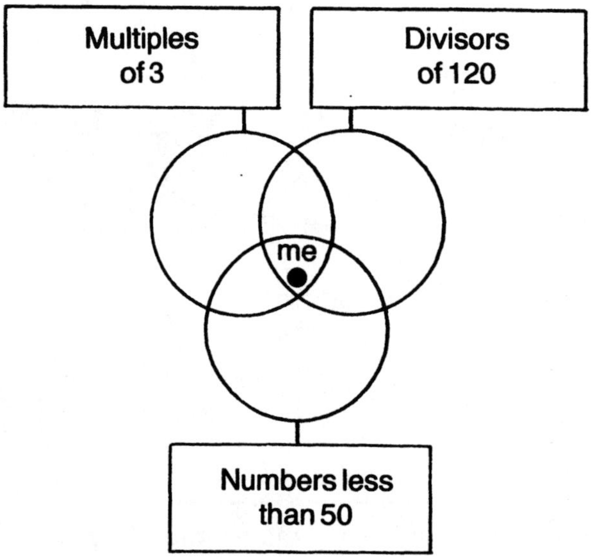

______, ______, ______, ______, ______, ______

CLUE 2: If you add 1 to me, your answer will be a prime number.

CLUE 3: If you square me, you will get an answer which is between 100 and 200.

Who am I? ______

Case W-59

CLUE 1: I am represented by the dot in the picture below.

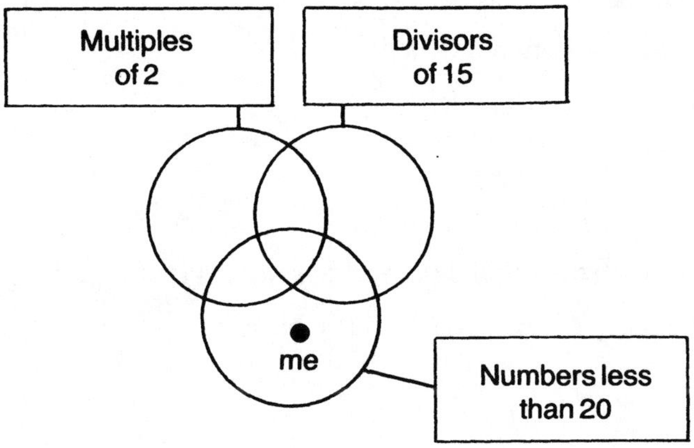

_____, _____, _____, _____, _____, _____

CLUE 2: If you multiply me by 2 your answer is greater than 30.

CLUE 3: I am not 170 ÷ 10.

Who am I? ______

Case W-60

CLUE 1: I am represented by the dot in the picture below.

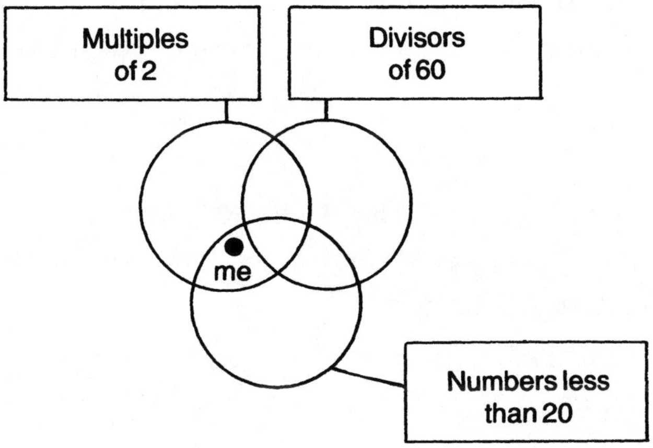

_____, _____, _____, _____, _____

CLUE 2: If you add one to me, the answer will be a prime number.

CLUE 3: I am not a multiple of 3.

Who am I? ______

The next six detective stories are about three-digit numbers. Again you must identify the unit's, ten's and hundred's digit. However, now you won't necessarily be able to identify each digit with one clue. You may need to put several clues together to identify some digits. Whenever you find what one of the digits is, write it in the appropriate blank.

Case W-61

CLUE 1: My hundred's digit and my unit's digit are the same.

CLUE 2: The sum of my hundred's digit and my unit's digit is 8.

CLUE 3: The sum of all my digits is 14.

I am __ __ __ .

Case W-62

CLUE 1: My ten's digit is 77 ÷ 11.

CLUE 2: The sum of my unit's digit and my hundred's digit is 12.

CLUE 3: My unit's digit is 4 more than my hundred's digit.

I am __ __ __ .

Case W-63

CLUE 1: The sum of my unit's digit and my ten's digit is 13.

CLUE 2: My units digit is 3 less than my ten's digit.

CLUE 3: My hundred's digit is half my ten's digit.

I am __ __ __ .

Case W-64

CLUE 1: The sum of all my digits is 11.

CLUE 2: All my digits are odd.

CLUE 3: The sum of my hundred's digit and my unit's digit is 4.

CLUE 4: My hundred's digit is bigger than my unit's digit.

I am __ __ __ .

Case W-65

CLUE 1: The sum of my unit's digit and my ten's digit is 12.

CLUE 2: My ten's digit is greater than my unit's digit and my ten's digit is odd.

CLUE 3: My ten's digit is not 9.

CLUE 4: The sum of all my digits is 14.

I am __ __ __ .

Case W-66

CLUE 1: My unit's digit is 3 more than my ten's digit.

CLUE 2: The sum of my unit's digit and twice my ten's digit is 15.

CLUE 3: My hundred's digit is one more than my ten's digit.

I am __ __ __ .

In the next two detective stories you are to find two mystery numbers. In these two cases, you should complete the table provided so that you will have a list of possible solutions and then eliminate suspects as you have done in previous detective stories.

Case W-67

CLUE 1: Zim is a divisor of 12.

CLUE 2: Zim and Zam are represented by dots in the diagram.

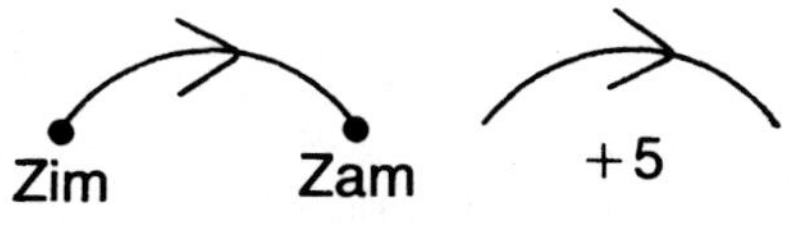

Zim						
Zam						

CLUE 3: Zam is odd.

CLUE 4: Zam is less than 10.

CLUE 5: Zim is not 2.

Who is Zim? ______Who is Zam? ______

Case W-68

CLUE 1: Zoom is a prime number less than 12.

CLUE 2: Zoom and Zum are represented by the dots in the diagram.

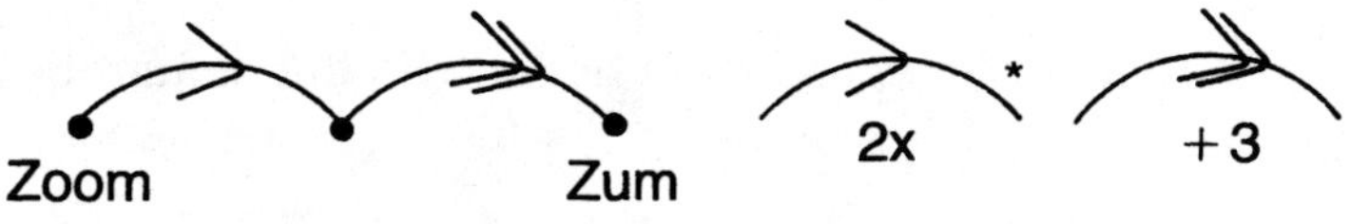

Zoom					
Zum					

CLUE 3: Zum is three times Zoom.

Who is Zoom? ______Who is Zum? ______

---

*This arrow indicates that the number is **multiplied** by 2.

In the next six detective stories **all** of the suspects are to be placed on the diagram pictured. Then you will be able to find the mystery number.

Case W-69

NUMBER SUSPECTS: 7, 12, 18, 45

CLUE 1: The number is pictured below.

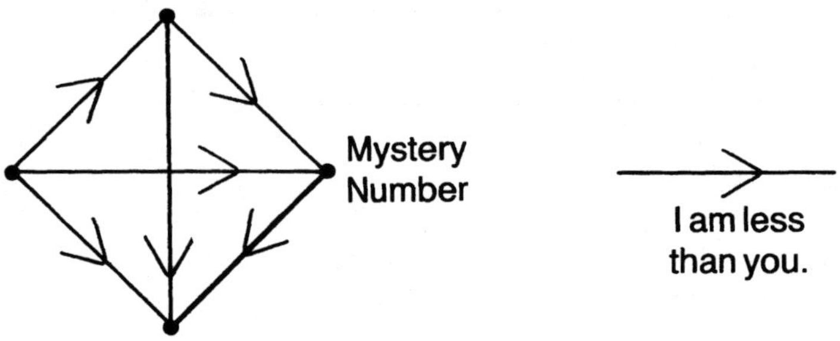

The number is ______.

Case W-70

NUMBER SUSPECTS: 5, 13, 18, 19

CLUE 1: The number is represented by a dot in the picture below.

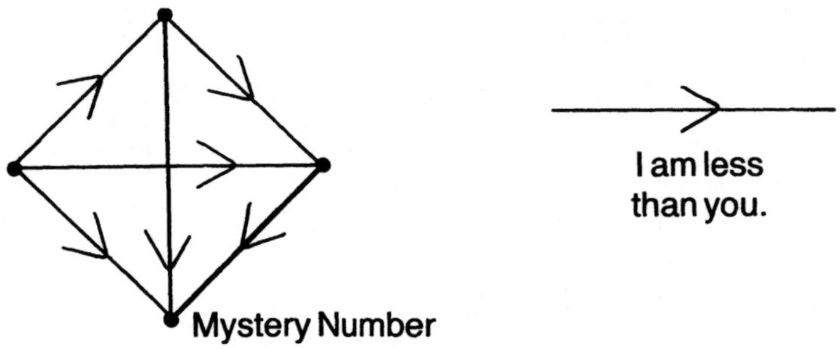

The number is ______.

Case W-71

NUMBER SUSPECTS: *1, 8, 11, 28*

CLUE 1: The number is represented by a dot in the picture below.

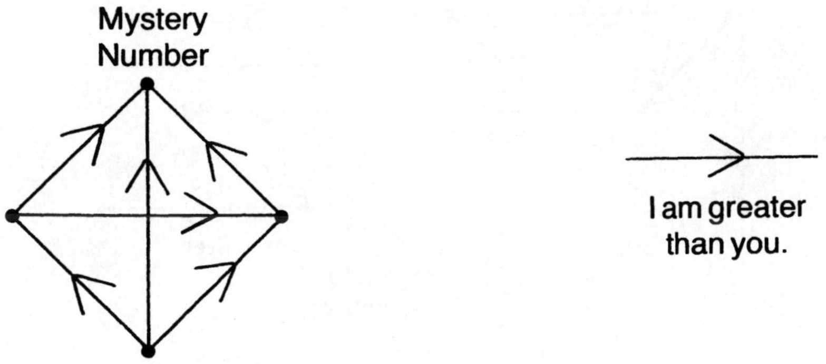

The number is ______.

Case W-72

NUMBER SUSPECTS: *7, 10, 12, 13, 14, 16*

CLUE 1: The number is represented by a dot in the picture below.

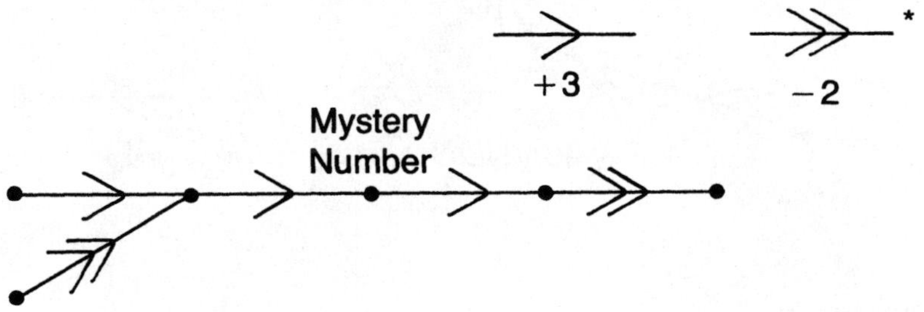

The number is ______.

---

*The double arrow indicates that 2 is to be **subtracted** from the number.

Case W-73

NUMBER SUSPECTS: 10, 25, 40, 55, 70

CLUE 1: The number is represented by a dot in the picture below.

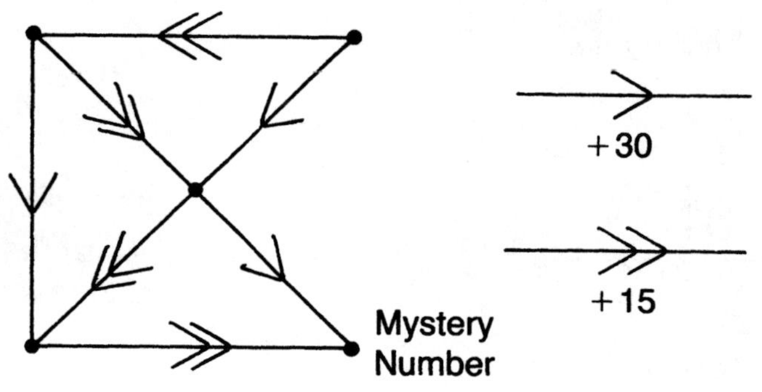

The number is ______.

Case W-74

NUMBER SUSPECTS: 4, 7, 8, 10, 13, 16

CLUE 1: The number is represented by a dot in the picture below.

The number is ______.

In the next three detective stories, you are again to find two mystery numbers. In these cases you should list the possible solutions in the blanks provided and then eliminate suspects using other clues.

Case W-75

CLUE 1: Fee is represented by a dot in the picture below.

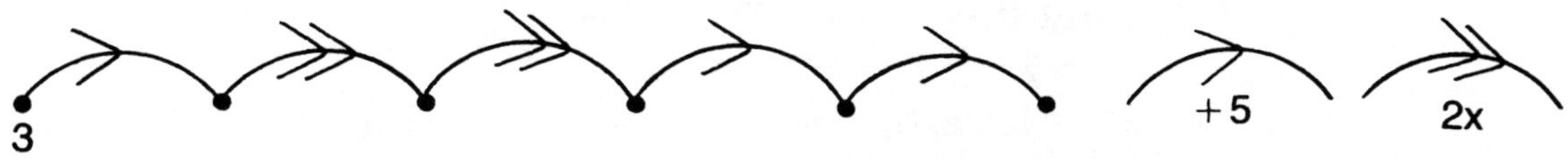

_____, _____, _____, _____, _____, _____

CLUE 2: Fi is represented by a dot in the picture below.

_____, _____, _____, _____, _____

CLUE 3: Fi is a divisor of Fee.

CLUE 4: Fi is an odd number.

Who is Fee? _____ Who is Fi? _____

The position of symbols of grouping often has a decided effect on the result of computation involving more than two numbers, and the person writing the problem can control the results through the placement of these symbols. For instance, concerning $7 + 3 \times 2$,
$(7 + 3) \times 2 = 10 \times 2 = 20$ while
$7 + (3 \times 2) = 7 + 6 = 13$.
Notice that when **PARENTHESES** (or other **symbols** of **grouping**) are used, computation should be completed **inside** parentheses **first**.

The next two detective stories involve determining possible placement of symbols of grouping.

Case W-76

CLUE 1: Tip can be found by placing grouping symbols in $3 \times 5 - 2$.

_____, _____

CLUE 2: Rip can be found by placing grouping symbols in $5 \times 2 + 4$.

_____, _____

CLUE 3: The greatest common divisor of Tip and Rip is 3.

Who is Tip? _____ Who is Rip? _____

Case W-77

CLUE 1: Pip can be found by placing grouping symbols in
$6 + 4 \times 5 - 3$.

_____, _____, _____, _____

CLUE 2: Kip can be found by placing grouping symbols in
$8 \times 4 + 6 \div 2$.

_____, _____, _____, _____

CLUE 3: Kip is a multiple of Pip.

CLUE 4: Pip is greater than 15.

Who is Pip? _____ Who is Kip? _____

Case W-78

NUMBER SUSPECTS: 4, 5, 6, 7, 8, 9, 10, 11, 12, 13, 14, 15, 16

CLUE 1: The number has exactly 4 divisors.

CLUE 2: The number is not 7×2.

CLUE 3: The number is not a multiple of 5.

CLUE 4: The number is not the greatest common divisor of 16 and 24.

The number is _____.

Case W-79

CLUE 1: Top is a divisor of 36. (Write all possibilities for Top in the table below.)

CLUE 2: Sop is a divisor of Top. (Write all possibilites for Sop in the table after each possible value for Top. The divisors of 9 are given to you.)

Top	Sop
9	1, 3, 9

CLUE 3: Top has four divisors.

CLUE 4: Sop has two divisors.

CLUE 5: Sop is an odd number.

Who is Top? _____ Who is Sop? _____

Case W-80

CLUE 1: I am a whole number between 22 and 34.

____, ____, ____, ____, ____, ____, ____, ____, ____, ____, ____

CLUE 2: I am the ending number of one of the roads pictured below.

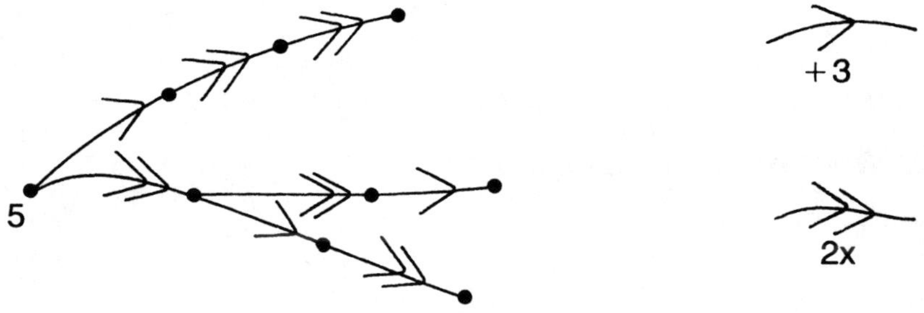

CLUE 3: I am not a prime number.

CLUE 4: 13 is not one of my **factors.***

Who am I? ____

Case W-81

CLUE 1: I am a whole number between 9 and 20.

____, ____, ____, ____, ____, ____, ____, ____, ____, ____

CLUE 2: I am the ending number of a single arrow-double road which starts at 2 and has two double arrows and one single arrow where the double arrow stands for the +3 relation and the single arrow stands for 2x. (Draw the roads. There are three of them.)

CLUE 3: I am not considered to be an unlucky number.

CLUE 4: I do not have 5 factors.

Who am I? ____

---

*The **divisors** and the **FACTORS** of counting numbers are the **same**.

Case W-82

CLUE 1: I am one of the cards below.

A	B	C	D
$n + 3$	$n + 5$	$2n - 4$	$9 - n$

CLUE 2: When $n = 3$, my value is 6.

CLUE 3: When $n = 2$, my value is 7.

Which card am I? ______

Case W-83

CLUE 1: I am one of the cards below.

A	B	C	D	E
$n - 5$	$n/2$	$2n - 18$	$n/3$	$12 - n$

CLUE 2: When $n = 12$, my value is 6.

CLUE 3: When $n = 10$, my value is 5.

Which card am I? ______

Case W-84

CLUE 1: I am one of the cards below.

A	B	C	D	E	F
$2n - 3$	$7 - n$	$9 - n$	$12/n$	$10 - 2n$	$2n + 1$

CLUE 2: When $n = 3$, my value is 4.

CLUE 3: When $n = 4$, my value is 3.

CLUE 4: When $n = 2$, my value is not 6.

Which card am I? ______

Case W-85

CLUE 1: I am one of the cards below.

A	B	C	D	E
n^2	$5n - 4$	$2n + 3$	2^n	$2n - 1$

CLUE 2: When n = 4, my value is 16.
CLUE 3: When n = 1, my value is 1.
CLUE 4: When n = 3, my value is not 11.
Which card am I? ______

Case W-86

CLUE 1: I am one of the cards below.

A	B	C	D	E
$40/n$	$n + 7$	$3n - 3$	3^n	$5n - 1$

CLUE 2: When n = 2, my value is 9.
CLUE 3: When n = 3, my value is not 14.
CLUE 4: When n = 1, my value is less than 6.
Which card am I? ______

Case W-87

CLUE 1: I am one of the cards below.

A	B	C	D	E
2^n	$8/n$	$2n + 1$	$4n - 3$	n^3

CLUE 2: When n = 4, my value is greater than 10.
CLUE 3: When n = 2, my value is not 8.
CLUE 4: When n = 3, my value is not 8.
Which card am I? ______

CHAPTER II

FRACTIONS

This chapter is very similar to Chapter 1. The only significant difference is that the detective stories in this chapter are about fractions.

Case F-1

CLUE 1: My **numerator*** is a prime number between 7 and 13.

CLUE 2: My **denominator*** is a whole number less than 14.

CLUE 3: My denominator is an even whole number greater than my numerator.

Who am I? ______

Case F-2

CLUE 1: My denominator is represented by the dot in the picture below.

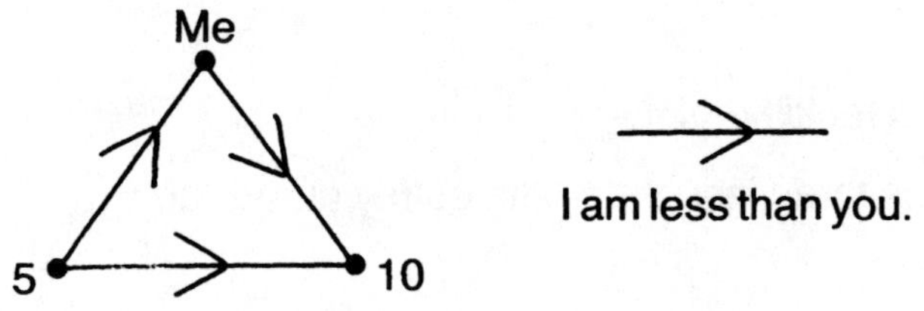

CLUE 2: My denominator is a multiple of 3.

CLUE 3: My denominator is an odd number.

CLUE 4: My numerator is 2 less than my denominator.

Who am I? ______

---

*For example, in the fraction $2/5$, 2 is the **NUMERATOR** and 5 is the **DENOMINATOR**.

Case F-3

CLUE 1: My numerator is represented by one of the dots below.

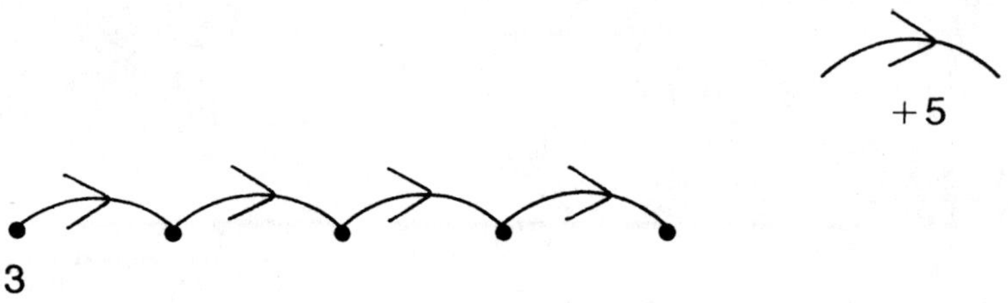

CLUE 2: My numerator is a multiple of 4.

CLUE 3: My denominator is one more than twice my numerator.

Who am I? ______

Case F-4

CLUE 1: My numerator is represented by the dot below.

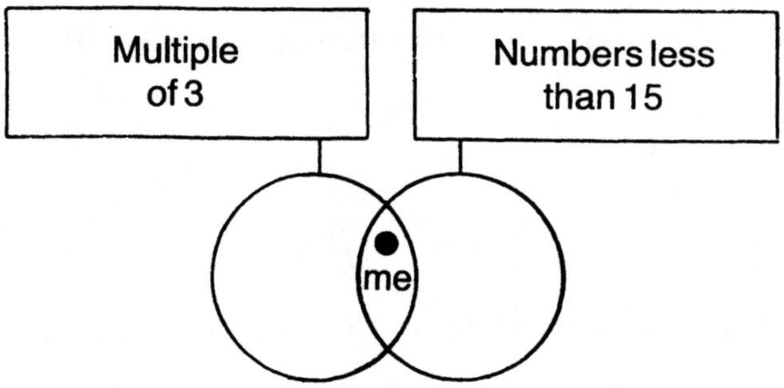

CLUE 2: My numerator is a multiple of 4.

CLUE 3: My denominator is three less than 5 times my numerator.

Who am I? ______

Case F-5

NUMBER SUSPECTS: 1/6, 2/6, 3/6, 4/6, 5/6.

CLUE 1: I am a fraction which is not in **simplest form***.

CLUE 2: I am not equal to 1/2.

CLUE 3: I am not the greatest (largest) of the two number suspects left.

Who am I? ______

---

*A fraction is in **SIMPLEST FORM** only when the **only common divisor** that its numerator and denominator have is **1**. For instance, 9/12 is not in simplest form since 3 is a divisor of both 9 and 12. However, 9/12 = 3/4 and 3/4 is in simplest form.

Case F-6

NUMBER SUSPECTS: $\frac{1}{4}$, $\frac{2}{4}$, $\frac{5}{7}$, $\frac{2}{11}$, $\frac{5}{12}$, $\frac{2}{14}$.

CLUE 1: My denominator is not 4.

CLUE 2: My numerator is not 5.

CLUE 3: I am not in simplest form.

Who am I? ______

Case F-7

NUMBER SUSPECTS: $\frac{4}{9}$, $\frac{6}{9}$, $\frac{5}{11}$, $\frac{5}{12}$, $\frac{5}{15}$, $\frac{7}{28}$.

CLUE 1: I am not in simplest form.

CLUE 2: I am not equal to $\frac{2}{3}$.

CLUE 3: I am not equal to $\frac{1}{4}$.

Who am I? ______

Case F-8

NUMBER SUSPECTS: $\frac{5}{2}$, $\frac{3}{7}$, $\frac{9}{8}$, $\frac{11}{9}$, $\frac{11}{12}$, $\frac{12}{17}$.

CLUE 1: I am less than 1.

CLUE 2: I am not equal to $\frac{300}{700}$.

CLUE 3: My numerator is not 12.

Who am I? ______

Case F-9

NUMBER SUSPECTS: $\frac{3}{5}$, $\frac{1}{6}$, $\frac{2}{7}$, $\frac{6}{9}$, $\frac{3}{11}$, $\frac{6}{14}$, $\frac{3}{15}$.

CLUE 1: I am in simplest form.

CLUE 2: I am not equal to $\frac{3}{18}$.

CLUE 3: I am not equal to $\frac{12}{20}$.

CLUE 4: I am not the **reciprocal*** of $\frac{11}{3}$.

Who am I? ______

Case F-10

NUMBER SUSPECTS: $\frac{1}{2}$, $\frac{2}{3}$, $\frac{3}{4}$, $\frac{5}{4}$, $\frac{9}{4}$, $\frac{5}{6}$, $\frac{11}{7}$.

CLUE 1: I am represented by one of the dots in the picture below.

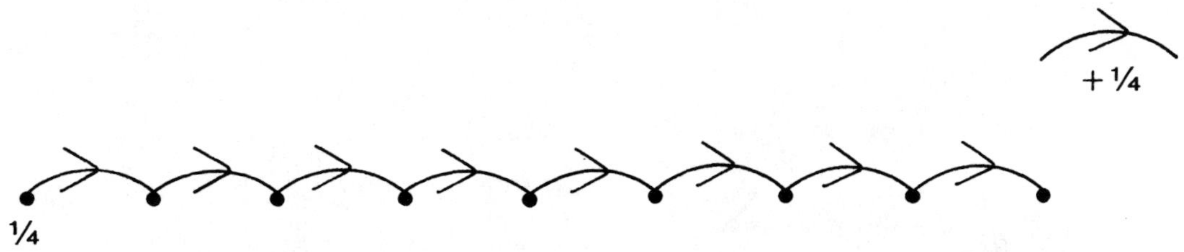

CLUE 2: I am greater than 1.

CLUE 3: I am not equal to $2\frac{1}{4}$.

Who am I? ______

---

*For example, the **RECIPROCAL** of $\frac{3}{7}$ is $\frac{7}{3}$.

Case F-11

NUMBER SUSPECTS: $5/2$, $2/3$, $3/7$, $9/8$, $11/9$, $12/17$.

CLUE 1: *I am greater than 1.*

CLUE 2: I am not equal to $1 + 1/8$.

CLUE 3: I am not equal to $2\frac{1}{2}$.

Who am I? ______

Case F-12

NUMBER SUSPECTS: $3/7$, $3/8$, $3/9$, $4/11$, $5/12$.

CLUE 1: I am not equal to $3/4 \cdot 1/2$.

CLUE 2: I am not equal to $1/3$.

CLUE 3: I am not equal to $7/12 - 2/12$.

CLUE 4: I am not equal to $1/7 + 2/7$.

Who am I? ______

Case F-13

NUMBER SUSPECTS: $3/7$, $4/15$, $3/20$, $7/25$, $6/35$.

CLUE 1: I am not equal to $2/5 \cdot 2/3$.

CLUE 2: I am not equal to $3/5 \cdot 2/7$.

CLUE 3: I am not equal to $5/20 - 2/20$.

CLUE 4: My reciprocal is not $7/3$.

Who am I? ______

Case F-14

NUMBER SUSPECTS: $1/3$, $2/3$, $1/4$, $3/5$, $3/8$, $5/8$.

CLUE 1: I am represented by the dot in the picture below.

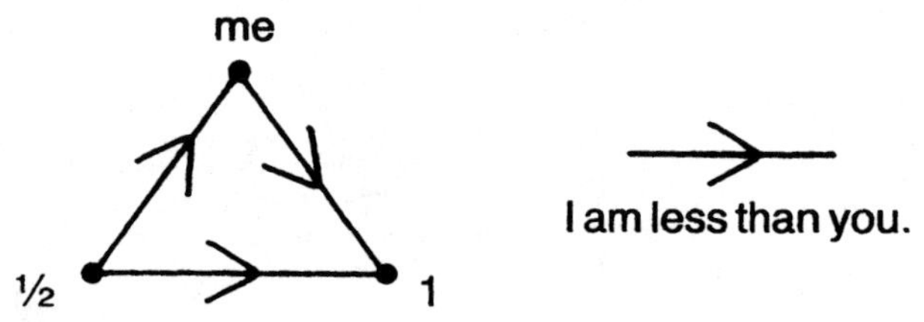

CLUE 2: My denominator is not equal to 2^3.

CLUE 3: I am not equal to $3/4 \cdot 8/9$.

Who am I? ______

Case F-15

NUMBER SUSPECTS: $\frac{1}{2}$, $\frac{1}{3}$, $\frac{1}{4}$, $\frac{1}{6}$, $\frac{1}{8}$, $\frac{1}{9}$, $\frac{1}{11}$.

CLUE 1: If you multiply me by 3 you get a number less than 1.

CLUE 2: I am not $\frac{3}{4} - \frac{1}{2}$.

CLUE 3: I am not $\frac{1}{2} - \frac{1}{3}$.

CLUE 4: I am not $1 \div 11$.

CLUE 5: I am not $\frac{1}{3} - \frac{2}{9}$.

Who am I? ______

Case F-16

NUMBER SUSPECTS: $\frac{1}{2}$, $\frac{1}{3}$, $\frac{2}{3}$, $\frac{1}{4}$, $\frac{1}{5}$, $\frac{1}{6}$, $\frac{2}{7}$, $\frac{2}{9}$, $\frac{2}{11}$.

CLUE 1: My reciprocal is greater than 4.

CLUE 2: I am not equal to $\frac{1}{3} - \frac{1}{9}$.

CLUE 3: I am not equal to $\frac{1}{2} \div 3$.

CLUE 4: I am not equal to $\frac{4}{20}$.

Who am I? ______

The next several detective stories involve decimal names for fractions. You will probably remember that $\frac{1}{2}$ means $1 \div 2$ and $1 \div 2 = .5$, so $\frac{1}{2} = .5$. Notice that .5 **TERMINATES (ends)**. Consider $\frac{1}{3} = 1 \div 3 = .3333 \ldots$. Notice that .333 ... is **NONTERMINATING**. To get ready for detective stories which relate to decimal names you will profit from completing the following table. You may want to use a calculator to help you.

TABLE OF DECIMAL NAMES FOR FRACTIONS

Fraction	Decimal Name
$\frac{1}{2}$	.5
$\frac{1}{3}$	.3333...
$\frac{2}{3}$	
$\frac{1}{4}$	
$\frac{3}{4}$	
$\frac{1}{5}$	
$\frac{2}{5}$	
$\frac{1}{6}$	
$\frac{5}{6}$	
$\frac{1}{7}$	
$\frac{5}{7}$	
$\frac{1}{8}$	
$\frac{3}{8}$	
$\frac{5}{8}$	
$\frac{7}{8}$	
$\frac{1}{9}$	
$\frac{2}{9}$	
$\frac{4}{9}$	

As you solve cases involving decimal names, refer back to this table.

Case F-17

NUMBER SUSPECTS: $1/2$, $3/4$, $2/5$, $3/5$, $5/8$, $7/10$, $12/11$.

CLUE 1: I am greater than .5.

CLUE 2: I am not equal to .75.

CLUE 3: If you multiply me by 2 you get a number which is less than 2.

CLUE 4: My denominator is a prime number.

Who am I? ______

Case F-18

NUMBER SUSPECTS: $1/2$, $3/4$, $5/4$, $2/5$, $7/5$, $5/8$, $11/8$.

CLUE 1: I am greater than 1.

CLUE 2: I am not equal to 1.25.

CLUE 3: I am not equal to 1.375.

Who am I? ______

Case F-19

NUMBER SUSPECTS: $1/2$, $1/3$, $2/3$, $3/4$, $1/6$, $5/6$, $7/8$, $8/7$.

CLUE 1: I am represented by the dot in the picture below.

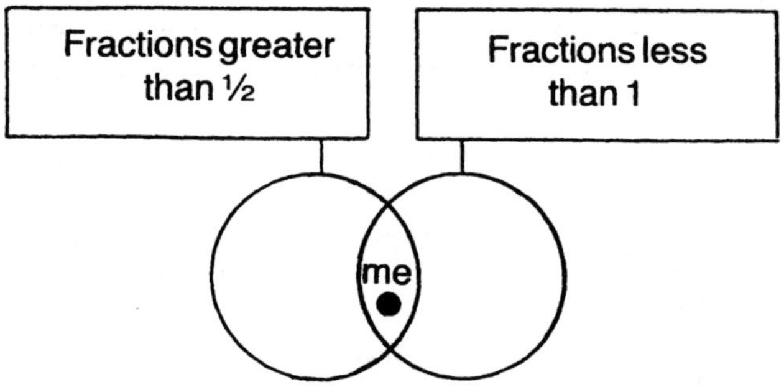

CLUE 2: I am not equal to .6666 ... .

CLUE 3: I am not equal to .75.

CLUE 4: I am not equal to .875.

Who am I? ______

Case F-20

NUMBER SUSPECTS: $2/3$, $4/3$, $1/4$, $5/4$, $5/6$, $11/6$, $7/10$, $13/10$.

CLUE 1: I am less than 1.

CLUE 2: My decimal name terminates (ends).

CLUE 3: I am not equal to .4 + .3.

Who am I? ______

Case F-21

NUMBER SUSPECTS: $\frac{1}{2}$, $\frac{1}{4}$, $\frac{3}{4}$, $\frac{1}{6}$, $\frac{5}{6}$, $\frac{3}{8}$, $\frac{5}{8}$, $\frac{7}{8}$, $\frac{5}{9}$, $\frac{8}{9}$.

CLUE 1: I am greater than $\frac{1}{2}$.

CLUE 2: My decimal name is nonterminating.

CLUE 3: I am not represented by a dot in the picture below.

Who am I? ______

Case F-22

NUMBER SUSPECTS: $\frac{1}{2}$, $\frac{1}{3}$, $\frac{2}{3}$, $\frac{1}{4}$, $\frac{3}{4}$, $\frac{2}{5}$, $\frac{5}{6}$, $\frac{1}{8}$.

CLUE 1: My decimal name terminates.

CLUE 2: I am not equal to $\frac{1}{4} - \frac{1}{8}$.

CLUE 3: I am not equal to $4 \div 8$.

CLUE 4: I am not equal to $\frac{1}{2} + \frac{1}{4}$.

CLUE 5: I am not equal to $\frac{1}{8} + \frac{1}{8}$.

Who am I? ______

Case F-23

NUMBER SUSPECTS: $\frac{1}{2}$, $\frac{1}{3}$, $\frac{2}{3}$, $\frac{1}{4}$, $\frac{3}{4}$, $\frac{2}{5}$, $\frac{5}{6}$, $\frac{1}{8}$.

CLUE 1: My decimal name is nonterminating.

CLUE 2: I am not equal to $\frac{1}{2} + \frac{1}{3}$.

CLUE 3: I am not equal to $\frac{4}{7} \div \frac{6}{7}$.

Who am I? ______

Case F-24

NUMBER SUSPECTS: $\frac{1}{3}$, $\frac{2}{3}$, $1\frac{1}{3}$, $1\frac{1}{4}$, $\frac{4}{5}$, $1\frac{2}{5}$, $1\frac{4}{5}$, $1\frac{1}{6}$, $2\frac{1}{8}$.

CLUE 1: I am represented by the dot in the picture below.

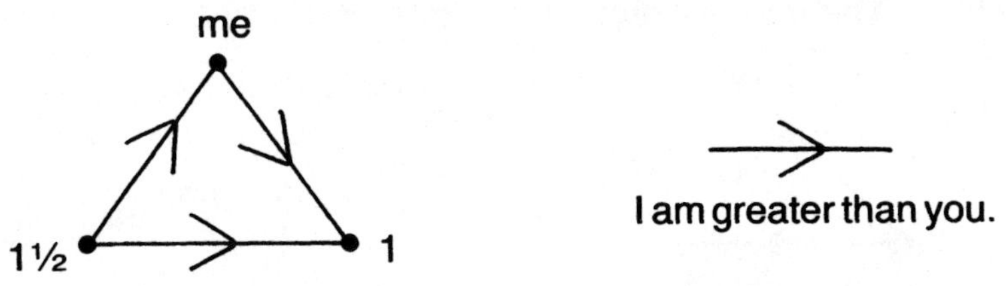

CLUE 2: I am not equal to $\frac{3}{4} + \frac{1}{2}$.

CLUE 3: I am not equal to $2\frac{1}{5} - \frac{4}{5}$.

CLUE 4: I am not equal to $4 \div 3$.

Who am I? ______

Case F-25

NUMBER SUSPECTS: $2\frac{1}{3}$, $2\frac{3}{5}$, $3\frac{1}{4}$, $3\frac{7}{8}$, $5\frac{4}{9}$, $5\frac{7}{9}$, $7\frac{1}{5}$, $7\frac{4}{5}$.

CLUE 1: I am less than 6.

CLUE 2: I am greater than 3.

CLUE 3: I am not equal to $\frac{20}{9} + \frac{29}{9}$.

CLUE 4: I am not equal to $4\frac{1}{8} - \frac{1}{4}$.

CLUE 5: I am not equal to $1\frac{1}{2} + 1\frac{3}{4}$.

Who am I? ______

Case F-26

NUMBER SUSPECTS: $1\frac{1}{4}$, $1\frac{3}{4}$, $2\frac{1}{7}$, $2\frac{5}{7}$, $3\frac{1}{8}$, $3\frac{7}{8}$, $4\frac{1}{7}$, $4\frac{5}{7}$.

CLUE 1: I am represented by the dot in the picture below.

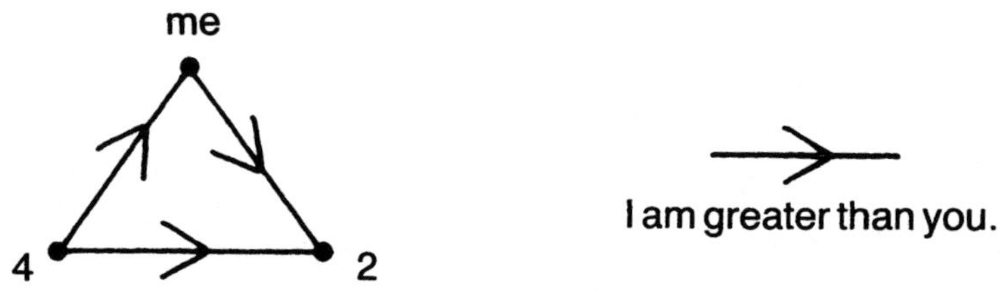

CLUE 2: I am not equal to $1\frac{2}{7} + \frac{6}{7}$.

CLUE 3: I am not equal to $4\frac{1}{4} - \frac{3}{8}$.

CLUE 4: I am not equal to $\frac{5}{2} \div \frac{4}{5}$.

Who am I? ______

In the next five detective stories, *all* of the number suspects are to be placed on the given diagram. Then you will be able to find the mystery number.

Case F-27

NUMBER SUSPECTS: $\frac{1}{2}$, $\frac{1}{3}$, $\frac{1}{4}$, $\frac{1}{6}$.

CLUE 1: The mystery number is represented by a dot in the picture below.

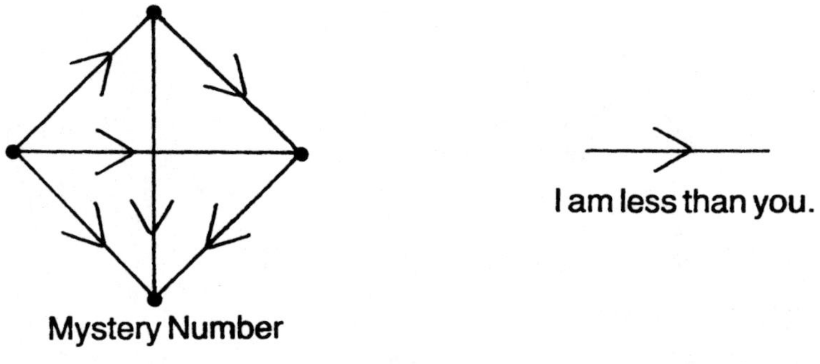

The number is ______.

Case F-28

NUMBER SUSPECTS: $\frac{1}{7}$, $\frac{2}{7}$, $\frac{3}{7}$, $\frac{4}{7}$.

CLUE 1: The mystery number is represented by a dot in the picture below.

The number is ______.

Case F-29

NUMBER SUSPECTS: $\frac{1}{2}$, $\frac{2}{3}$, $\frac{3}{4}$, $\frac{4}{5}$.

CLUE 1: The mystery number is represented by a dot in the picture below.

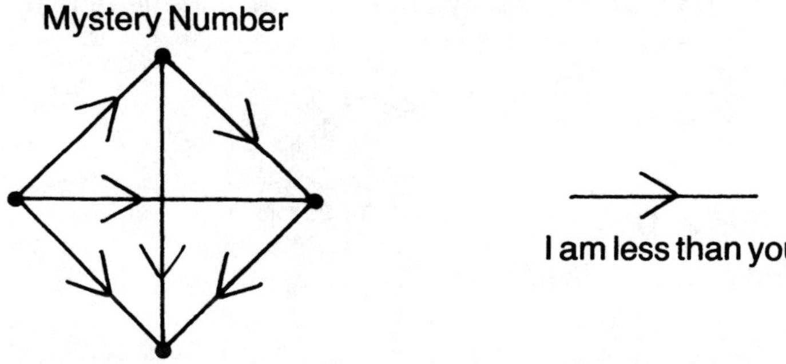

The number is ______.

Case F-30

NUMBER SUSPECTS: $\frac{1}{2}$, $\frac{1}{3}$, $\frac{1}{4}$, $\frac{1}{8}$.

CLUE 1: The mystery number is represented by a dot in the picture below.

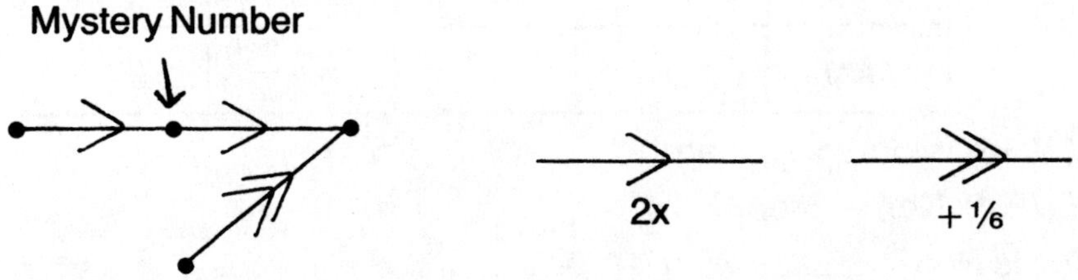

The number is ______.

Case F-31

NUMBER SUSPECTS: $1/7$, $3/7$, $6/7$, $9/7$, $3/14$, $1/21$.

CLUE 1: The mystery number is represented by a dot in the picture below.

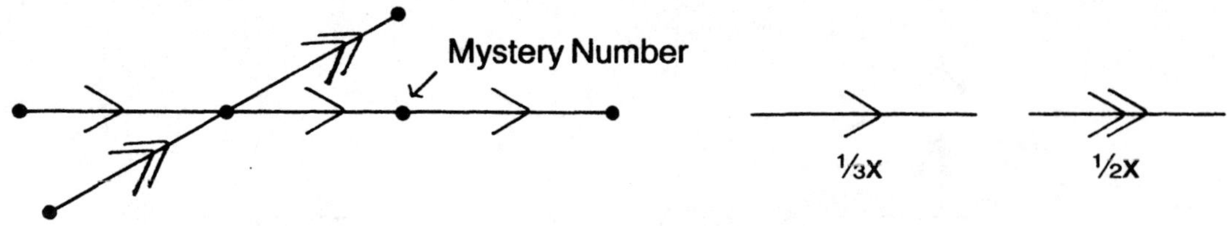

The number is ______.

In the next three detective stories you are to find two mystery numbers.

Case F-32

CLUE 1: Bip is represented by one of the dots in the picture below.

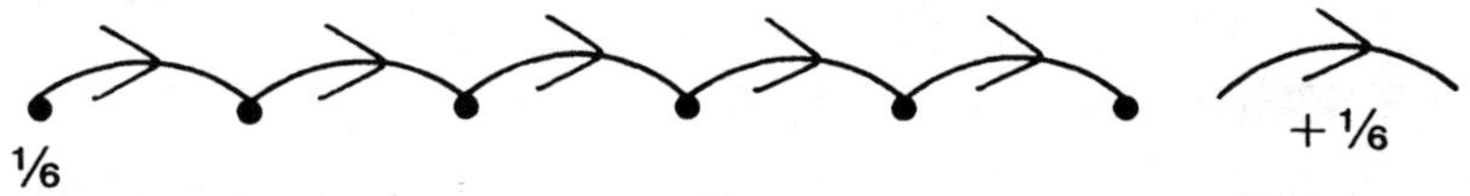

CLUE 2: Dip is represented by one of the dots in the picture below.

CLUE 3: Bip + Dip = $7/8$.

Who is Bip? ______ Who is Dip? ______

Case F-33

CLUE 1: Nop is represented by a dot in the picture below.

CLUE 2: Mop is the **double*** of Nop.

Nop				
Mop				

CLUE 3: Mop is less than 1.

CLUE 4: Nop + Mop $\neq$ $1/5$**.

Who is Nop? ______ Who is Mop? ______

11

*If for example Nop is $2/7$, then Mop is $\mathbf{2} \cdot 2/7$ or $4/7$.

The symbol $\neq$ means is **not equal to.

Case F-34

CLUE 1: Kip is represented by a dot in the picture below.

CLUE 2: Rip + Kip = 3.

Kip				
Rip				

CLUE 3: Rip − Kip = $\frac{1}{3}$.

Who is Kip? ______ Who is Rip? ______

The next four detective stories involve **PERCENTS.** Remember, for instance, that ¼ **= 1 ÷ 4 = .25 = 25%.**

Case F-35

NUMBER SUSPECTS: ½, ⅓, ⅔, ¼, ¾, ⅘.

CLUE 1: The number is greater than 50%.

CLUE 2: The number is not equal to 75%.

CLUE 3: The number is not equal to 80%.

The number is ______.

Case F-36

NUMBER SUSPECTS: ¼, ¾, ⅖, ⅗, ⅘, ⅒, 7/10.

CLUE 1: The number is less than .7.

CLUE 2: The number is greater than 30%.

CLUE 3: The number is not equal to 40%.

The number is ______.

Case F-37

NUMBER SUSPECTS: ¾, ⅕, ⅗, ⅘, ⅒, 3/10, 7/10, 9/10.

CLUE 1: The number is less than 50%.

CLUE 2: The number is not equal to .2.

CLUE 3: The number is not equal to 10%.

The number is ______.

Case F-38

NUMBER SUSPECTS: $1/2$, $1/3$, $1/4$, $3/4$, $2/5$, $3/5$, $4/5$, $1/8$, $3/10$.

CLUE 1: The mystery number is represented by the dot in the picture below.

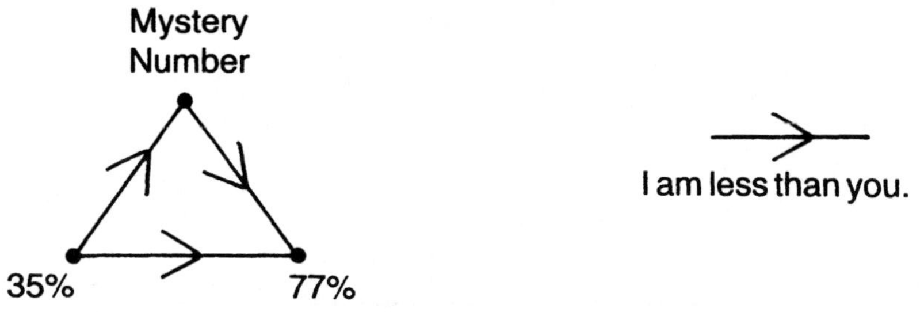

CLUE 2: The number is not 50%.

CLUE 3: The number is not 60%.

CLUE 4: The number is not 75%.

The number is ______.

Case F-39

CLUE 1: I am represented by the dot in the picture below.

Who am I? ______

Case F-40

CLUE 1: I am represented by the dot in the picture below.

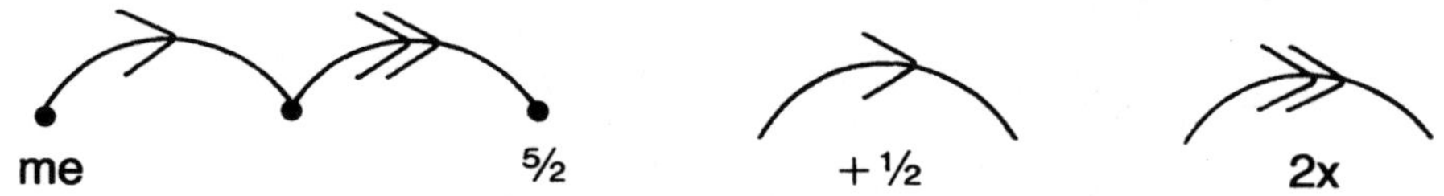

Who am I? ______

Case F-41

CLUE 1: I am represented by the dot in the picture below.

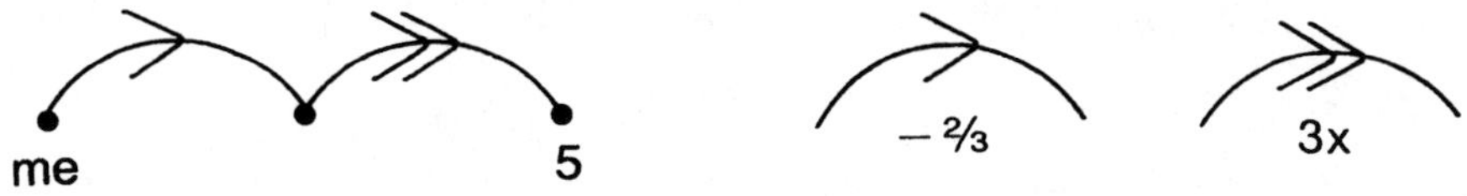

Who am I? ______

Case F-42

CLUE 1: I am represented by the dot in the picture below.

Who am I? ______

Case F-43

CLUE 1: I am represented by the dot in the picture below.

Who am I? ______

Case F-44

CLUE 1: I am represented by the dot in the picture below.

Who am I? ______

Case F-45

CLUE 1: I am one of the cards below.

A	B	C
$\frac{n}{5}$	$\frac{3}{4n}$	$\frac{12}{n} + 1$

CLUE 2: When n = 1 my value is less than 1.

CLUE 3: When n = 3 my value is greater than $\frac{1}{2}$.

Which card am I? ______

Case F-46

CLUE 1: I am one of the cards below.

A	B	C	D
$\frac{2}{3n}$	$\frac{n}{6}$	$n - \frac{5}{3}$	$\frac{5}{2} - \frac{n}{4}$

CLUE 2: When n = 2 my value is $\frac{1}{3}$.

CLUE 3: When n = 3 my value is not $\frac{2}{9}$.

CLUE 4: When n = 4 my value is not $\frac{7}{3}$.

Which card am I? ______

Case F-47

CLUE 1: I am one of the cards below.

A	B	C	D
$\frac{n+1}{5}$	$\frac{1}{3} + \frac{n}{2}$	$\frac{7}{n}$	$2 - \frac{2n}{3}$

CLUE 2: When n = 2 my value is greater than 1.

CLUE 3: When n = 5 my value is less than 2.

Which card am I? ______

CHAPTER III

DECIMALS AND PERCENT

The detective stories in this chapter concern decimals and percent. As in the first two chapters, you should use the clues to eliminate suspects. As you work with decimals, you must remember there are two basic kinds of decimals, those which terminate (end) and those which are nonterminating. For example, in Chapter II you found the decimal name for $\frac{3}{4}$ is 0.75 and 0.75 terminates, while the decimal name for $\frac{2}{3}$ is 0.6666... and 0.666... is nonterminating.

In the first three cases of this chapter, the mystery number has three places, a unit's (one's) place, a tenth's place, and a hundredth's place. For these cases, as soon as you identify the digit for any of these places, write the digit in the blank provided.

Case D-1

CLUE 1: The digit in the unit's place is 44 ÷ 11.

CLUE 2: The tenth's digit is 5 greater than the unit's digit.

CLUE 3: The sum of the tenth's digit and the hundredth's digit is 12.

The number is ___.______.

Case D-2

CLUE 1: The number is between 7 and 8.

CLUE 2: The hundredth's digit is 5 less than the unit's digit.

CLUE 3: The sum of the hundredth's digit and the tenth's digit is 8.

The number is ___.______.

Case D-3

CLUE 1: The sum of all three digits is 3.

CLUE 2: The digits are all different.

CLUE 3: The tenth's digit is less than the other two.

CLUE 4: The hundredth's digit is even.

The number is ___.___ ___.

Case D-4

NUMBER SUSPECTS: 2.7, 4.7, 5.6, 7.5, 9.3

CLUE 1: I am represented by the dot in the picture below.

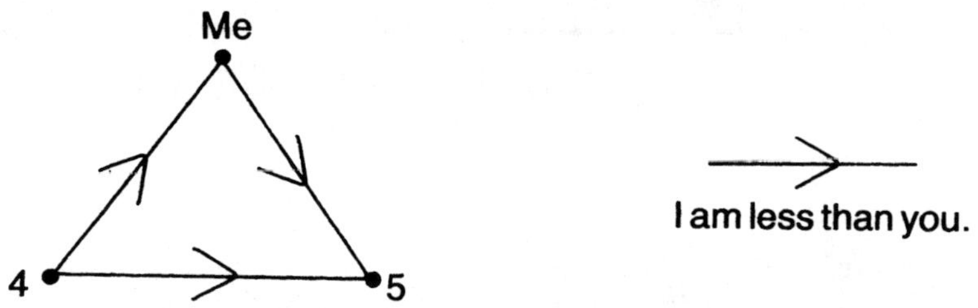

Who am I? ______

Case D-5

NUMBER SUSPECTS: 1.9, 3.8, 7.6, 11.4.

CLUE 1: I am represented by the dot in the picture below.

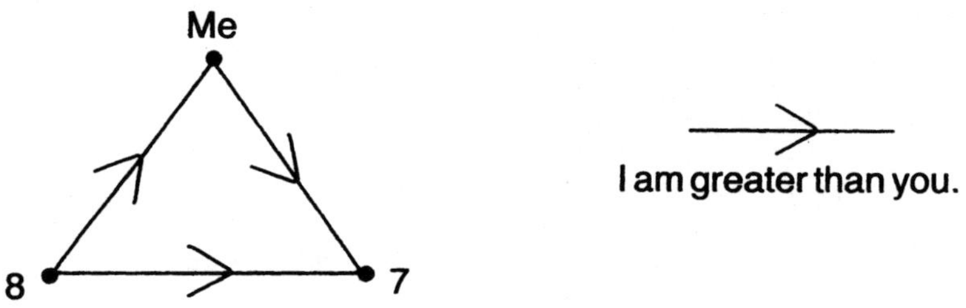

Who am I? ______

Case D-6

NUMBER SUSPECTS: 2.32, 2.49, 2.51, 2.71, 2.79, 2.81.

CLUE 1: I am represented by the dot in the picture below.

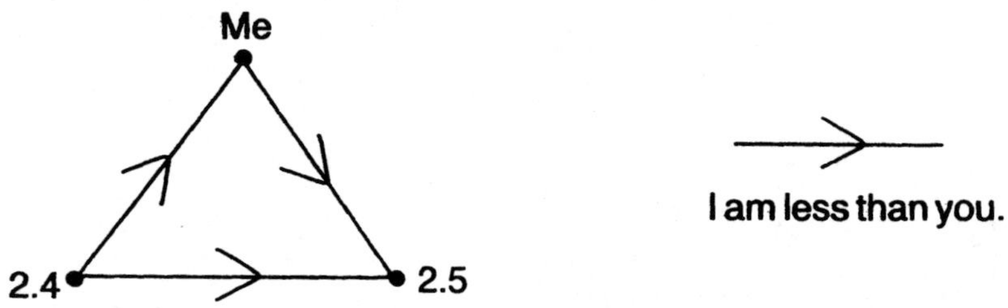

Who am I? ______

Case D-7

NUMBER SUSPECTS: 2.32, 2.49, 2.51, 2.71, 2.79, 2.81.

CLUE 1: I am represented by the dot in the picture below.

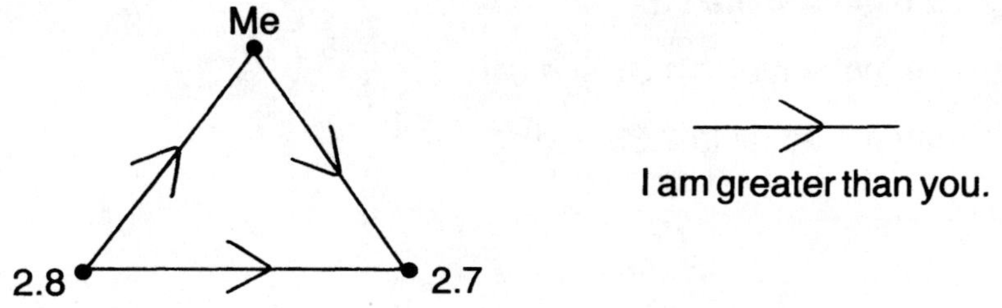

CLUE 2: I am not $^{279}/_{100}$.

Who am I? ______

Case D-8

NUMBER SUSPECTS: 0.35, 0.72, 1.36, 1.54, 1.777..., 1.81, 3.51.

CLUE 1: I am greater than 1.

CLUE 2: I am less than 2.

CLUE 3: I am a terminating decimal.

CLUE 4: My tenth's digit is prime.

CLUE 5: My hundredth's digit is not 4.

Who am I? ______

Case D-9

NUMBER SUSPECTS: 0.4, 0.6666..., 0.72, 0.75, 1.31, 1.46.

CLUE 1: I am less than 1.

CLUE 2: I am not equal to $^3/_4$.

CLUE 3: I am not equal to $^2/_3$.

CLUE 4: I am greater than $^1/_2$.

Who am I? ______

Case D-10

NUMBER SUSPECTS: 1.51, 2.61, 2.73, 3.74, 4.89.

CLUE 1: I am less than 4.

CLUE 2: I am greater than 2.

CLUE 3: I am not equal to $2 + {}^{73}/_{100}$.

CLUE 4: I am not equal to $^{374}/_{100}$.

Who am I? ______

Case D-11

NUMBER SUSPECTS: *0.46, 1.41, 1.48, 2.32, 3.49, 5.96.*

CLUE 1: I am greater than 2.

CLUE 2: I am not equal to 1.31 + 1.01.

CLUE 3: I am not equal to 2.36 + 1.13.

Who am I? ______

Case D-12

NUMBER SUSPECTS: *0.46, 1.95, 3.56, 4.85, 5.26, 8.14.*

CLUE 1: I am less than 4.

CLUE 2: I am not equal to 2.38 + 1.18.

CLUE 3: I am not equal to 4.65 − 2.70.

Who am I? ______

Case D-13

NUMBER SUSPECTS: *4.21, 4.63, 4.76, 4.87, 4.98.*

CLUE 1: I am greater than 4.6.

CLUE 2: I am not equal to 1.56 + 3.31.

CLUE 3: I am not equal to 9.74 − 5.11.

CLUE 4: I am not equal to 8.93 − 4.17.

Who am I? ______

Case D-14

NUMBER SUSPECTS: *1.7, 3.8, 4.2, 6.1, 8.3.*

CLUE 1: I am represented by the dot in the picture below.

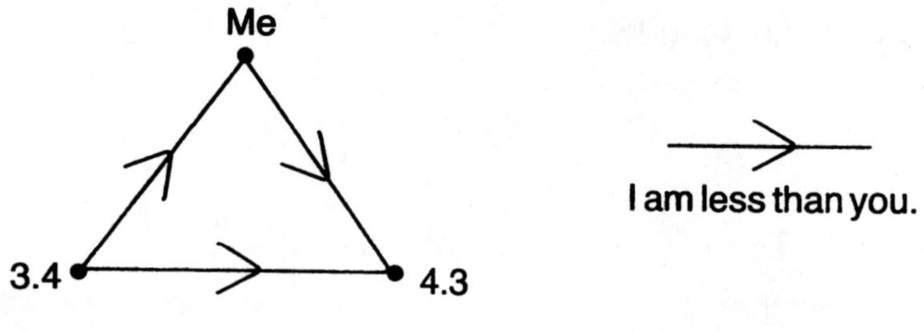

CLUE 2: I am not equal to 2.7 + 1.5.

Who am I? ______

Case D-15

NUMBER SUSPECTS: 0.3333..., 0.4, 0.616161..., 0.8, 1.3333..., 4.9.

CLUE 1: I am represented by the dot in the picture below.

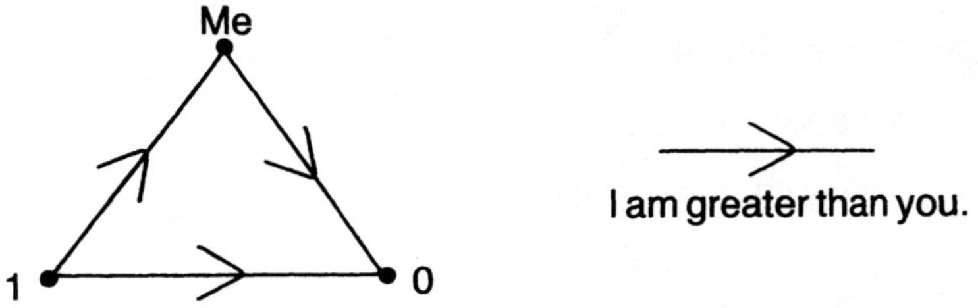

CLUE 2: I am a nonterminating decimal.

CLUE 3: I am not equal to ⅓.

Who am I? ______

Case D-16

NUMBER SUSPECTS: 0.25, 0.3333..., 0.5, 0.6, 0.6666..., 0.75, 0.875.

CLUE 1: I am greater than ½.

CLUE 2: I am a terminating decimal.

CLUE 3: I am not equal to ⅗.

CLUE 4: I am not equal to ⅞.

Who am I? ______

Case D-17

NUMBER SUSPECTS: 0.25, 0.3333..., 0.5, 0.6, 0.75, 0.875.

CLUE 1: I am less than ¾.

CLUE 2: I am not equal to 50%.

CLUE 3: I am not equal to ¼.

CLUE 4: I am a terminating decimal.

Who am I? ______

Case D-18

NUMBER SUSPECTS: 0.1, 0.2, 0.25, 0.3333..., 0.5, 0.6666..., 0.75, 0.875.

CLUE 1: I am greater than ¼.

CLUE 2: I am not equal to ⅓.

CLUE 3: I am less than ⅘.

CLUE 4: I am not equal to ¾.

CLUE 5: I am not equal to ½.

Who am I? ______

Case D-19

NUMBER SUSPECTS: 0.31, 0.37, 0.42, 0.46, 0.82, 0.95, 1.02.

CLUE 1: I am less than 90%.

CLUE 2: I am greater than 40%.

CLUE 3: I am not equal to $\frac{21}{50}$.

CLUE 4: I am not equal to 46 ÷ 100.

Who am I? ______

Case D-20

NUMBER SUSPECTS: 0.73, 0.79, 0.84, 0.97, 1.04, 1.25, 1.34.

CLUE 1: I am greater than 100%.

CLUE 2: I am not equal to $\frac{134}{100}$.

CLUE 3: I am not equal to $1\frac{1}{4}$.

Who am I? ______

Case D-21

NUMBER SUSPECTS: 0.2, 0.45, 0.62, 0.75, 0.93, 2.89.

CLUE 1: I am greater than 50%.

CLUE 2: I am less than 200%.

CLUE 3: I am not equal to $\frac{3}{4}$.

CLUE 4: I am not equal to 93%.

Who am I? ______

Case D-22

NUMBER SUSPECTS: 0.232323..., 0.54, 0.7777..., 0.851851851... .

CLUE 1: I am a nonterminating decimal.

CLUE 2: I do not have 3 digits in my **repeating block***.

CLUE 3: I am not equal to $\frac{23}{99}$.

Who am I? ______

---

*For example, the nonterminating decimal .858585... has **two** digits in the **REPEATING BLOCK** since 85 is repeated over and over again, while .777... has **one** digit in the repeating block.

Case D-23

NUMBER SUSPECTS: 0.434343..., 0.5555.... 0.72, 0.731731731..., 0.818181..., 0.82.

CLUE 1: I am a nonterminating decimal.

CLUE 2: I have two digits in my repeating block.

CLUE 3: I am not equal to $\frac{9}{11}$.

Who am I? ______

Case D-24

NUMBER SUSPECTS: 3.92, 4.61, 5.24, 7.53, 8.26.

CLUE 1: I am not equal to $7 + 5(0.1) + 3(0.01)$.

CLUE 2: I am not equal to $4 + 6(0.1) + 1(0.01)$.

CLUE 3: I am not equal to $8 + 2(0.1) + 6(0.01)$.

CLUE 4: I am greater than 4.

Who am I? ______

Case D-25

NUMBER SUSPECTS: 2.58, 3.64, 5.24, 7.43, 9.16.

CLUE 1: I am not equal to $5 + (2 \times \frac{1}{10}) + (4 \times \frac{1}{100})$.

CLUE 2: I am not equal to $9 + (1 \times \frac{1}{10}) + (6 \times \frac{1}{100})$.

CLUE 3: I am not equal to $3 + (6 \times \frac{1}{10}) + (4 \times \frac{1}{100})$.

CLUE 4: I am greater than 3.

Who am I? ______

Case D-26

NUMBER SUSPECTS: 1.32, 3.12, 3.78, 5.91, 6.73.

CLUE 1: I am less than $1.92 + 4.81$.

CLUE 2: I am not equal to $(5 \times 10^0) + (9 \times 10^{-1}) + (1 \times 10^{-2})$.*

CLUE 3: I am not equal to 1.1×1.2.

CLUE 4: I am not equal to 2.1×1.8.

Who am I? ______

***Remember** $10^0 = 1$, $10^{-1} = \frac{1}{10}$ **and** $10^{-2} = \frac{1}{10^2}$.

Case D-27

NUMBER SUSPECTS: 1.4, 2.7, 4.8, 8.3, 11.2.

CLUE 1: I am greater than 3.

CLUE 2: I am not equal to 24 × 0.2.

CLUE 3: I am not equal to 0.249 ÷ 0.03.

Who am I? ______

Case D-28

NUMBER SUSPECTS: 2.81, 3.47, 3.85, 4.76, 5.21.

CLUE 1: I am not equal to 28.1 × 0.1.

CLUE 2: I am not equal to .952 ÷ 0.2.

CLUE 3: I am not equal to 15.63 ÷ 3.

CLUE 4: I am not equal to 0.77 × 5.

Who am I? ______

Case D-29

CLUE 1: I am represented by one of the dots pictured below.

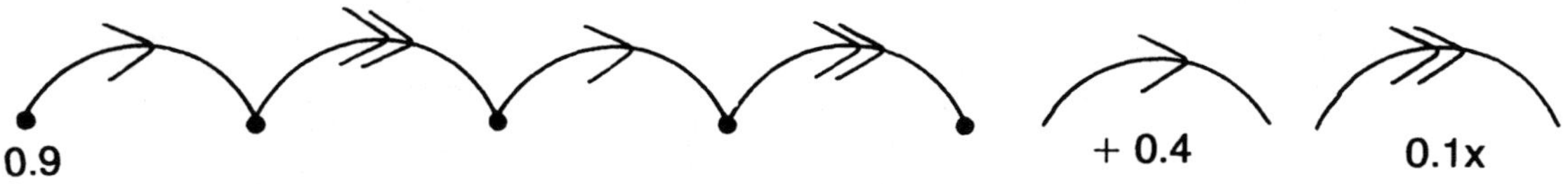

CLUE 2: I am less than 1.

CLUE 3: I am greater than 0.2

CLUE 4: I am not equal to 90%.

Who am I? ______

In the next two cases, you are to place each number suspect on the arrow picture and then find the mystery number.

Case D-30

NUMBER SUSPECTS: 0.1, 0.6, 0.8, 0.9, 1.1.

CLUE 1: I am represented by the dot in the picture below.

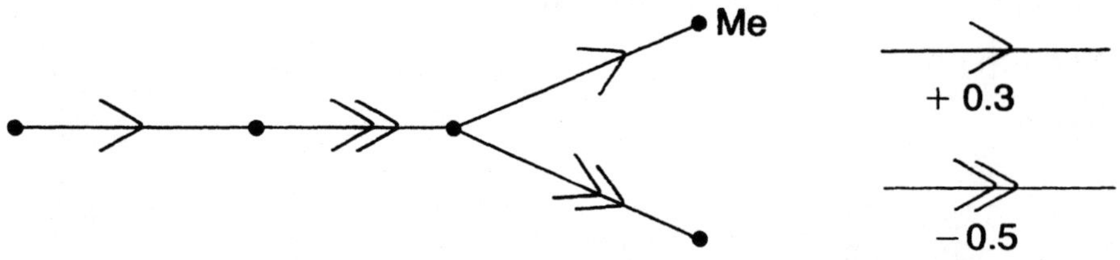

Who am I? ______

Case D-31

NUMBER SUSPECTS: 0.3, 0.5, 0.6, 0.7, 0.8, 0.9.

CLUE 1: I am represented by the dot in the picture below.

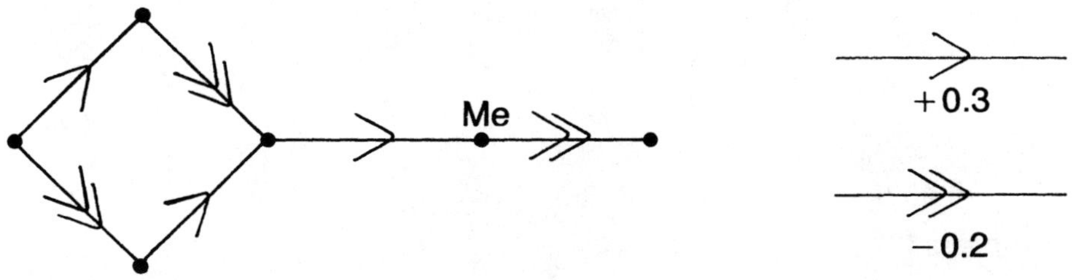

Who am I? ______

Case D-32

CLUE 1: I am represented by the dot in the picture below.

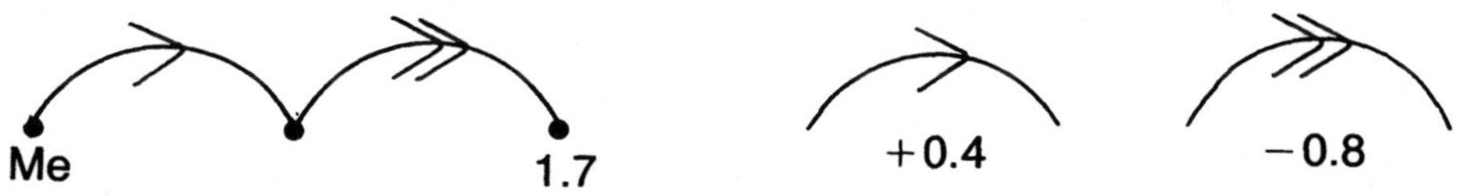

Who am I? ______

Case D-33

CLUE 1: I am represented by the dot in the picture below.

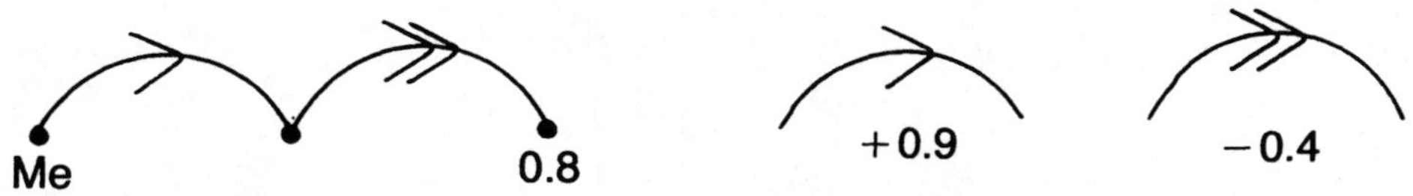

Who am I? ______

Case D-34

CLUE 1: I am represented by the dot in the picture below.

Who am I? ______

Case D-35

CLUE 1: I am represented by the dot in the picture below.

Who am I? ______

Case D-36

CLUE 1: I am represented by the dot in the picture below.

Who am I? ______

Case D-37

CLUE 1: I am represented by the dot in the picture below.

Who am I? ______

Case D-38

CLUE 1: I am represented by the dot in the picture below.

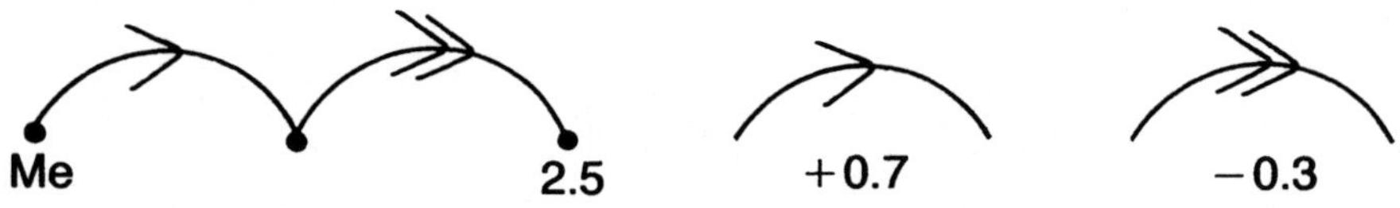

Who am I? ______

Case D-39

CLUE 1: I am represented by the dot in the picture below.

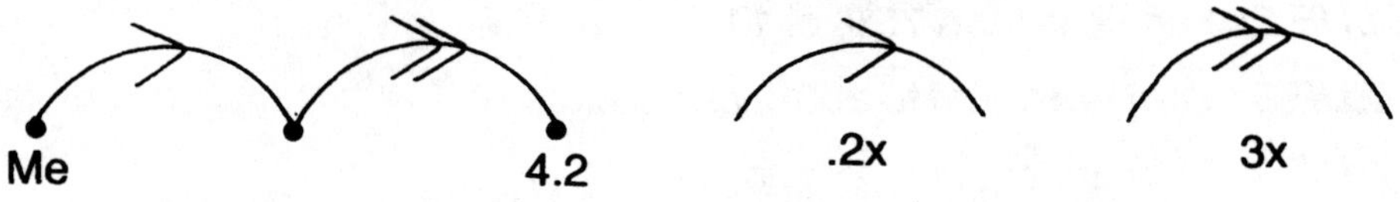

Who am I? ______

Case D-40

CLUE 1: I am represented by the dot in the picture below.

Who am I? ______

Case D-41

NUMBER SUSPECTS: 2.3, 3.5, 3.6.

CLUE 1: I am not 50% of 7.

CLUE 2: I am not 75% of 4.8.

Who am I? ______

Case D-42

NUMBER SUSPECTS: 2.8, 3.9, 5.2, 6.6, 7.5.

CLUE 1: I am greater than 80% of 5.

CLUE 2: I am not equal to 150% of 5.

CLUE 3: I am not equal to 200% of 3.3.

Who am I? ______

Case D-43

NUMBER SUSPECTS: 1.6, 3.7, 5.2, 7.1.

CLUE 1: I am less than 50% of 10.

CLUE 2: I am not equal to 50% of 3.2.

Who am I? ______

Case D-44

NUMBER SUSPECTS: 1.4, 2.5, 3.9, 5.4, 8.5.

CLUE 1: I am greater than 50% of 3.

CLUE 2: I am less than 75% of 10.

CLUE 3: I am not equal to 200% of 1.25.

CLUE 4: I am not equal to 25% of 21.6.

Who am I? ______

In the next four cases you are to identify two mystery numbers.

Case D-45

CLUE 1: Kae is represented by a dot in the picture below.

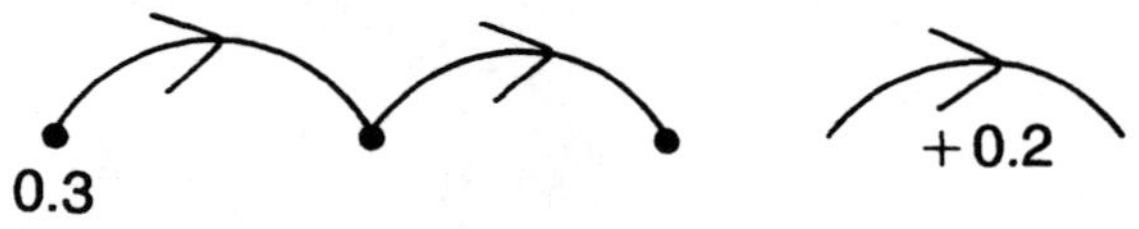

_____, _____, _____

CLUE 2: Fae is represented by a dot in the picture below.

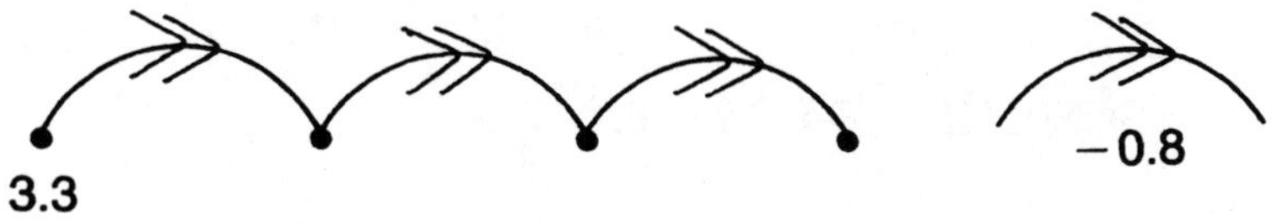

_____, _____, _____, _____

CLUE 3: Fae − Kae = 2.

Who is Kae? ______ Who is Fae? ______

Case D-46

CLUE 1: Moe is represented by a dot in the picture below.

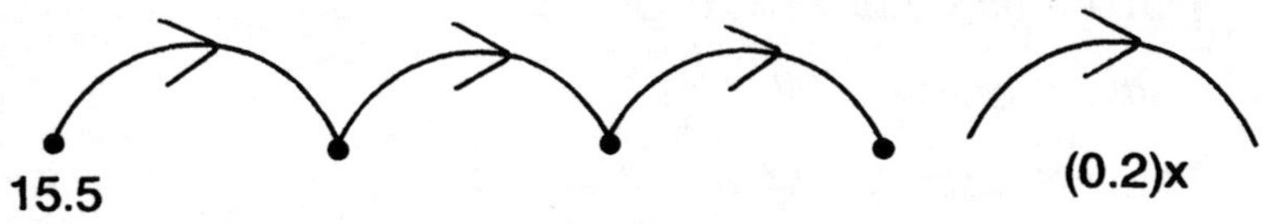

CLUE 2: Joe = Moe + 1

Moe				
Joe				

CLUE 3: Moe + Joe = 7.2.

Who is Moe? ______ Who is Joe? ______

Case D-47

CLUE 1: Rob is represented by a dot in the picture below.

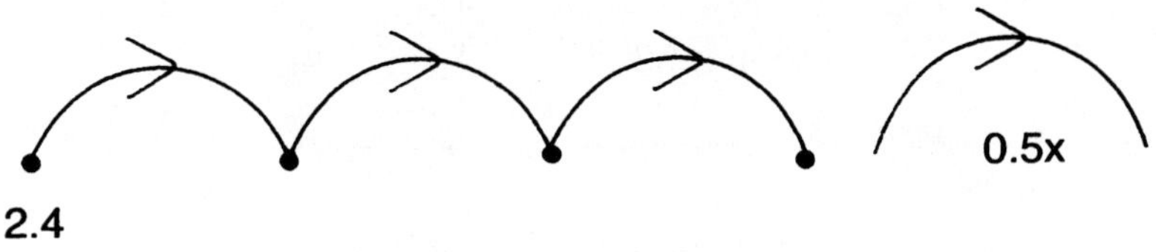

____, ____, ____, ____

CLUE 2: Bob is represented by a dot in the picture below.

____, ____, ____, ____, ____

CLUE 3: Bob $>$1.

CLUE 4: Rob $<$ 1.

CLUE 5: Rob $+$ Bob $<$ 2.

Who is Rob? ______ Who is Bob? ______

Case D-48

CLUE 1: Dop is represented by a dot in the picture below.

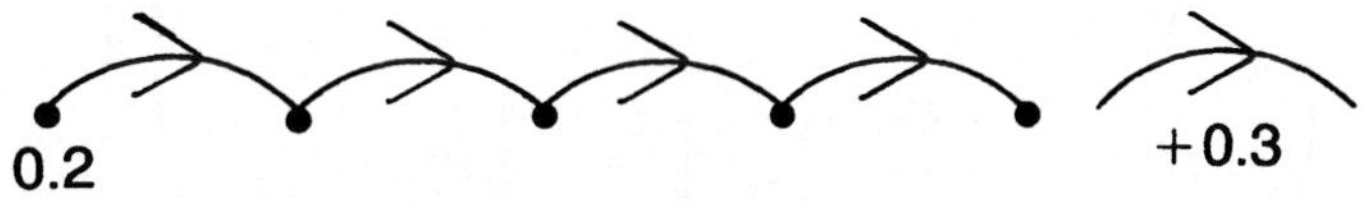

____, ____, ____, ____, ____

CLUE 2: Fop $=$ 2 Dop.

Dop					
Fop					

CLUE 3: Dop $>$ 1.

CLUE 4: Dop $+$ Fop $\neq$ 4.2.

Who is Dop? ______ Who is Fop? ______

Case D-49

CLUE 1: I am one of the cards below.

A	B	C
$.21/n$	$n + 0.03$	$n/0.3$

CLUE 2: When $n = 3$, my value is greater than 1.

CLUE 3: When $n = 6$, my value is less than 10.

Which card am I? ______

Case D-50

CLUE 1: I am one of the cards below.

A	B	C
$0.13 + n$	$4/n$	$0.0014/n$

CLUE 2: When $n = 0.01$, my value is 0.14.

CLUE 3: When $n = 0.02$, my value is greater than 0.14.

Which card am I? ______

Case D-51

CLUE 1: I am one of the cards below.

A	B	C	D
$0.2/n$	$1 - n/2$	$n/0.001$	$3 + n$

CLUE 2: When $n = 0.1$, my value is less than 100.

CLUE 3: When $n = 0.2$, my value is not 1.

CLUE 4: When $n = 0.4$, my value is not 0.8.

Which card am I? ______

Case D-52

NUMBER SUSPECTS: 14%, 23%, 45%, 68%, 90%.

CLUE 1: I am greater than 0.5.

CLUE 2: I am less than 0.7.

Who am I? ______

Case D-53

NUMBER SUSPECTS: 25%, 35%, 47%, 49%, 57%, 62%.

CLUE 1: I am less than 50%.

CLUE 2: I am not equal to $^{49}/_{100}$.

CLUE 3: I am not equal to 0.25.

CLUE 4: I am not equal to 0.35.

Who am I? ______

Case D-54

NUMBER SUSPECTS: 14%, 29%, 43%, 53%, 71%, 94%.

CLUE 1: I am greater than 30%.

CLUE 2: I am less than 90%.

CLUE 3: I am not equal to 0.53.

CLUE 4: I am not equal to $^{71}/_{100}$.

Who am I? ______

Case D-55

NUMBER SUSPECTS: 13%, 27%, 45%, 75%, 80%, 93%.

CLUE 1: I am greater than $^{1}/_{2}$.

CLUE 2: I am not equal to $^{3}/_{4}$.

CLUE 3: I am not equal to $^{4}/_{5}$.

Who am I? ______

Case D-56

NUMBER SUSPECTS: 28%, 72%, 95%, 114%, 125%, 150%.

CLUE 1: I am greater than 1.

CLUE 2: I am not equal to $^{5}/_{4}$.

CLUE 3: I am not equal to $^{3}/_{2}$.

Who am I? ______

Case D-57

NUMBER SUSPECTS: 4%, 17%, 29%, 56%, 73%, 85%, 97%, 101%.

CLUE 1: I am represented by the dot in the picture below.

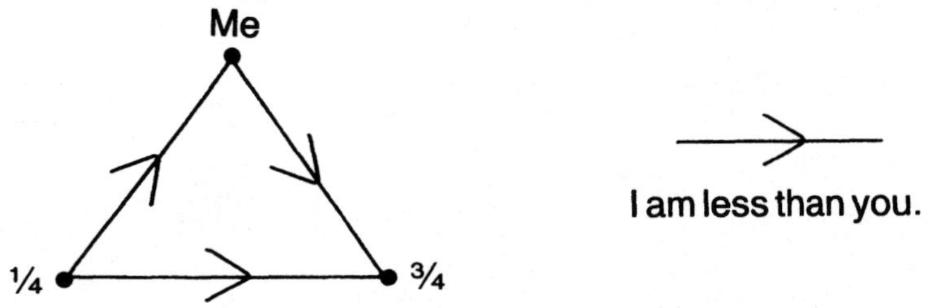

CLUE 2: I am not equal to $^{56}/_{100}$.

CLUE 3: I am not equal to 0.29.

Who am I? ______

Case D-58

NUMBER SUSPECTS: 17%, 23%, 41%, 56%, 87%, 93%.

CLUE 1: I am represented by the dot in the picture below.

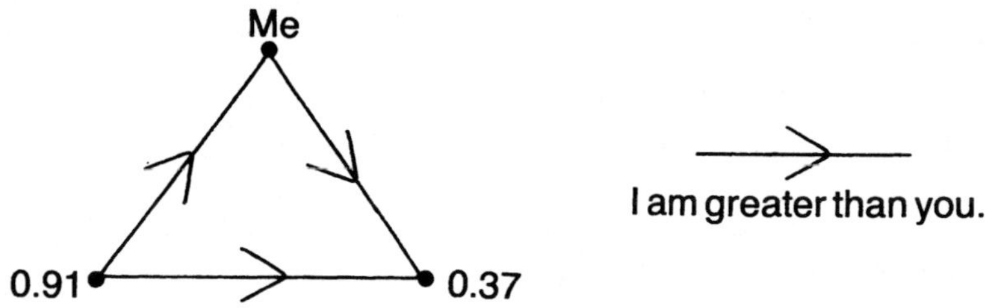

CLUE 2: I am not equal to 42% + 45%.

CLUE 3: I am not equal to 112% ÷ 2.

Who am I? ______

Case D-59

NUMBER SUSPECTS: 40%, 60%, 75%, 80%, 90%.

CLUE 1: I am not the percent that 12 is of 16.

CLUE 2: I am not the percent that 18 is of 20.

CLUE 3: I am greater than 0.62.

Who am I? ______

Case D-60

NUMBER SUSPECTS: 25%, 40%, 50%, 75%, 90%.

CLUE 1: I am not the percent that 3 is of 12.

CLUE 2: I am not the percent that 9 is of 12.

CLUE 3: I am not the percent that 6 is of 12.

CLUE 4: I am less than 80%.

Who am I? ______

CHAPTER IV

INTEGERS

The integers are the numbers ... $-3, -2, -1, 0, 1, 2, 3, \ldots$. Each case in this chapter will refer to integers and the mystery number or numbers will be integers.

Case I-1

CLUE 1: I am an integer between -4 and 2.

____, ____, ____, ____, ____

CLUE 2: I am not equal to $-7 + 4$.

CLUE 3: I am not equal to $6 + (-5)$.

CLUE 4: I am not the identity number for addition.

CLUE 5: I am not equal to $2 - 3$.

Who am I? ______

Case I-2

CLUE 1: I am a negative integer greater than -6.

____, ____, ____, ____, ____

CLUE 2: I am less than -2.

CLUE 3: I am not equal to $-2 + (-1)$.

CLUE 4: I am not equal to $2 - 6$.

Who am I? ______

Case I-3

CLUE 1: I am an integer between -3 and 3.

____, ____, ____, ____, ____

CLUE 2: My **additive inverse (opposite)*** is a negative integer.

CLUE 3: I am not the identity number for multiplication.

Who am I? ______

***The sum of a number and its ADDITIVE INVERSE is 0**. For instance, the additive inverse of -3 is 3 because $-3 + 3 = 0$.

Case I-4

CLUE 1: I am represented by one of the dots in the picture below.

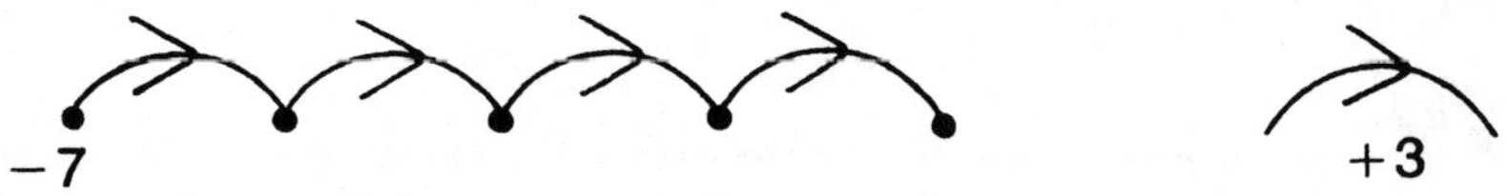

______, ______, ______, ______, ______

CLUE 2: My additive inverse is a positive number.

CLUE 3: I am not equal to $-3 + (-1)$.

CLUE 4: I am not equal to $-4 - 3$.

Who am I? ______

Case I-5

CLUE 1: I am an integer between -3 and 3.

______, ______, ______, ______, ______

CLUE 2: I am not a negative integer.

CLUE 3: I am not a positive integer.

Who am I? ______

Case I-6

CLUE 1: I am represented by one of the dots in the picture below.

______, ______, ______, ______, ______, ______

CLUE 2: I am greater than $20 \div (-4)$.

CLUE 3: I am less than $(-18) \div 9$.

Who am I? ______

Case I-7

CLUE 1: I am represented by one of the dots in the picture below.

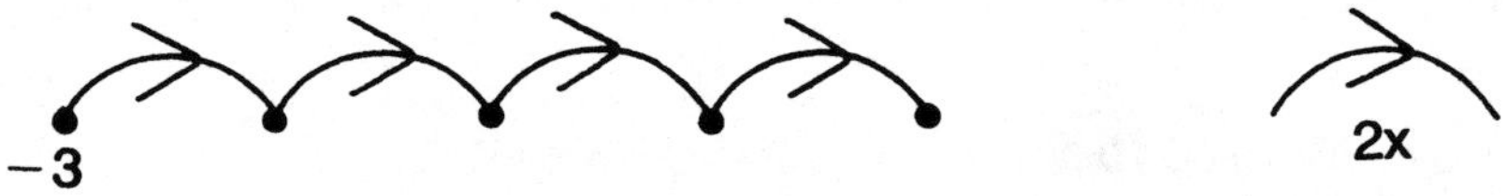

______, ______, ______, ______, ______

CLUE 2: I am not equal to $(-6) \times 4$.

CLUE 3: I am not equal to $(-36) \div 12$.

CLUE 4: I am not equal to $4 \times (-3)$.

CLUE 5: I am greater than -25.

Who am I? ______

Case I-8

CLUE 1: I am an even integer between -5 and 3.

_____, _____, _____, _____

CLUE 2: I am not the identity number for addition.

CLUE 3: I am not $-(-2)$.

CLUE 4: I am greater than -3.

Who am I? ______

Case I-9

NUMBER SUSPECTS: -6, -5, -2, -1, 5, 7.

CLUE 1: The number is represented by one of the dots in the picture below.

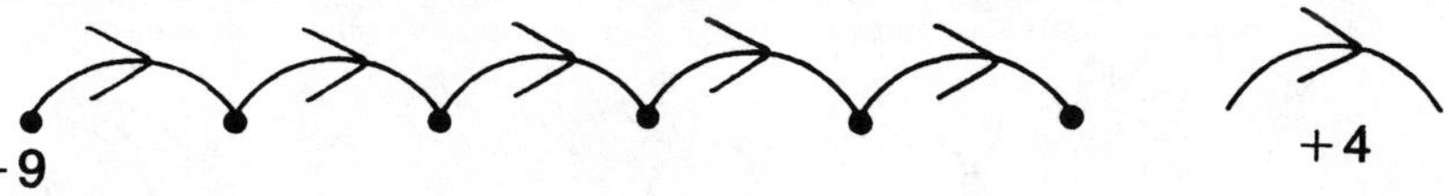

CLUE 2: The number is not equal to $-(-7)$.

CLUE 3: The additive inverse of the number is not 1.

The number is ______.

Case I-10

NUMBER SUSPECTS: -8, -7, -4, -3, 1, 2, 5.

CLUE 1: The number is represented by one of the dots in the picture below.

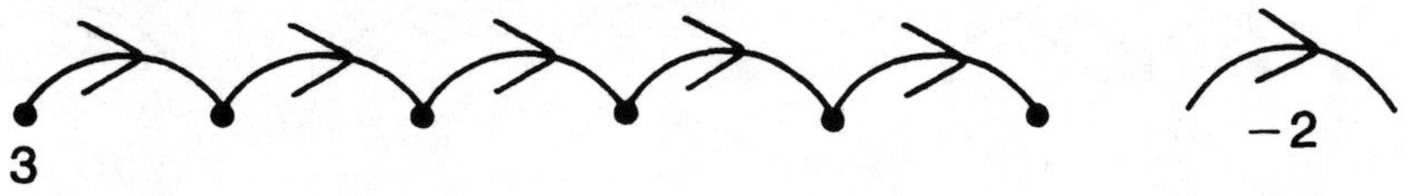

CLUE 2: The additive inverse of the number is greater than 2.

CLUE 3: The number is greater than -6.

The number is ______.

Case I-11

CLUE 1: I am represented by the dot in the picture below.

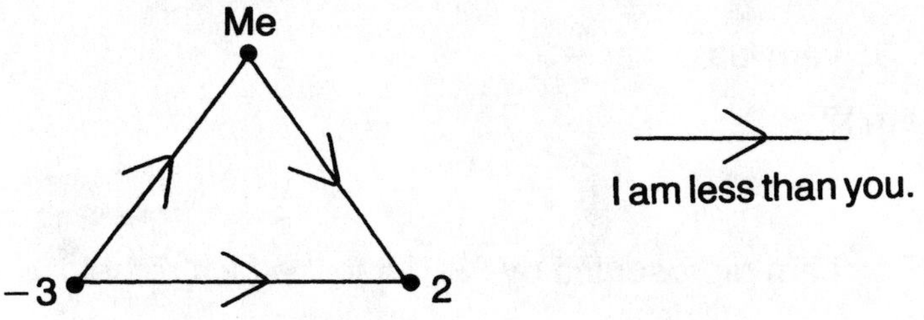

_____, _____, _____, _____

CLUE 2: I am a negative integer.

CLUE 3: I am not equal to $756 \div (-756)$.

Who am I? ______

Case I-12

CLUE 1: I am represented by the dot in the picture below.

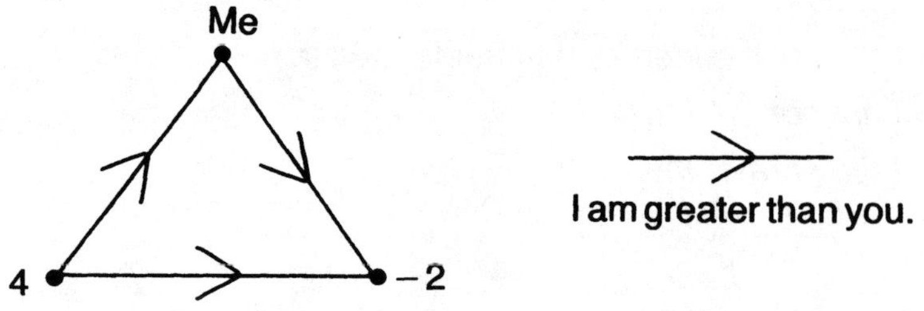

____, ____, ____, ____, ____

CLUE 2: I am represented by a dot in the picture below.

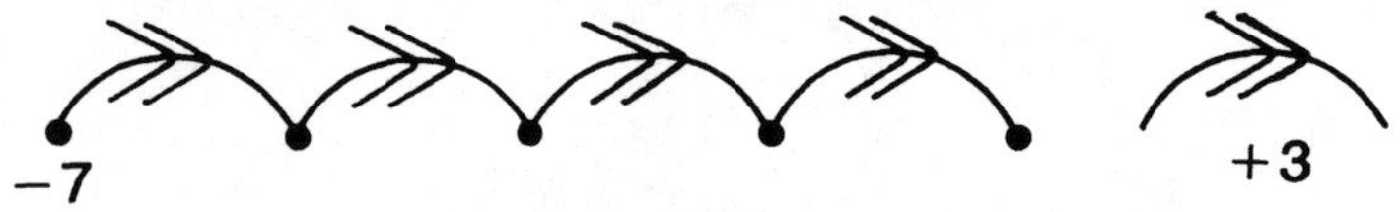

CLUE 3: My additive inverse is not 1.

Who am I? ______

Case I-13

CLUE 1: I am represented by one of the dots in the picture below.

____, ____, ____, ____, ____, ____

CLUE 2: I am represented by one of the dots in the picture below.

CLUE 3: I am less than −3.

Who am I? ______

Case I-14

CLUE 1: I am represented by the dot in the picture below.

Who am I? ______

Case I-15

CLUE 1: I am represented by the dot in the picture below.

Who am I? ______

Case I-16

CLUE 1: I am represented by the dot in the picture below.

Who am I? ______

Case I-17

CLUE 1: I am represented by the dot in the picture below.

Who am I? ______

The next five cases all require you to identify properties concerning addition and multiplication of integers. Here is a list of these properties.

PROPERTIES OF INTEGERS

For any integer **a**, for any integer **b**, for any integer **c**,

$a + b = b + a$	Commutative Property of Addition
$ab = ba$	Commutative Property of Multiplication
$(a + b) + c = a + (b + c)$	Associative Property of Addition
$(ab)c = a(bc)$	Associative Property of Multiplication
$a + 0 = a$	Identity Property of Addition
$a \cdot 1 = a$	Identity Property of Multiplication
$a + -a = 0$	Additive Inverse Property
$a(b + c) = ab + ac$	Distributive Property

A particular sentence which fits the pattern of a property is called an instance of that property. For example, $7 + 2 = 2 + 7$ is an instance of the Commutative Property of Addition.

Case I-18

CLUE 1: I am one of the properties named below.
Associative Property of Addition (APA)
Identity Property of Addition (IPA)
Additive Inverse Property (AIP)
Distributive Property (DP)

CLUE 2: The following sentence is an instance of me.
$11 + (-11) = 0$

Which property am I? ______

Case I-19

CLUE: 1: I am one of the properties named below.
Associative Property of Addition (APA)
Commutative Property of Addition (CPA)
Distributive Property (DP)

CLUE 2: The following sentence is an instance of me.
$3 + (4 + 2) = (3 + 4) + 2$

Which property am I? ______

Case I-20

CLUE I: I am one of the properties named below.
Commutative Property of Multiplication (CPM)
Associative Property of Multiplication (APM)
Identity Property of Multiplication (IPM)

CLUE 2: The following sentence is not an instance of me.
$(-7)1 = -7$

CLUE 3: The following sentence is not an instance of me.
$(3 \cdot 7)11 = 3(7 \cdot 11)$

Which property am I? ______

Case I-21

CLUE 1: I am one of the properties named below.
Commutative Property of Addition (CPA)
Identity Property of Addition (IPA)
Additive Inverse Property (AIP)

CLUE 2: The following sentence is not an instance of me.
$-9 + 0 = -9$

CLUE 3: The following sentence is not an instance of me.
$7 + (-7) = 0$

Which property am I? ______

Case I-22

CLUE 1: I am one of the properties named below.
Associative Property of Multiplication (APM)
Commutative Property of Multiplication (CPM)
Distributive Property (DP)

CLUE 2: The following sentence is not an instance of me.
$7[2 + (-3)] = 7 \cdot 2 + 7(-3)$

CLUE 3: The following sentence is not an instance of me.
$7(2 \cdot 6) = (2 \cdot 6)7$

Which property am I? ______

In the next four cases, place all the number suspects on the arrow picture and then determine the mystery number.

Case I-23

NUMBER SUSPECTS: −9, −6, −3, 3, 12, 18.

CLUE 1: I am represented by the dot in the picture below.

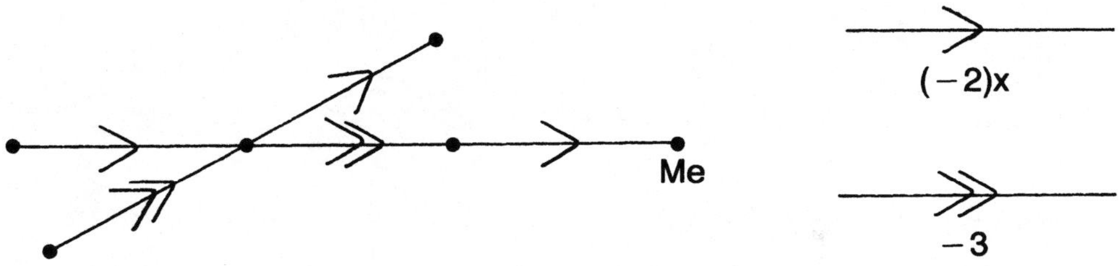

Who am I? ______

Case I-24

NUMBER SUSPECTS: −25, −3, −1, 1, 5, 9.

CLUE 1: I am represented by the dot in the picture below.

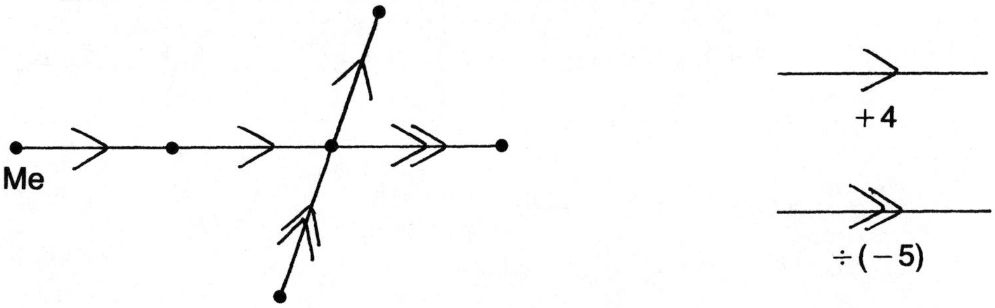

Who am I? ______

Case I-25

NUMBER SUSPECTS: $-10, -5, 0, 5, 10.$

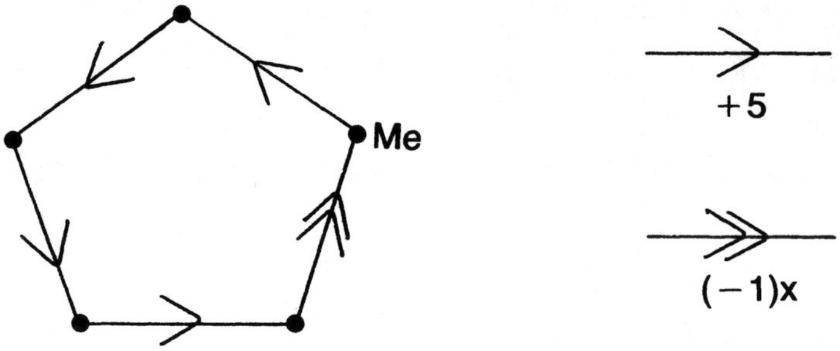

Who am I? ______

Case I-26

NUMBER SUSPECTS: $-10, -7, -4, -1, 2, 8, 11.$

CLUE 1: I am represented by the dot in the picture below.

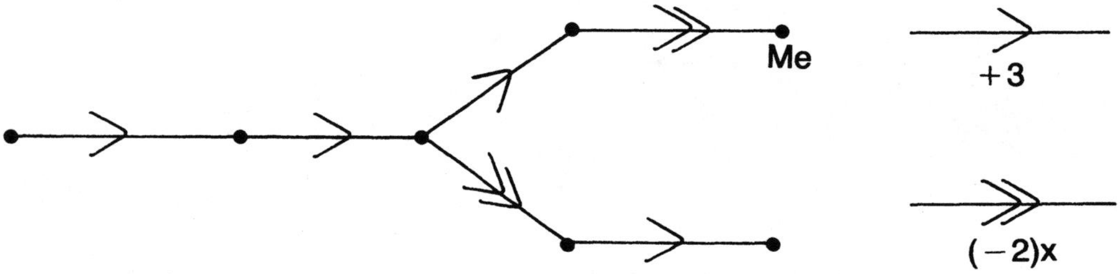

Who am I? ______

Case I-27

CLUE 1: I am one of the cards below.

A	B	C	D
$n - 2$	$7 - n$	$n/2$	$2n + 1$

CLUE 2: When $n = 2$, my value is 5.

CLUE 3: When $n = -3$, my value is -5.

Which card am I? ______

Case I-28

CLUE 1: I am one of the cards below.

A	B	C	D	E
$9 - n$	$\frac{n+1}{2}$	$3n + 2$	$2n - 1$	$4(n + 1)$

CLUE 2: When $n = -3$, my value is -7.

CLUE 3: When $n = -2$, my value is -4.

Which card am I? ______

Case I-29

CLUE 1: I am one of the cards below.

A	B	C	D
$n + 3$	$n - 3$	$2n - 1$	$4 - 6n$

E	F
$4/n$	$9 - 2n$

CLUE 2: When $n = 4$, my value is 1.

CLUE 3: When $n = -1$, my value is -4.

CLUE 4: When $n = -4$, my value is -1.

Which card am I? ______

Case I-30

CLUE 1: I am one of the cards below.

A	B	C	D	E
$9 - n$	$n + 5$	$2n - 3$	$14/n$	$5n$

CLUE 2: When $n = 2$, my value is 7.

CLUE 3: When $n = 7$, my value is 2.

CLUE 4: When $n = -7$, my value is -2.

Which card am I? ______

In the next six cases, you will be finding two numbers.

Case I-31

CLUE 1: Tam is represented by a dot in the picture below.

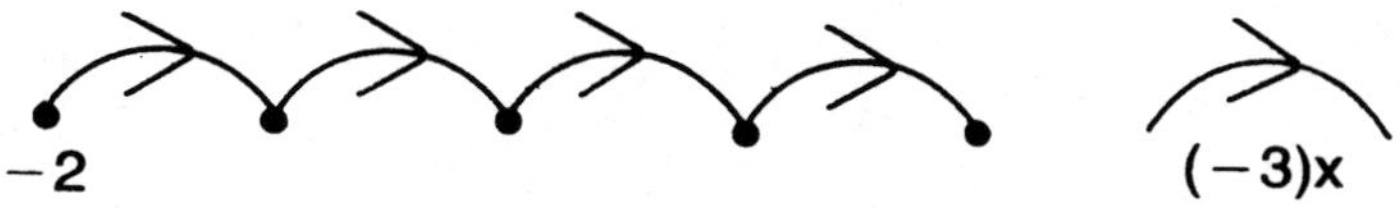

____, ____, ____, ____, ____, ____

CLUE 2: Sam is represented by a dot in the picture below.

____, ____, ____, ____, ____

CLUE 3: Sam + 10 = Tam

Who is Tam? ______ Who is Sam? ______

Case I-32

CLUE 1: Tock is represented by a dot in the picture below.

____, ____, ____, ____, ____

CLUE 2: Rock is represented by a dot in the picture below.

____, ____, ____, ____, ____

CLUE 3: Tock is a negative number.

CLUE 4: Rock is a positive number.

CLUE 5: Tock + Rock = 4

Who is Tock? ______ Who is Rock? ______

Case I-33

CLUE 1: Rick is an integer between -3 and 5.

CLUE 2: Nick is an integer such that Rick + Nick = 10.

Rick							
Nick							

CLUE 3: Nick is greater than 10.

CLUE 4: Nick − Rick $\neq$ 12

Who is Rick? ______ Who is Nick? ______

Case I-34

CLUE 1: Rae is represented by a dot in the picture below.

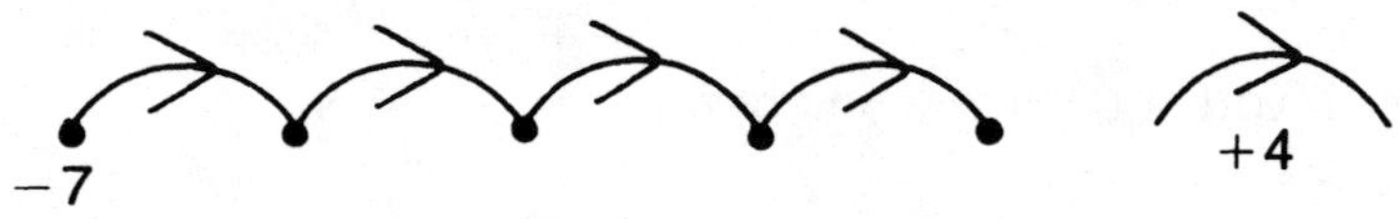

CLUE 2: Mae is an integer such that Rae + Mae = 0.

Rae					
Mae					

CLUE 3: Mae is a negative number.

CLUE 4: Mae is not -5.

CLUE 5: Rae is not 9.

Who is Rae? ______ Who is Mae? ______

Case I-35

CLUE 1: Moe is represented by a dot in the picture below.

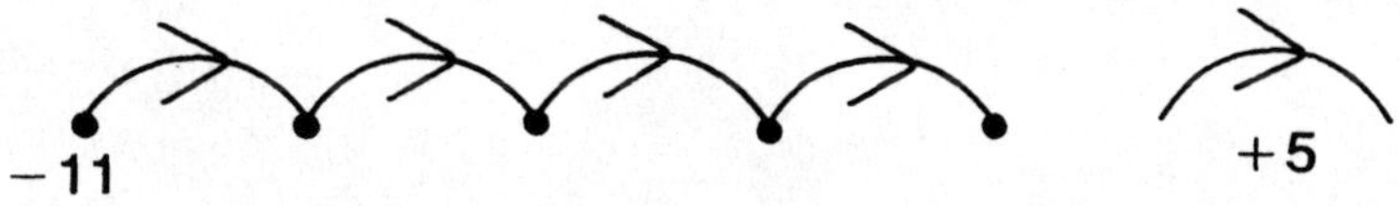

CLUE 2: Joe is a number such that Joe = Moe + 4.

Moe					
Joe					

CLUE 3: Joe is a positive number.

CLUE 4: Moe is a negative number.

Who is Moe? ______ Who is Joe? ______

Case I-36

CLUE 1: Nip is an integer between -4 and 4.

CLUE 2: Pip = 2 Nip

Nip							
Pip							

CLUE 3: (Nip) • (Pip) > 8

CLUE 4: Nip − Pip ≠ −3

Who is Nip? ______Who is Pip? ______

Case I-37

CLUE 1: When you square me, you get 4.

______, ______

CLUE 2: I am not equal to -2.

Who am I? ______

Case I-38

CLUE 1: When you square me, you get me again! ($x^2 = x$)

______, ______

CLUE 2: I am not equal to 0.

Who am I? ______

Case I-39

CLUE 1: When you square me and then subtract 9 you get 0.

______, ______

CLUE 2: I am not equal to 3.

Who am I? ______

In the next seven cases, the letter **x** will be used to represent the **mystery number.** In each instance, a sentence involving x will be given and you are to find the replacements for x which will make the sentence true. For example, for the sentence

$$x + 3 = 5,$$

the replacement of 2 for x gives

$$2 + 3 = 5,$$

which is a true sentence. For the sentence

$$x + 3 > 5,$$

the replacements which will make this sentence true are 3, 4, 5, 6, ...

On the first case below the previous approach is shown so that you can compare the two methods.

Case I-37

CLUE 1: When you square me, you get 4.

_____, _____

CLUE 2: I am not equal to -2.
Who am I? _____

Case I-38

CLUE 1: $x^2 = x$

_____, _____

CLUE 2: $x \neq 0$

Who is it? _____

Case I-39

CLUE 1: $x^2 - 9 = \phi$

_____, _____

CLUE 2: $x \neq 3$

Who is it? _____

Case I-40

CLUE 1: $x^2 = 4x$

_____, _____

CLUE 2: $x \neq 4$

Who is it? _____

Case I-41

NUMBER SUSPECTS: 1, 3, 5, 9.

CLUE 1: $x + 7 > 10$

CLUE 2: $x - 2 < 7$

Who is it? _____

Case I-42

NUMBER SUSPECTS: −5, −3, −1, 1, 3, 5.

CLUE 1: $2x - 1 < 0$

CLUE 2: $x + 3 > 1$

Who is it? _____

Case I-43

NUMBER SUSPECTS: $-3, -2, -1, 0, 1, 2, 3.$

CLUE 1: $3x - 1 > -3$

CLUE 2: $x + 1 < 4$

CLUE 3: $x \neq 786\,(-521) + 786\,(521)$

CLUE 4: $x \neq \dfrac{492 \cdot 751 + 492\,(-857)}{492\,(7\,(751 + -857)}$

Who is it? ______

CHAPTER V

GEOMETRY

Since this a geometry chapter, the suspects will be geometric things, such as points, lines, segments, angles, triangles and quadrilaterals. You should eliminate suspects just as you have in previous chapters.

The first seven detective stories involve **SEGMENTS.** Notice that points A and B are pictured below, together with the **shortest possible path** connecting A and B. This path is called a segment, **A** and **B** are its **endpoints** and we **write $\overline{AB}$** to name it. Also "$\overline{AB}$" is **read "segment AB."**

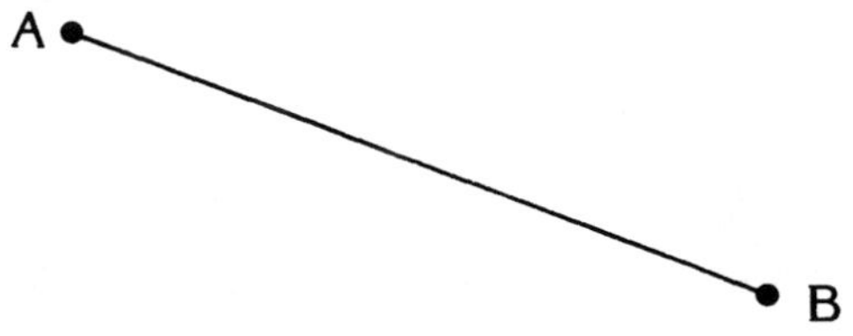

To solve these seven cases you will need to measure the lengths of the segments pictured. To do this, you will need a ruler which will enable you to measure in inches and in centimeters.

Case G-1

CLUE 1: I am one of the segments pictured below.

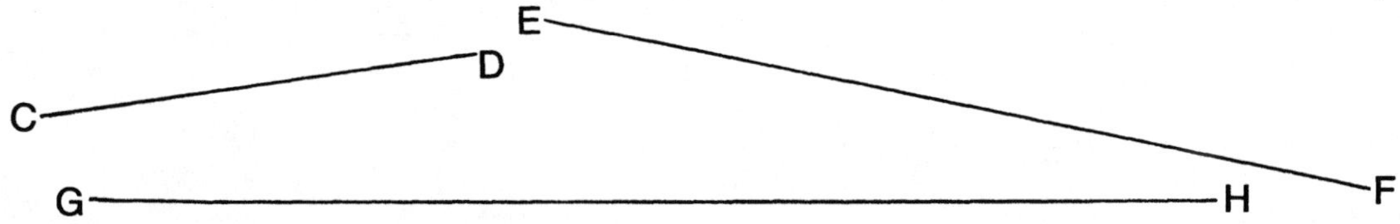

CLUE 2: I am shorter than 2 inches.

Which segment am I? ______

Case G-2

CLUE 1: I am one of the segments pictured below.

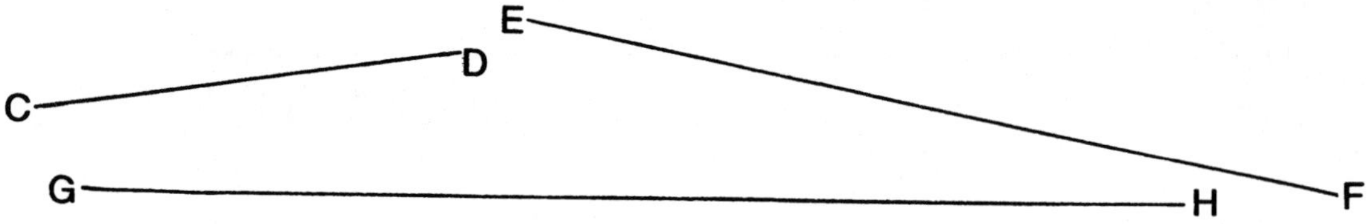

CLUE 2: I am longer than 4 inches.

Which segment am I? ______

Case G-3

CLUE 1: I am one of the segments of Case G-2.

CLUE 2: I am longer than 2 inches.

CLUE 3: I am shorter than 4 inches.

Which segment am I? ______

Case G-4

CLUE 1: I am one of the segments pictured below.

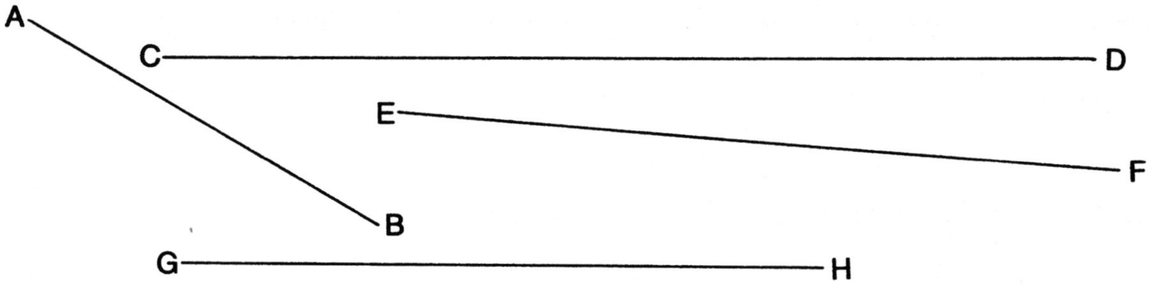

CLUE 2: I am longer than 10 centimeters.

Which segment am I? ______

Case G-5

CLUE 1: I am one of the segments pictured below.

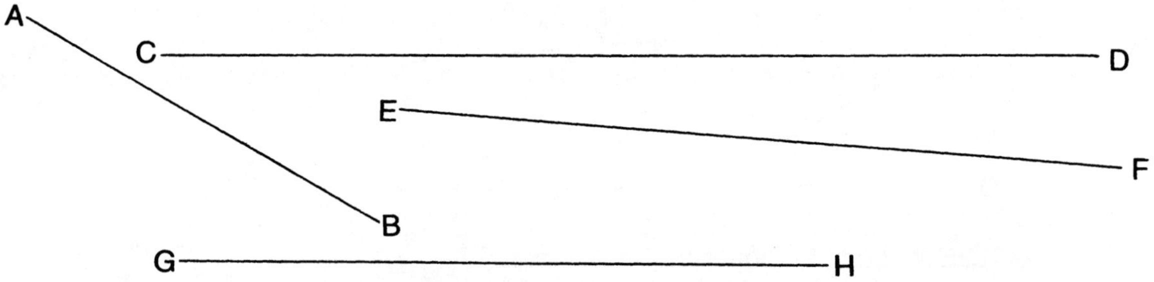

CLUE 2: I am shorter than 10 centimeters.

CLUE 3: I am longer than 8 centimeters.

Which segment am I? ______

Case G-6

CLUE 1: I am one of the segments pictured below.

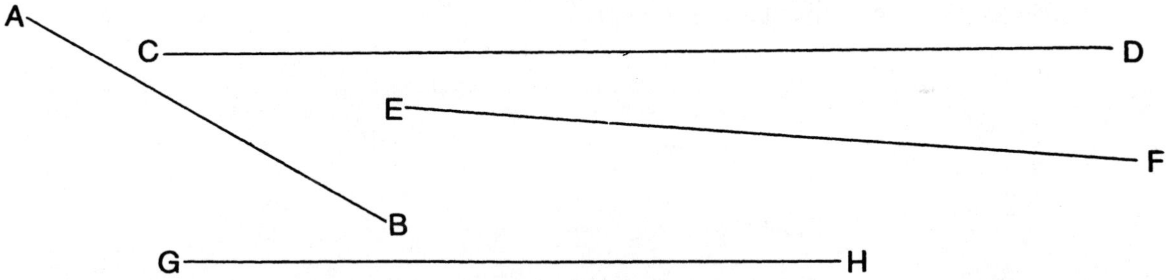

CLUE 2: I am longer than 6 centimeters.

CLUE 3: I am shorter than 9 centimeters.

Which segment am I? ______

Case G-7

CLUE 1: I am one of the segments pictured below.

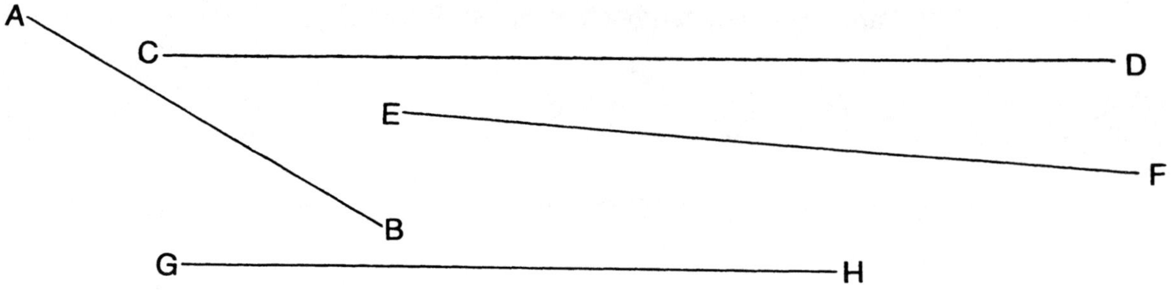

CLUE 2: I am shorter than 7 centimeters.

Which segment am I? ______

The next three detective stories involve **LINES**. Notice the picture below. This is a picture of a line and we **write** $\overleftrightarrow{AB}$ to name it ("$\overleftrightarrow{AB}$" is **read "line AB"**). The arrows mean that the line goes on indefinitely in the directions of the arrows.

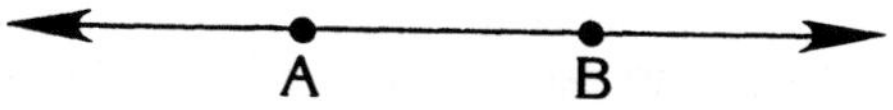

Pairs of lines which are on the **same surface** and which **do not intersect** are said to be **PARALLEL.** The two lines below are parallel.

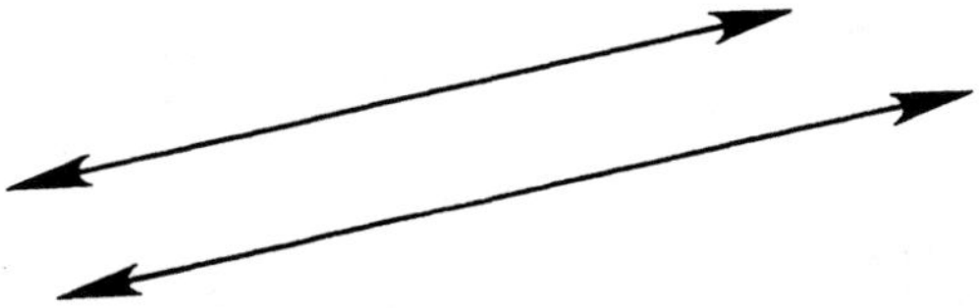

Lines which intersect to **form square corners** are said to be **PERPENDICULAR.** The two lines below are perpendicular.

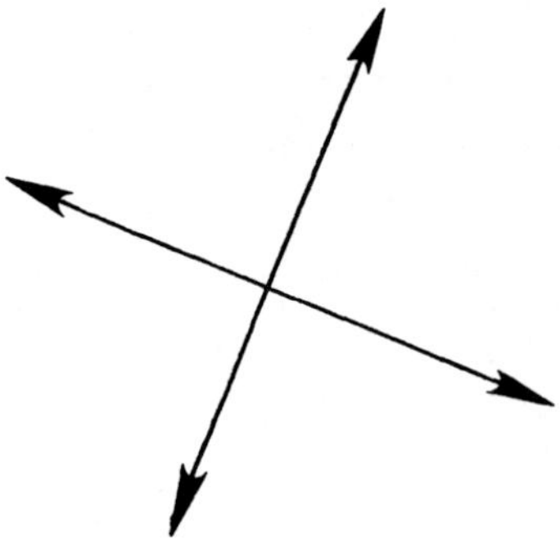

Case G-8

CLUE 1: I am one of the lines pictured below: $\overleftrightarrow{AB}$, $\overleftrightarrow{CD}$, $\overleftrightarrow{EF}$, or $\overleftrightarrow{GH}$.

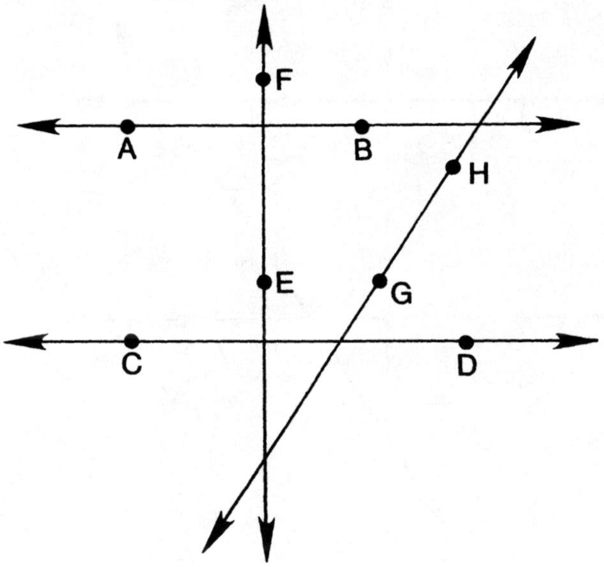

CLUE 2: I am perpendicular to $\overleftrightarrow{EF}$.

CLUE 3: I am not $\overleftrightarrow{AB}$.

Which line am I? ______

Case G-9

CLUE 1: I am one of the lines of Case G-8:

CLUE 2: I am not perpendicular to $\overleftrightarrow{CD}$.

CLUE 3: I am not parallel to $\overleftrightarrow{AB}$.

CLUE 4: I am not $\overleftrightarrow{AB}$.

Which line am I? ______

Case G-10

CLUE 1: I am one of the lines pictured below: $\overleftrightarrow{AB}$, $\overleftrightarrow{CD}$, $\overleftrightarrow{EF}$ or $\overleftrightarrow{GH}$.

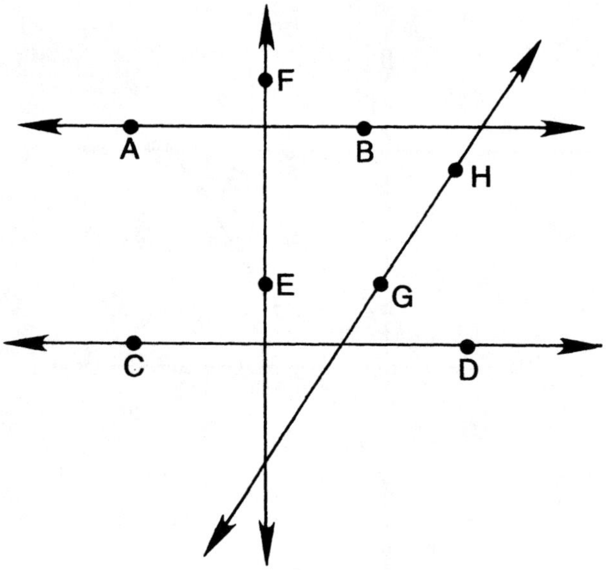

CLUE 2: I am perpendicular to $\overleftrightarrow{AB}$.

Which line am I? ______

The next five detective stories all involve **ANGLES**. When a **square corner** is formed, as in the picture below, you have a **RIGHT ANGLE**. The **corner point** for any angle is called its **VERTEX**, and an angle is often named for its vertex. For instance, to name the angle below we **write $\angle$A (read angle A)**.

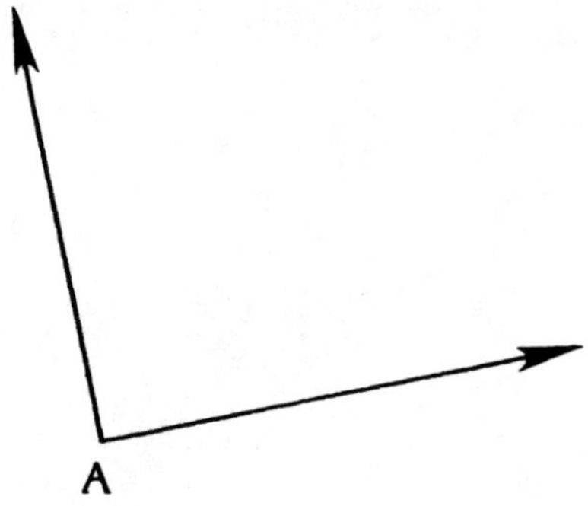

An angle that is **smaller than** a **right angle** is called an **ACUTE ANGLE.** Note that ∠B is an acute angle.

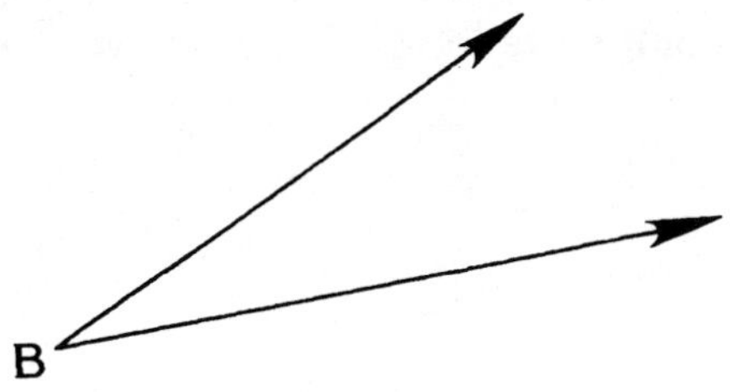

An angle **larger than** a **right angle** is said to be an **OBTUSE angle.** Note that ∠C is an obtuse angle.

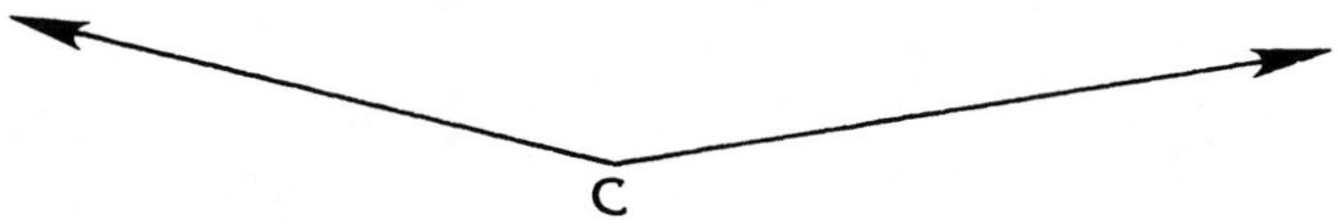

To be able to complete the cases in which the suspects are angles, you may need to get a protractor and measure the angles.

Case G-11

CLUE 1: I am one of the angles pictured below: ∠A, ∠B, ∠C, ∠D, or ∠E.

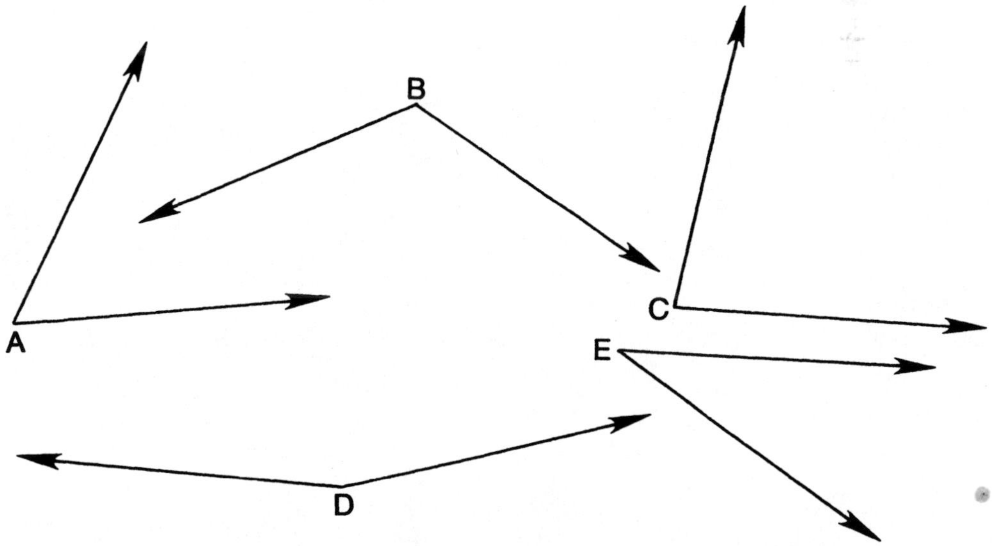

CLUE 2: I am the biggest of these angles.

Which angle am I? ______

Case G-12

CLUE 1: I am one of the angles pictured below: ∠A, ∠B, ∠C, ∠D, or ∠E.

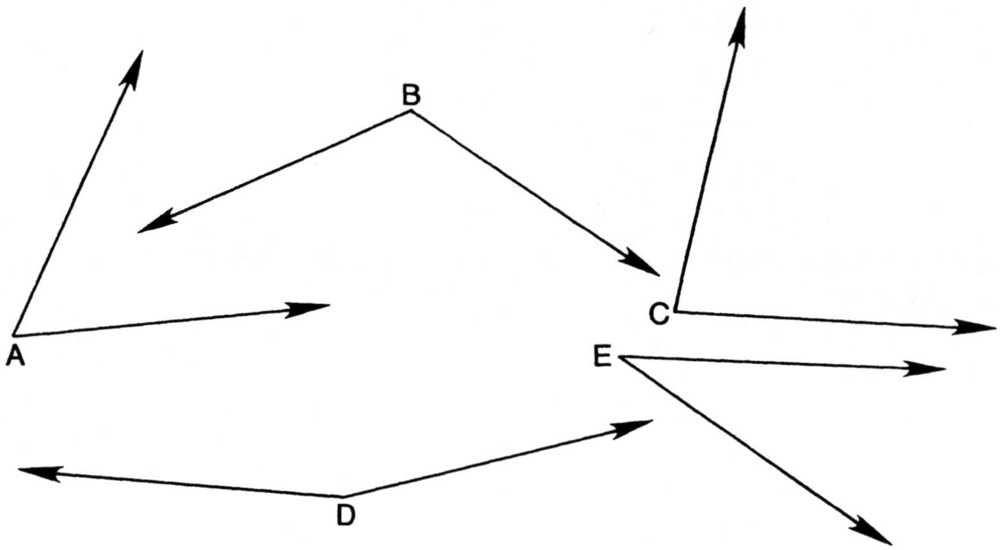

CLUE 2: I am the angle which is closest in size to a right angle.

Which angle am I? ______

Case G-13

CLUE 1: I am one of the angles of Case G-12: ∠A, ∠B, ∠C, ∠D, or ∠E.

CLUE 2: I am the smallest of these angles.

Which angle am I? ______

Case G-14

CLUE 1: I am one of the angles pictured below: ∠A, ∠B, ∠C, ∠D or ∠E.

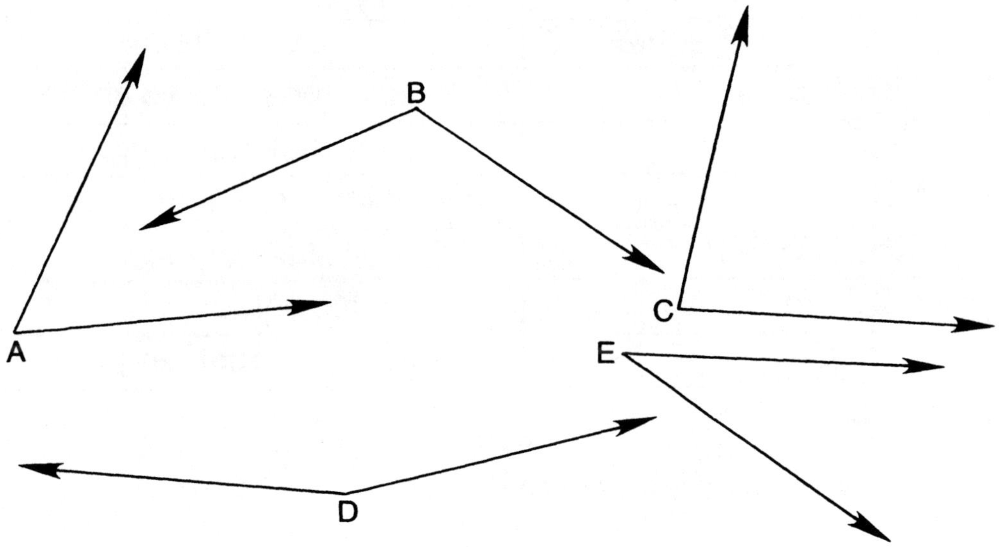

CLUE 2: I am an acute angle.

CLUE 3: Of the angles remaining, I am not the smallest angle and I am not the biggest angle.

Which angle am I? ______

Case G-15

CLUE 1: I am one of the angles of Case G-14: ∠A, ∠B, ∠C, ∠D, or ∠E.

CLUE 2: I am an obtuse angle.

CLUE 3: I am smaller than a 150° angle.

Which angle am I? ______

In order to solve the next few cases you will need to know about different kinds of triangles. **TRIANGLES** are classified in terms of their angles or the lengths of their sides.

TYPES OF TRIANGLES	
Name of Triangle	Conditions
OBTUSE	Contains one obtuse angle
RIGHT	Contains one right angle
ACUTE	Contains three acute angles
EQUILATERAL	All three sides equal
ISOSCELES	Two sides equal
SCALENE	All sides different lengths

Case G-16

CLUE 1: I am one of the triangles below: I, II, III, IV, V, or VI.

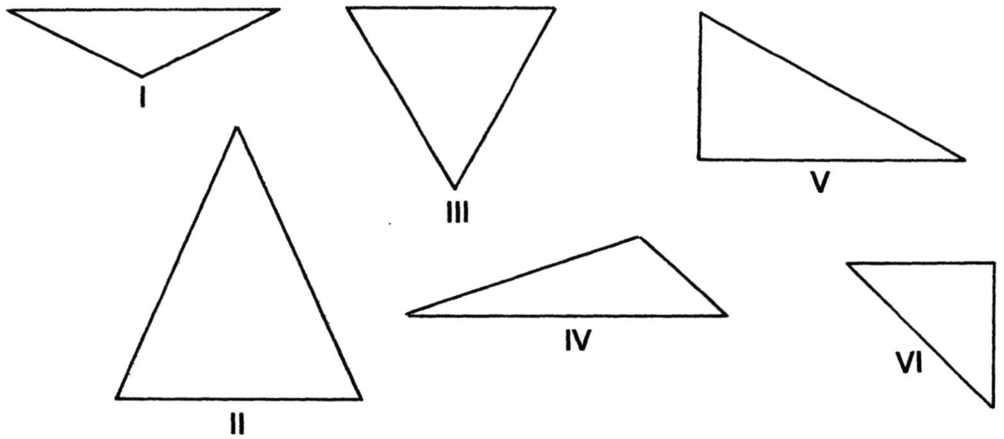

CLUE 2: I am a right triangle.

CLUE 3: I am not an isosceles triangle.

Which triangle am I? ______

Case G-17

CLUE 1: I am one of the triangles of Case G-16: I, II, III, IV, V, or VI.

CLUE 2: I am not a right triangle.

CLUE 3: I am not an obtuse triangle.

CLUE 4: I am not an equilateral triangle.

Which triangle am I? ______

Case G-18

CLUE 1: I am one of the triangles below: I, II, III, IV, V, or VI.

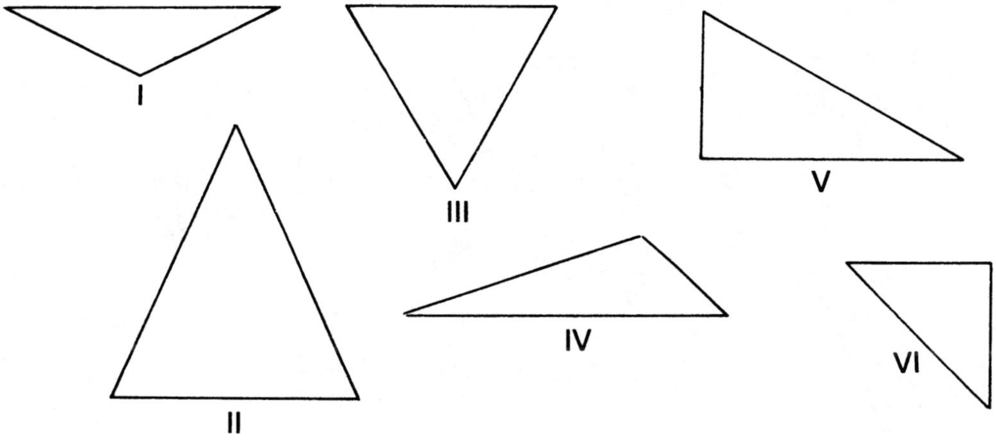

CLUE 2: I am an obtuse triangle.

CLUE 3: I am an isosceles triangle.

Which triangle am I? ______

Case G-19

CLUE 1: I am one of the triangles of Case G-18: I, II, III, IV, V, or VI.

CLUE 2: I am an isosceles triangle.

CLUE 3: I am a right triangle.

Which triangle am I? ______

Case G-20

CLUE 1: I am one of the triangles below: I, II, III, IV, V, or VI.

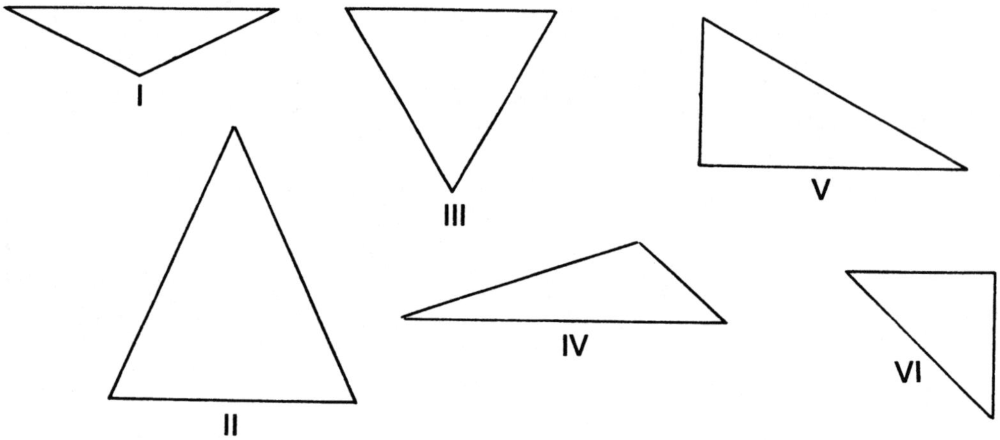

CLUE 2: I am not an acute triangle.

CLUE 3: I am not a right triangle.

CLUE 4: I am a scalene triangle.

Which triangle am I? ______

Case G-21

CLUE 1: I am one of the triangles of Case G-20: I, II, III, IV, V, or VI.

CLUE 2: I am not an obtuse triangle.

CLUE 3: I am not a right triangle.

CLUE 4: I am the smallest of the triangles left.

Which triangle am I? ______

Case G-22

CLUE 1: I am one of the points, G, H, I, J, K, L, or M, in the picture below.

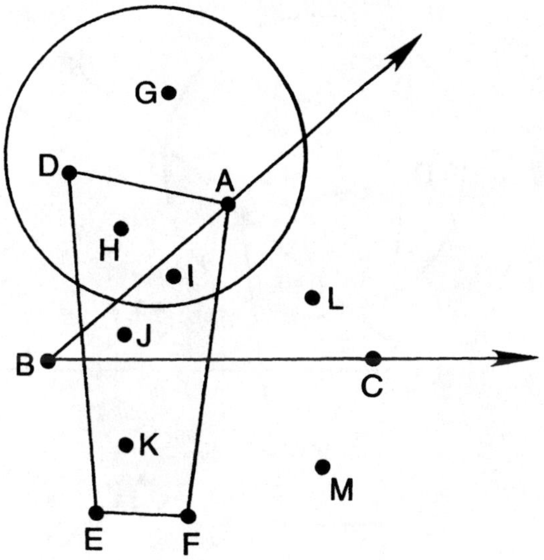

CLUE 2: I am in the **EXTERIOR (outside)** ∠B.

CLUE 3: I am in the exterior of the circle.

CLUE 4: I am in the **INTERIOR (inside)** of **QUADRILATERAL** ADEF. (A **QUADRILATERAL** is a four-sided figure.)

Which point am I? ______

Case G-23

CLUE 1: I am one of the of Case G-22: G, H, I, J, K, L, or M.

CLUE 2: I am in the interior of the circle.

CLUE 3: I am in the exterior of quadrilateral ADEF.

Which point am I? ______

Case G-24

CLUE 1: I am one of the points, G, H, I, J, K, L, or M, in the picture below.

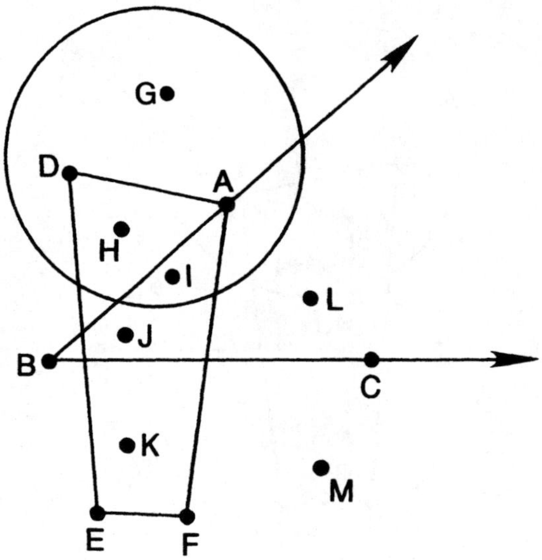

CLUE 2: I am in the exterior of the circle.

CLUE 3: I am in the exterior of ∠B.

CLUE 4: I am in the exterior of quadrilateral ADEF.

Which point am I? ______

Case G-25

CLUE 1: I am one of the points of Case G-24: G, H, I, J, K, L, or M.

CLUE 2: I am in the interior of ∠B.

CLUE 3: I am in the exterior of the circle.

CLUE 4: I am in the interior of quadrilateral ADEF.

Which point am I? ______

Case G-26

CLUE 1: I am one of the points, G, H, I, J, K, L, or M, in the picture below.

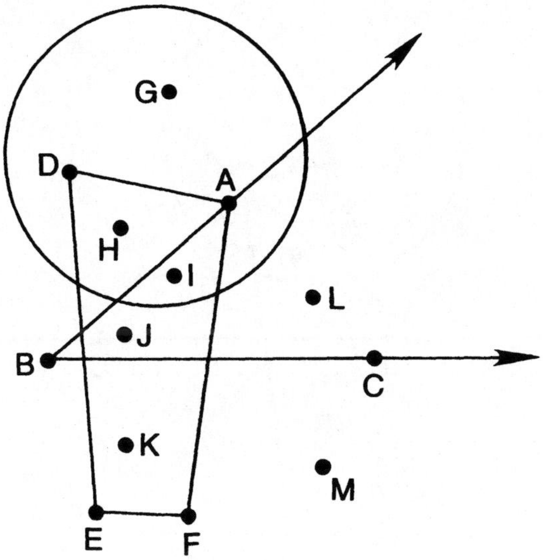

CLUE 2: I am in the interior of ∠B.

CLUE 3: I am in the interior of quadrilateral ADEF.

CLUE 4: I am in the interior of the circle.

Which point am I? ______

Case G-27

CLUE 1: I am one of the points of Case G-26: G, H, I, J, K, L, or M.

CLUE 2: I am in the interior of quadrilateral ADEF.

CLUE 3: I am in the interior of the circle.

CLUE 4: I am in the exterior of ∠B.

Which point am I? ______

Case G-28

CLUE 1: I am one of the points, G, H, I, J, K, L, or M, in the picture below.

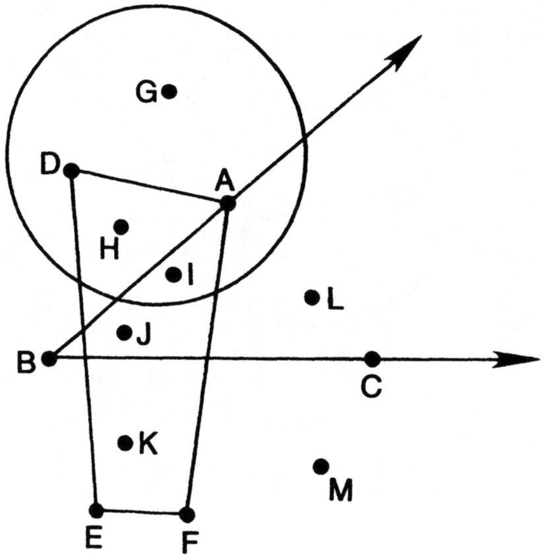

CLUE 2: I am in the interior of ∠ B.

CLUE 3: I am in the exterior of quadrilateral ADEF.

Which point am I? ______

Figures which are the **same size and shape** are said to be **CONGRUENT.** The following two triangles are congruent.

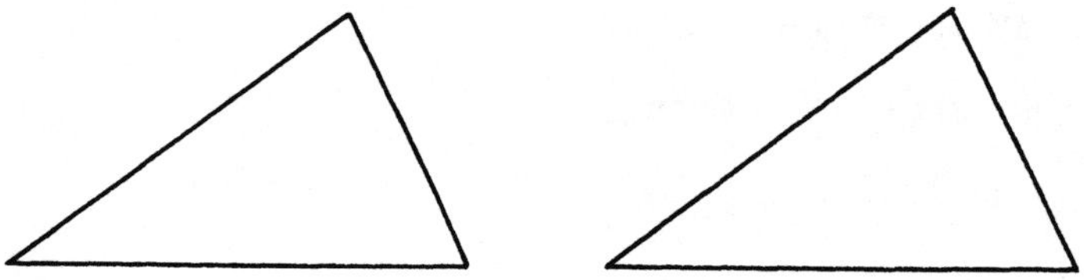

Notice, if we were to cut out one triangular shape, it would **exactly fit on top** of the other triangle. This is a nice way to think when you are trying to decide whether two figures are congruent. Notice that the two rectangles which follow are not congruent because one of them would not fit on the other. In particular, the rectangle on the left is bigger than the rectangle on the right.

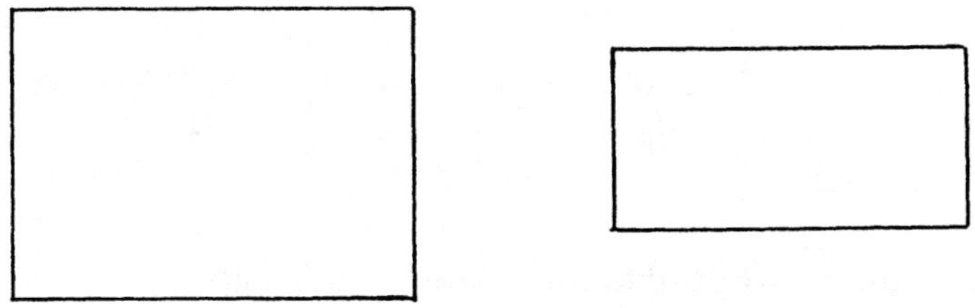

Case G-29

CLUE 1: I am one of the triangles below: I, II, III, IV, or V.

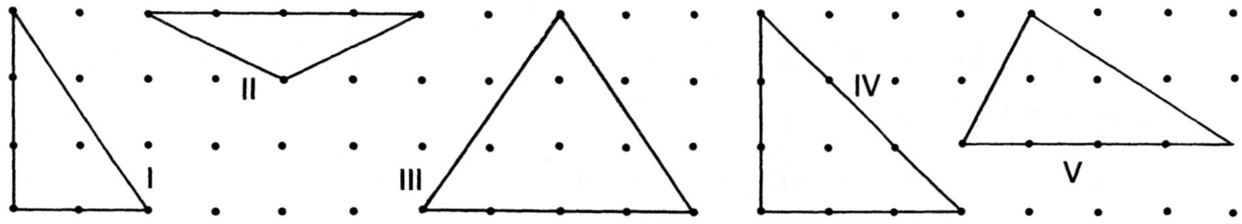

CLUE 2: I am congruent to the following triangle.

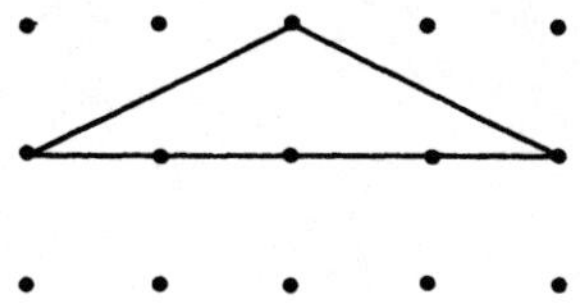

Which triangle am I? ______

Case G-30

CLUE 1: I am one of the triangles below: I, II, III, IV, or V.

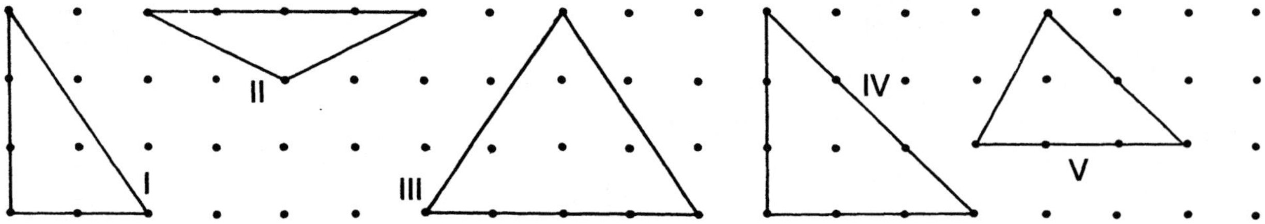

CLUE 2: I am congruent to the following triangle.

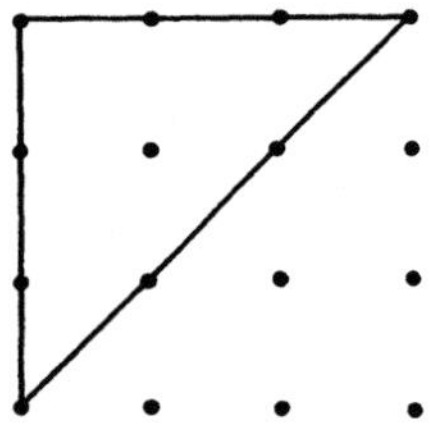

Which triangle am I? ______

Case G-31

CLUE 1: I am one of the triangles below: I, II, III, IV, or V.

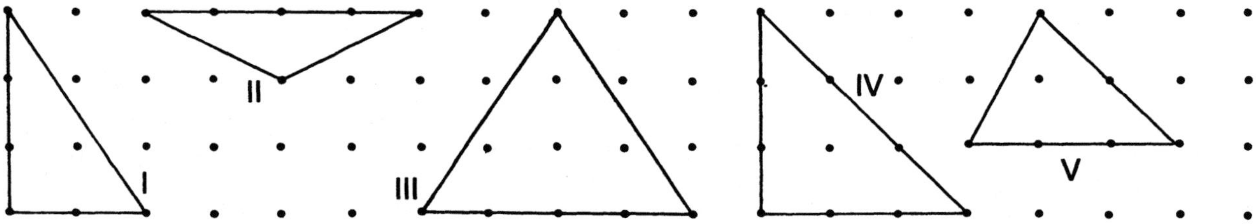

CLUE 2: I am congruent to the following triangle.

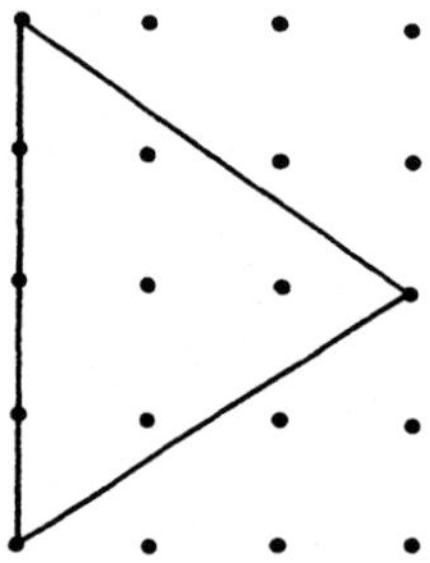

Which triangle am I? ______

Case G-32

CLUE 1: I am one of the triangles below: I, II, III, IV, or V.

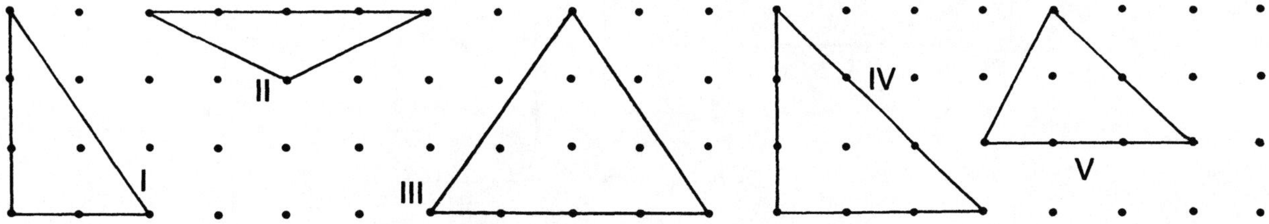

CLUE 2: I am congruent to the following triangle.

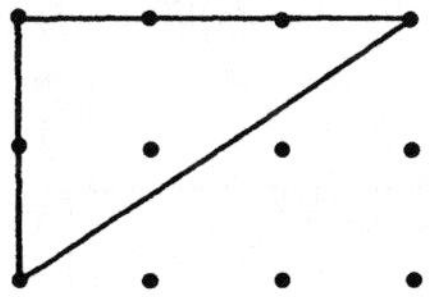

Which triangle am I? ______

Case G-33

CLUE 1: I am one of the rectangles below: I, II, or III.

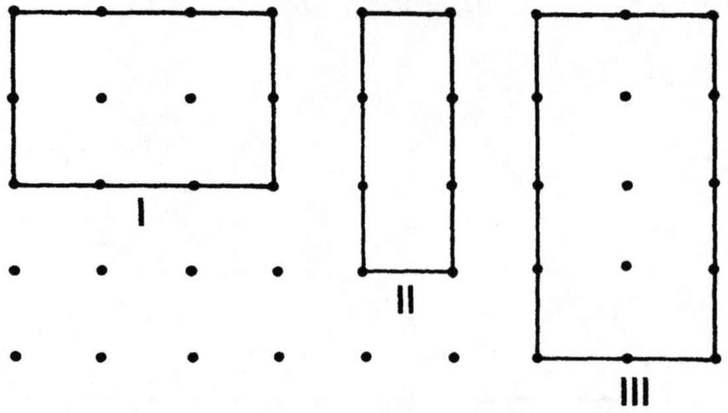

CLUE 2: I am not congruent to the following rectangle.

CLUE 3: I am not congruent to the following rectangle.

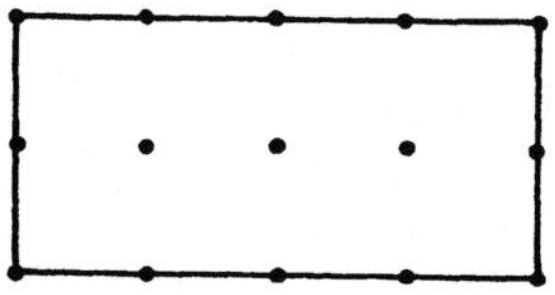

Which rectangle am I? ______

Case G-34

CLUE 1: I am one of the rectangles below: I, II, or III.

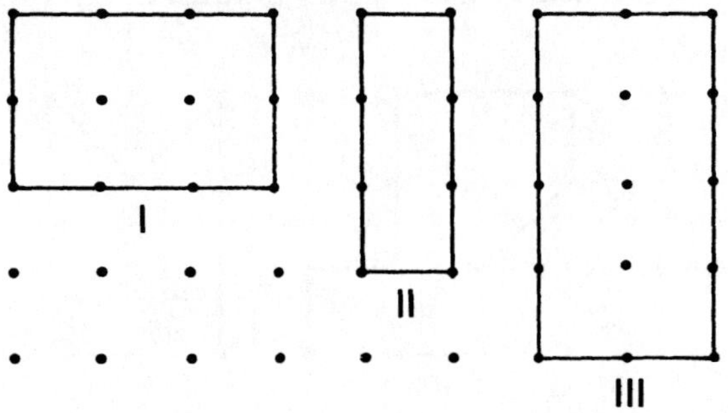

CLUE 2: I am not congruent to the following rectangle.

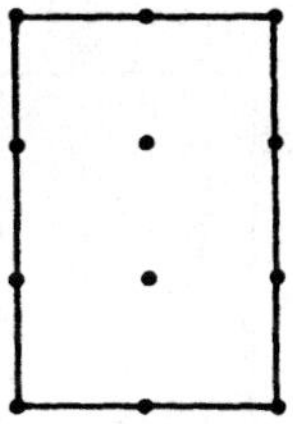

CLUE 3: I am not congruent to the following rectangle.

Which rectangle am I? ______

Case G-35

CLUE 1: I am one of the following figures: I, II, III, or IV.

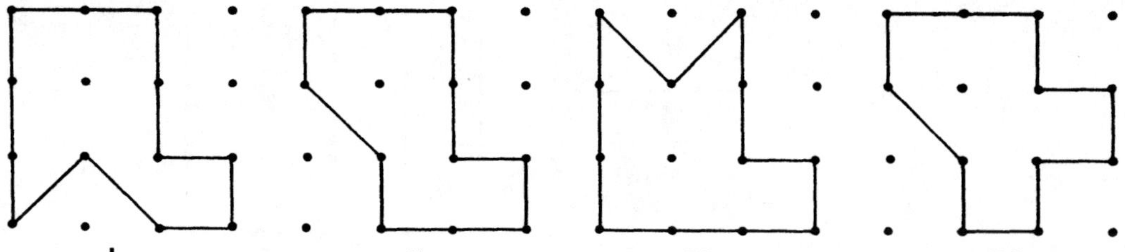

I II III IV

CLUE 2: I am congruent to the following figure.

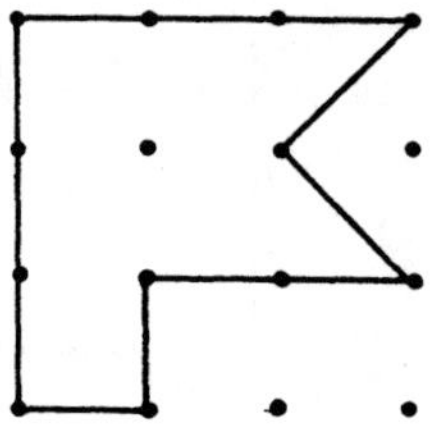

Which figure am I? ______

Case G-36

CLUE 1: I am one of the following figures: I, II, III, or IV.

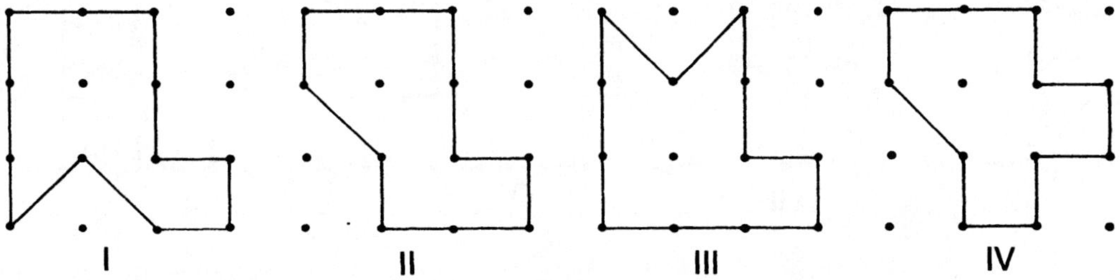

CLUE 2: I am congruent to the following figure.

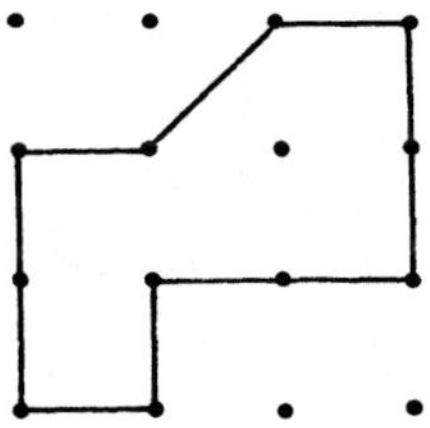

Which figure am I? ______

Case G-37

CLUE 1: I am one of the following figures: I, II, III, or IV.

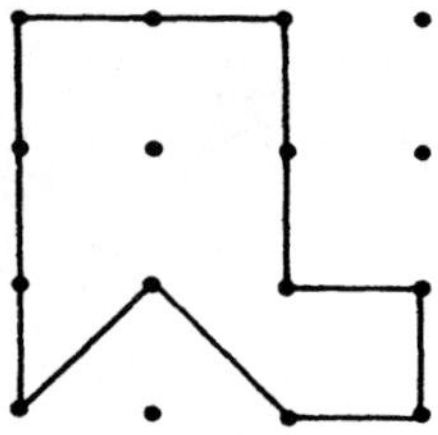

I

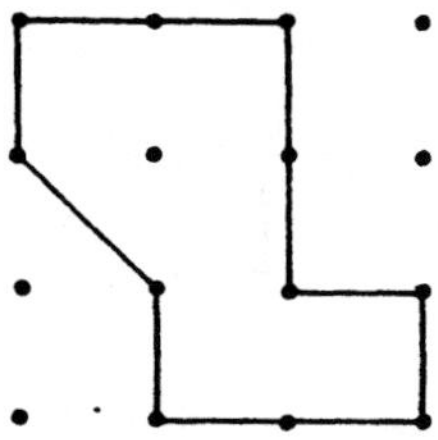

II

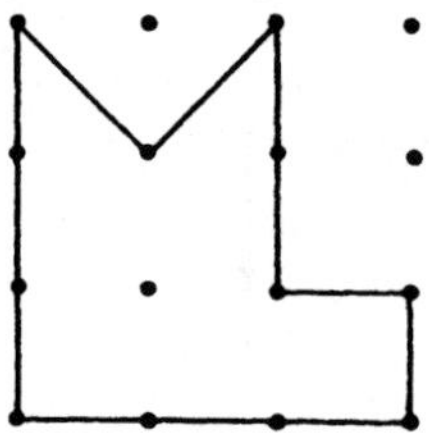

III

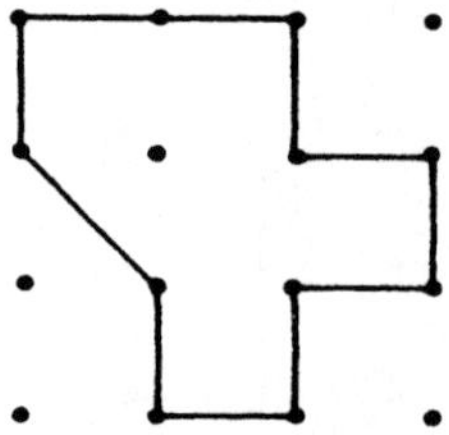

IV

CLUE 2: I am congruent to the following figure.

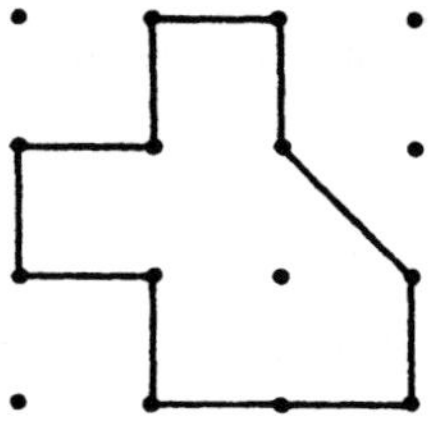

Which figure am I? ______

Case G-38

CLUE 1: I am one of the following figures: I, II, III, or IV.

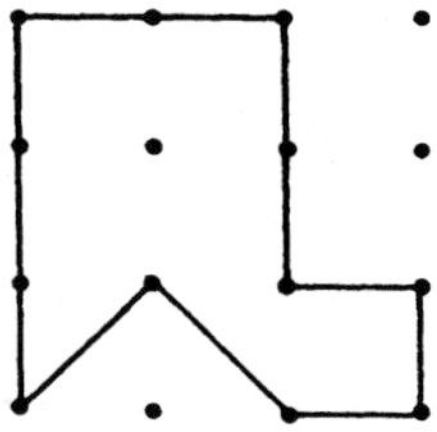

I

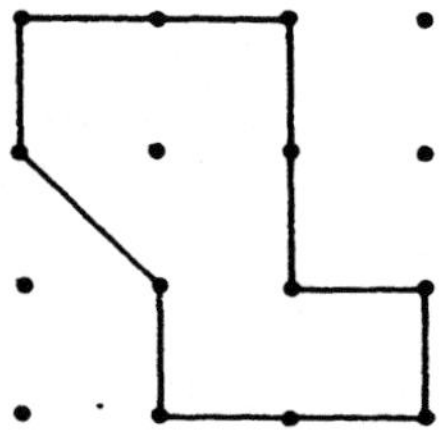

II

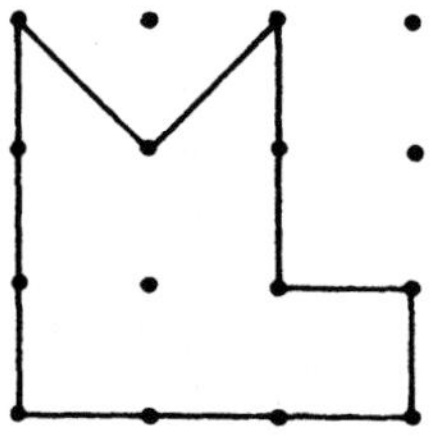

III

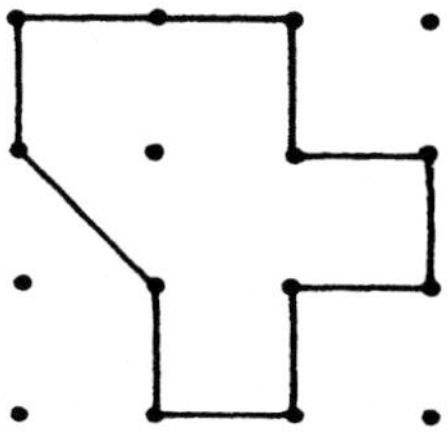

IV

CLUE 2: I am congruent to the following figure.

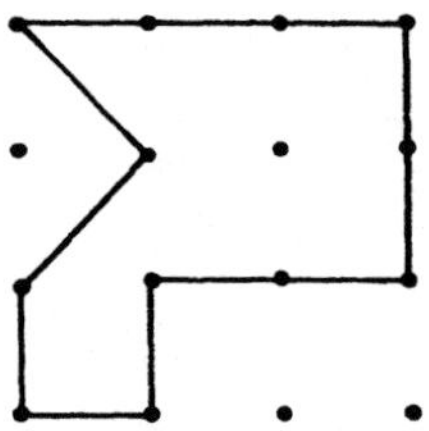

Which figure am I? ______

The next six cases involve **CURVES**. If you can **trace** a figure **without lifting** your pencil from the paper **or retracing** a path, the figure is said to be a curve. The following figures are curves,

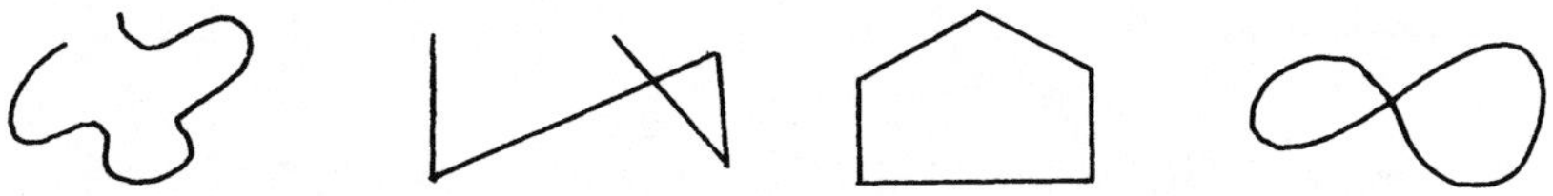

but

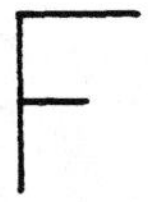

is not a curve. (You will not be able to trace the figure without either lifting your pencil or retracing a path.) Note that a curve **may have straight sides**. Of the four curves pictured, the first and the third **do not intersect themselves.** Such curves are called **SIMPLE CURVES**. In the case of the third and fourth curves, it is possible to pick a point and trace the curve **starting and ending at that point** without lifting the pencil or retracing a path. Curves with this property are called **CLOSED CURVES**.

Case G-39

CLUE 1: I am one of the figures below: I, II, III, IV, V, or VI.

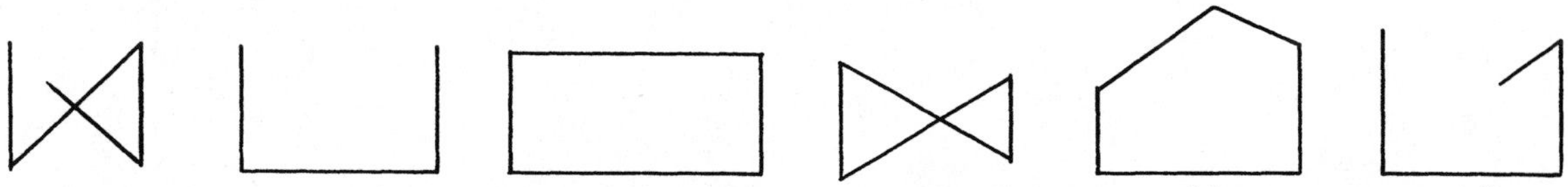

I II III IV V VI

CLUE 2: I am a simple curve.

CLUE 3: I am a closed curve.

CLUE 4: I do not have four sides.

Which figure am I? ______

Case G-40

CLUE 1: I am one of the figures below: I, II, III, IV, V, or VI.

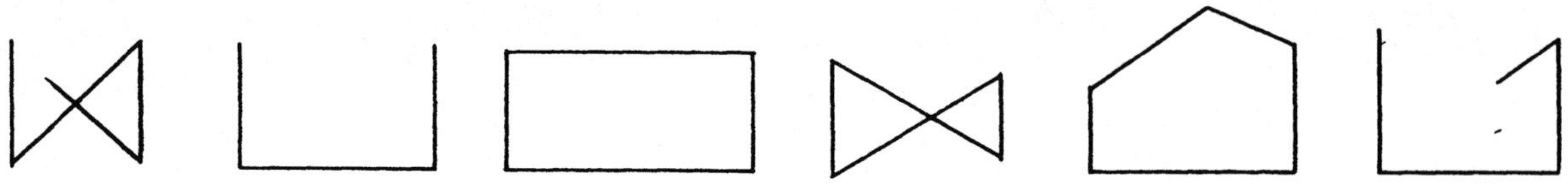

I II III IV V VI

CLUE 2: I am a simple curve.

CLUE 3: I am not a closed curve.

CLUE 4: I am made up of 4 segments.

Which figure am I? ______

Case G-41

CLUE 1: I am one of the figures below: I, II, III, IV, V, or VI.

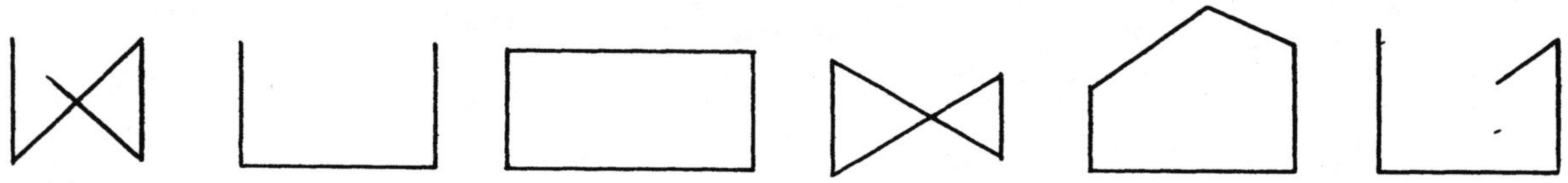

I II III IV V VI

CLUE 2: I am not a simple curve.

CLUE 3: I am not a closed curve.

Which figure am I? ______

Case G-42

CLUE 1: I am one of the figures below: I, II, III, IV, V, or VI.

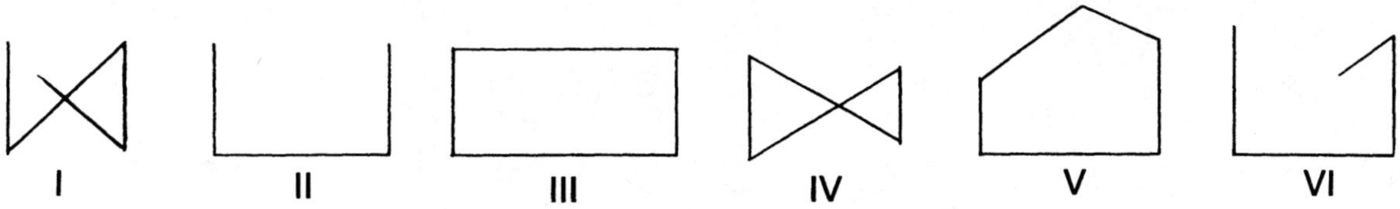

CLUE 2: I am a simple curve.

CLUE 3: I am a closed curve.

CLUE 4: I do not have 5 sides.

Which figure am I? ______

Case G-43

CLUE 1: I am one of the figures below: I, II, III, IV, V, or VI.

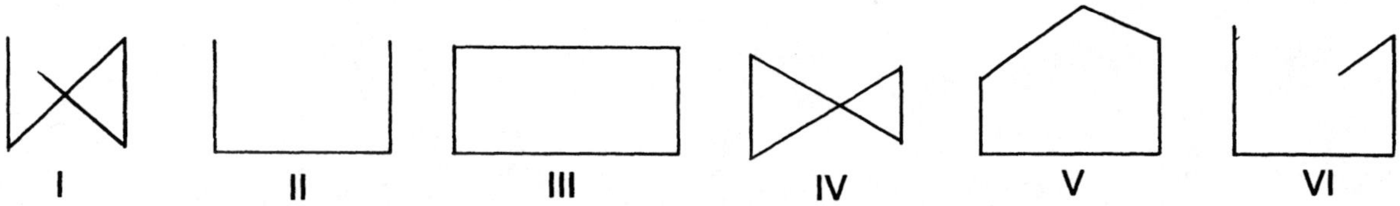

CLUE 2: I am a simple curve.

CLUE 3: I am not a closed curve.

CLUE 4: I am not made up of 4 segments.

Which figure am I? ______

Case G-44

CLUE 1: I am one of the figures below: I, II, III, IV, V, or VI.

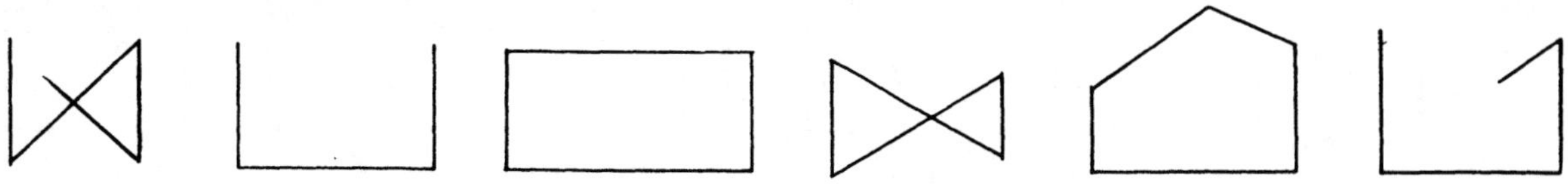

I II III IV V VI

CLUE 2: I am a closed curve.

CLUE 3: I am not a simple curve.

Which figure am I? ______

Case G-45

CLUE 1: I am one of the figures below: I, II, III, or IV.

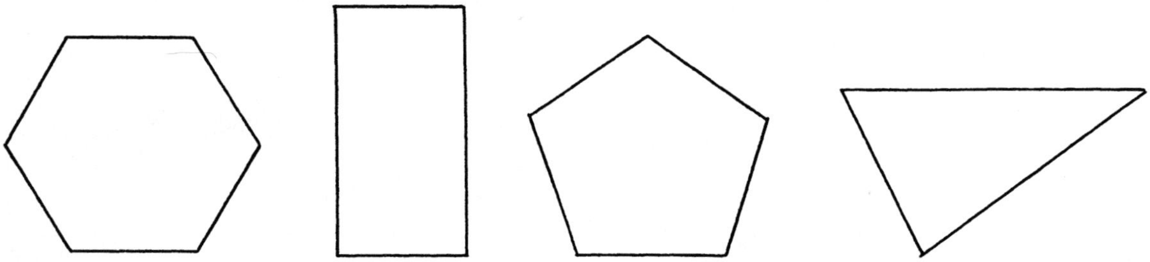

I II III IV

CLUE 2: I have more than 4 sides.

CLUE 3: I am not a **pentagon***.

Which figure am I? ______

---

*A **PENTAGON**, remember, has **5** sides.

Case G-46

CLUE 1: I am one of the figures below: I. II, III, or IV.

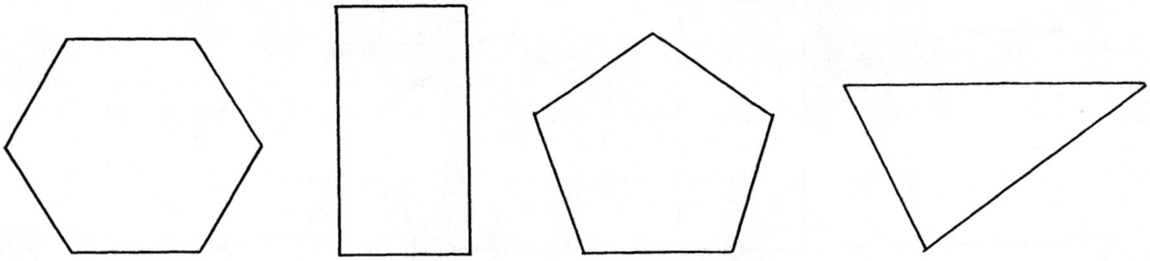

I II III IV

CLUE 2: I have fewer than 5 sides.

CLUE 3: I have no right angles.

Which figure am I? ______

Case G-47

CLUE 1: I am one of the figures below: I, II,III, or IV.

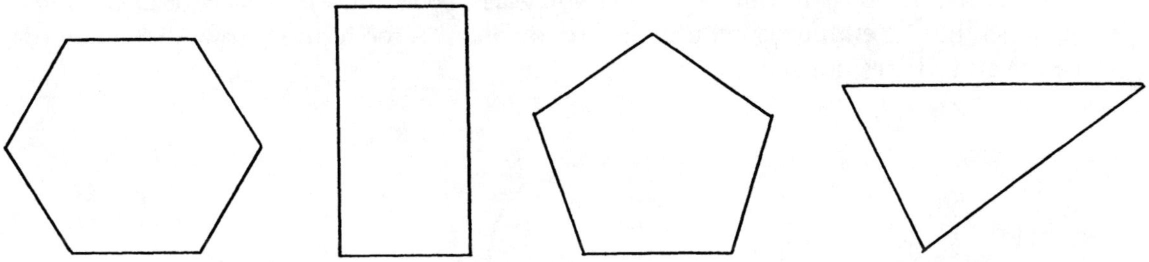

I II III IV

CLUE 2: I am not a triangle.

CLUE 3: I am not a **hexagon***.

CLUE 4: I am not a **quadrilateral***.

Which figure am I? ______

*A **QUADRILATERAL**, remember, has **4** sides, and a **HEXAGON** has **6** sides.

Case G-48

CLUE 1: I am one of the figures below: I, II, III, or IV.

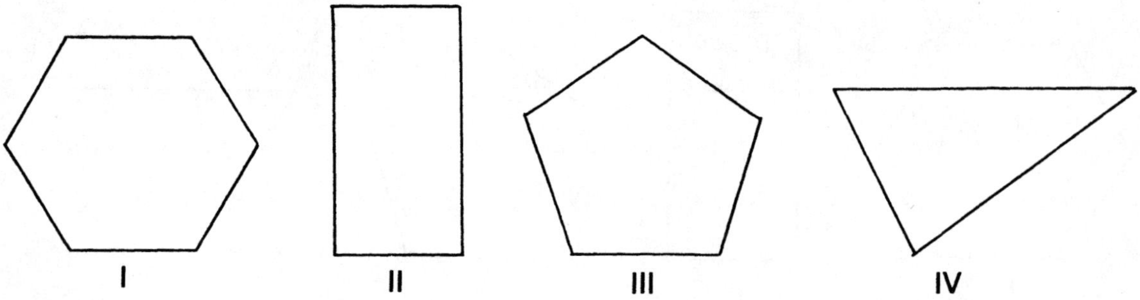

CLUE 2: I have more than 3 sides.

CLUE 3: I have fewer than 6 sides.

CLUE 4: I am not a pentagon.

Which figure am I? ______

In order to solve the next few cases, you will need to know that a **CHORD** is a **segment which has its endpoints on a circle.** For instance, in the figure below $\overline{AB}$ is a chord while $\overline{CD}$ and $\overline{EF}$ are not chords.

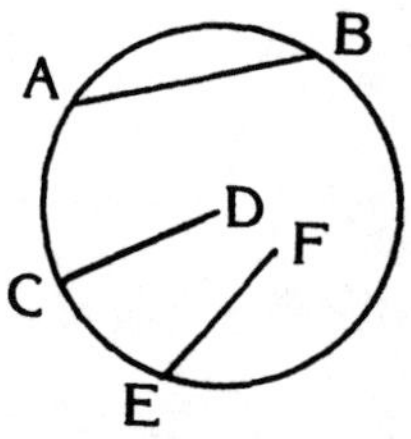

Case G-49

CLUE 1: I am one of the segments in the picture below: $\overline{OH}$, $\overline{JK}$, or $\overline{LM}$ (O is the center of the circle).

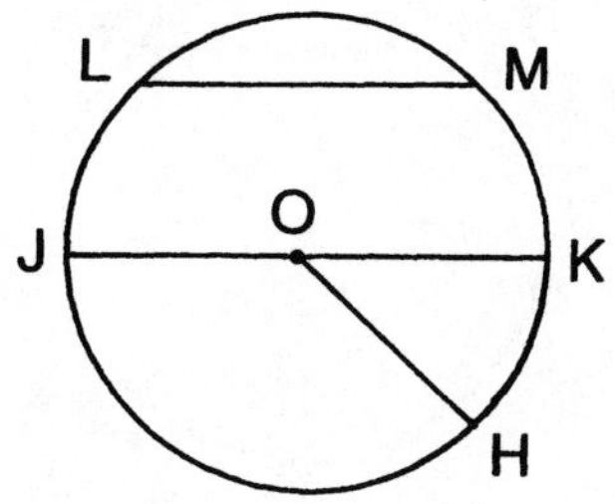

CLUE 2: I am not a chord.

Which segment am I? ______

Case G-50

CLUE 1: I am one of the segments in the picture below: $\overline{OH}$, $\overline{JK}$, or $\overline{LM}$.

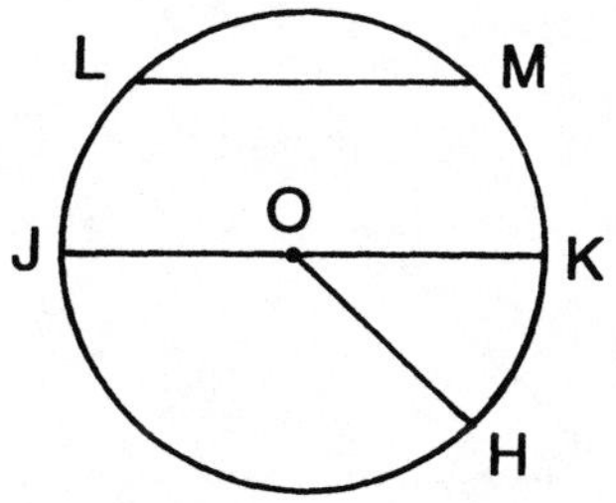

CLUE 2: I am a chord of the circle.

CLUE 3: I am not a **diameter*** of the circle.

Which segment am I? ______

*A diameter is a **chord** that passes through the **center** of a circle.

Case G-51

CLUE 1: I am one the segments in the picture below: $\overline{OH}$, $\overline{JK}$, or $\overline{LM}$.

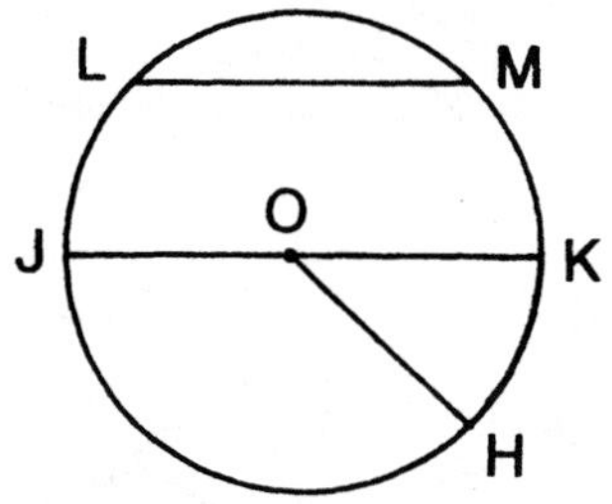

CLUE 2: I am not a **radius*** of the circle.

CLUE 3: I am not $\overline{LM}$.

Which segment am I? ______

Two geometric figures are said to be **SIMILAR** if they have the **same shape.** For instance, the two triangles below are similar. In particular, note that the sides of the triangle on the left are twice as long as the corresponding sides of the triangle on the right, and also the angles of the triangle on the left are the same size as the corresponding angles of the triangle on the right.

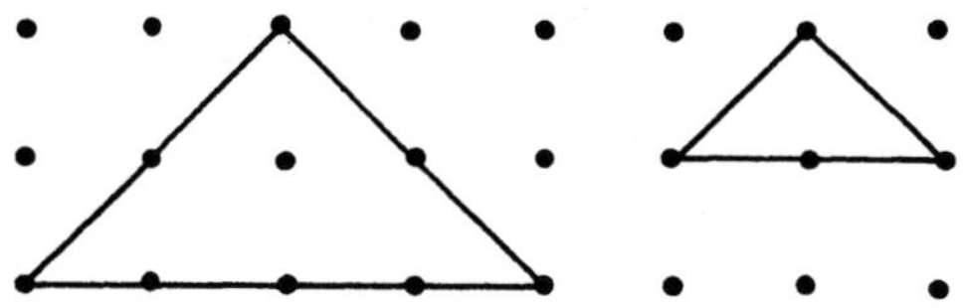

*A **radius** is a segment with one endpoint at the **center** of the circle and the other endpoint **on** the circle.

Case G-52

CLUE 1: I am one of the triangles below: I, II, III, or IV.

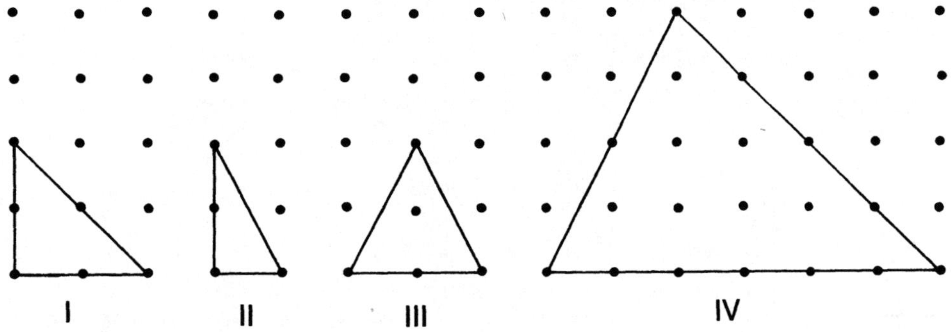

CLUE 2: I am similar to the following triangle.

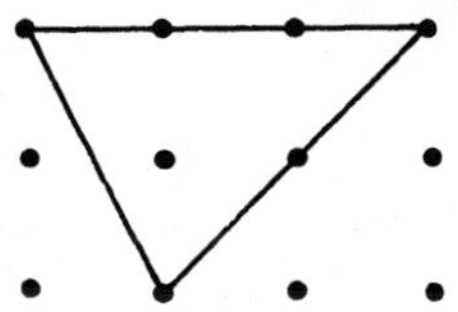

Which triangle am I? ______

Case G-53

CLUE 1: I am one of the triangles of Case G-52: I, II, III, or IV.

CLUE 2: I am similar to the following triangle.

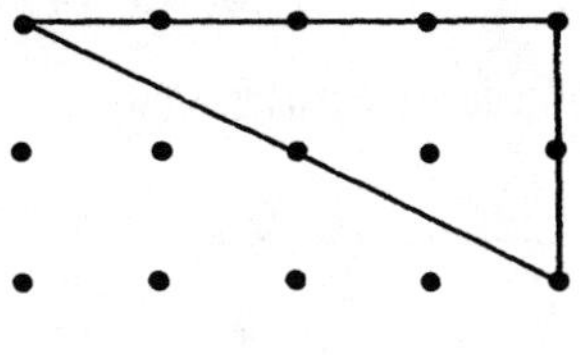

Which triangle am I? ______

Case G-54

CLUE 1: I am one of the triangles below: I, II, III, or IV.

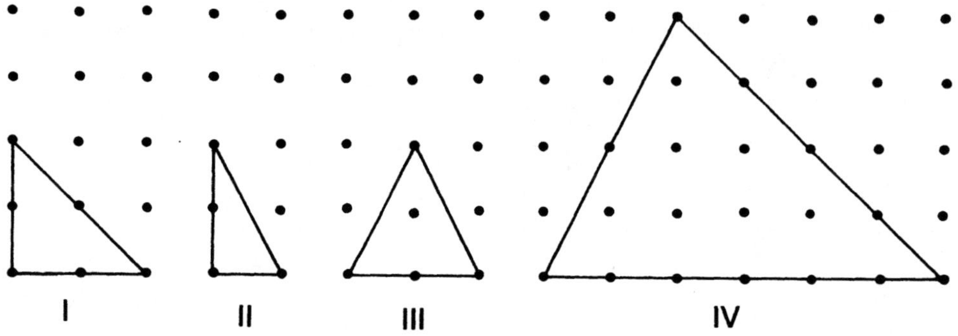

CLUE 2: I am similar to the following triangle.

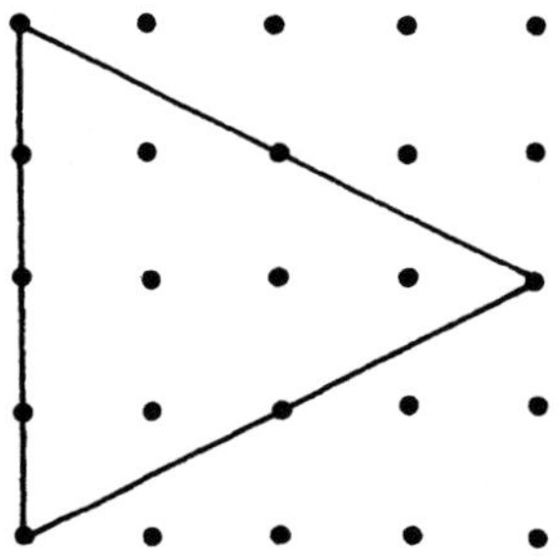

Which triangle am I? ______

Case G-55

CLUE 1: I am one of the triangles of Case G-54: I, II, III, or IV.

CLUE 2: I am similar to the following triangle.

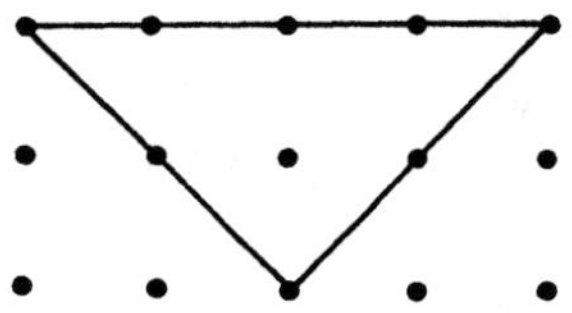

Which triangle am I? ______

Case G-56

CLUE 1: I am one of the rectangles below: I, II, III, or IV.

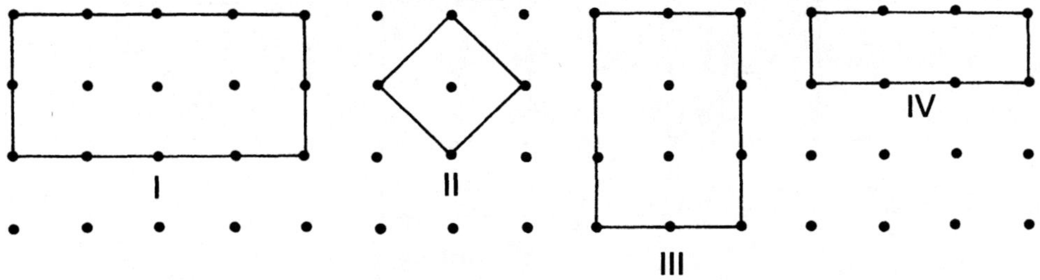

CLUE 2: I am similar to the following rectangle.

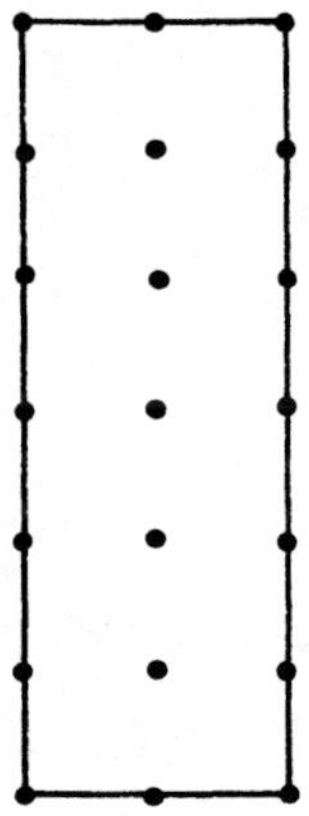

Which rectangle am I? ______

Case G-57

CLUE 1: I am one of the rectangles of Case G-56: I, II, III, or IV.

CLUE 2: I am similar to the following rectangle.

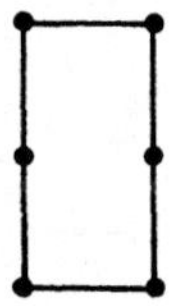

Which rectangle am I? ______

Case G-58

CLUE 1: I am one of the rectangles below: I, II, III, or IV.

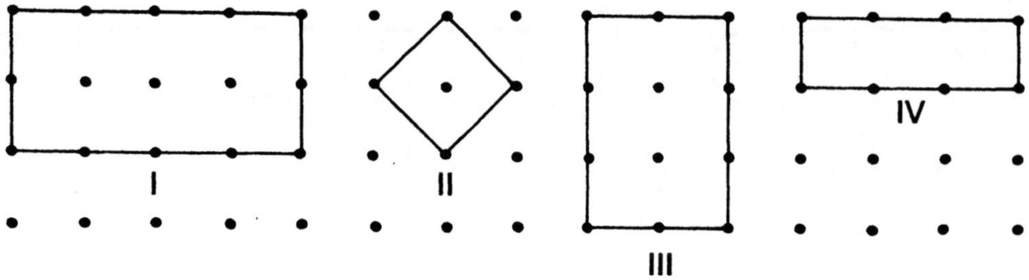

CLUE 2: I am similar to the following rectangle.

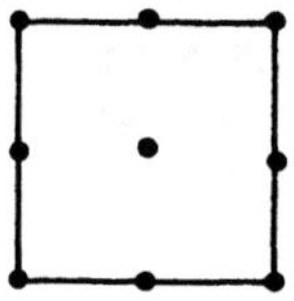

Which rectangle am I? ______

Case G-59

CLUE 1: I am one of the rectangles of Case G-58: I, II, III, or IV.

CLUE 2: I am similar to the following rectangle.

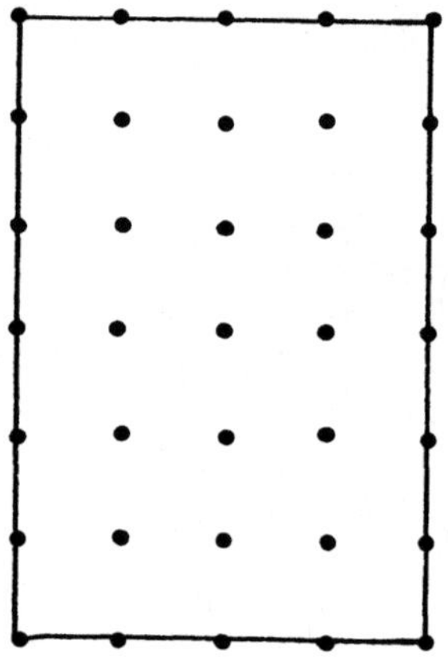

Which rectangle am I? ______

Case G-60

CLUE 1: I am one of the quadrilaterals pictured below. I, II, III, IV, V, VI, VII, or VIII.

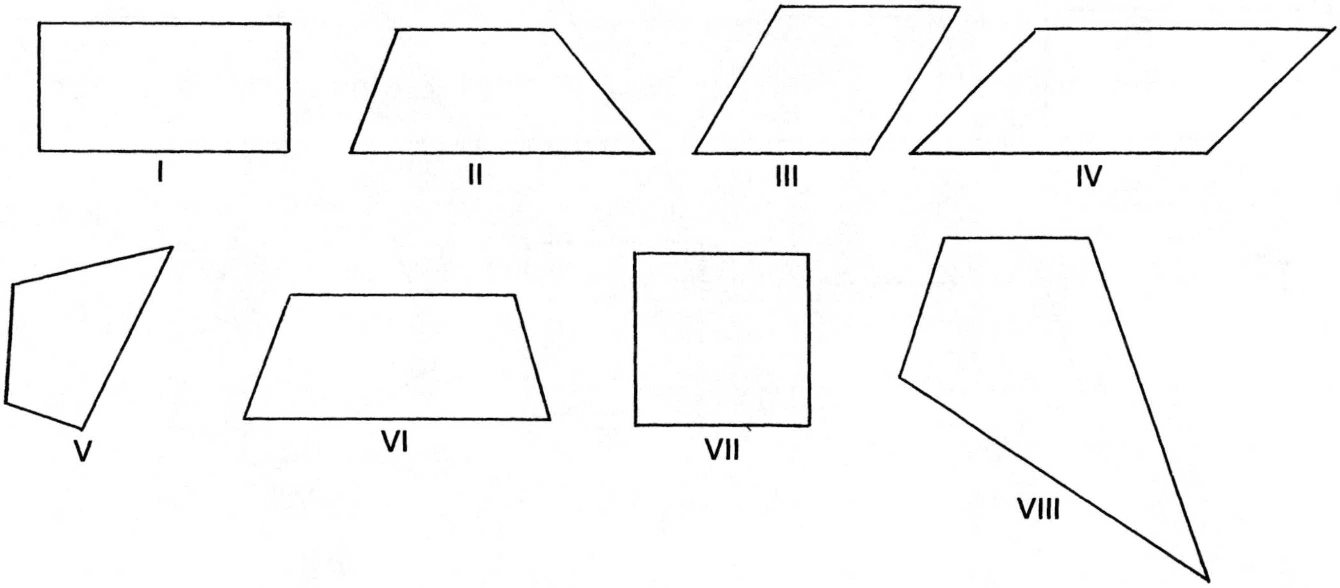

CLUE 2: I have exactly one pair of parallel sides.

CLUE 3: I have exactly one pair of **congruent*** sides.

Which quadrilateral am I? ______

Case G-61

CLUE 1: I am one of the quadrilaterals of Case G-60: I, II, III, IV, V, VI, VII or VIII.

CLUE 2: I have four right angles.

CLUE 3: My sides are all the same length.

Which quadrilateral am I? ______

---

*Two **SEGMENTS** are **CONGRUENT** if they are the **same length.**

Case G-62

CLUE 1: I am one of the quadrilaterals pictured below: I, II, III, IV, V, VI, VII, or VIII.

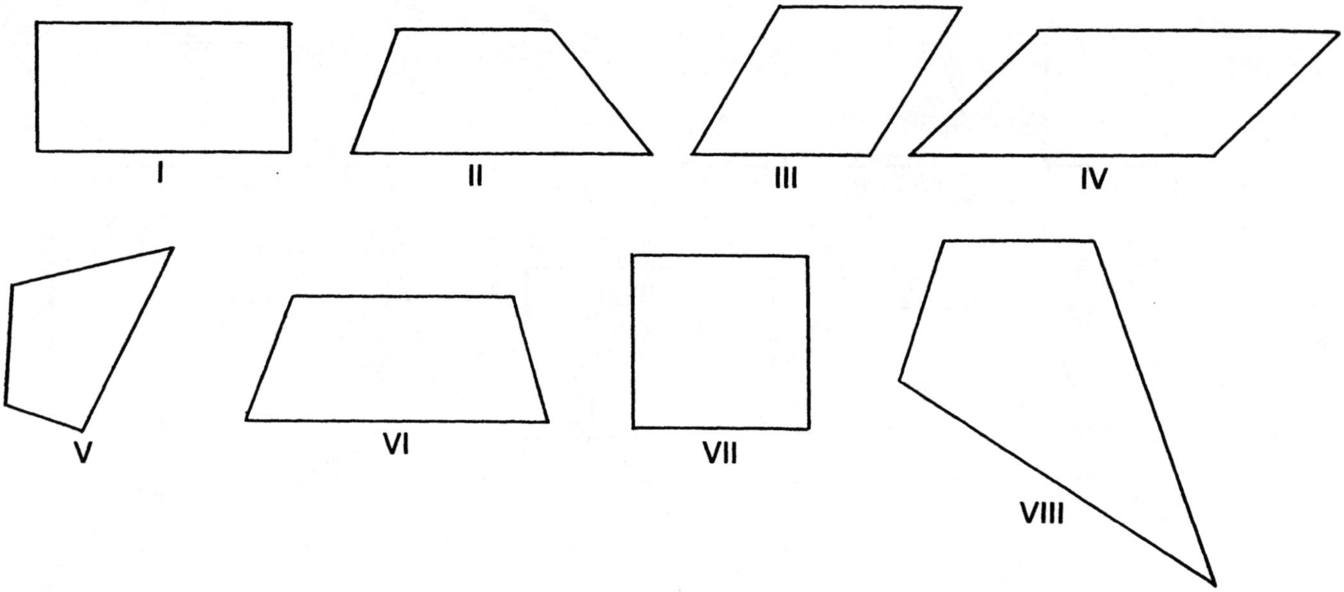

CLUE 2: I have no parallel sides.

CLUE 3: I have no congruent sides.

Which quadrilateral am I? ______

Case G-63

CLUE 1: I am one of the quadrilaterals of Case G-62: I, II, III, IV, V, VI, VII, or VIII.

CLUE 2: I am a **trapezoid***.

CLUE 3: I have no congruent sides.

Which quadrilateral am I? ______

---

*A **TRAPEZOID** is a **quadrilateral** with **exactly one pair** of **parallel sides.**

Case G-64

CLUE 1: I am one of the quadrilaterals pictured below: I, II, III, IV, V, VI, VII, or VIII.

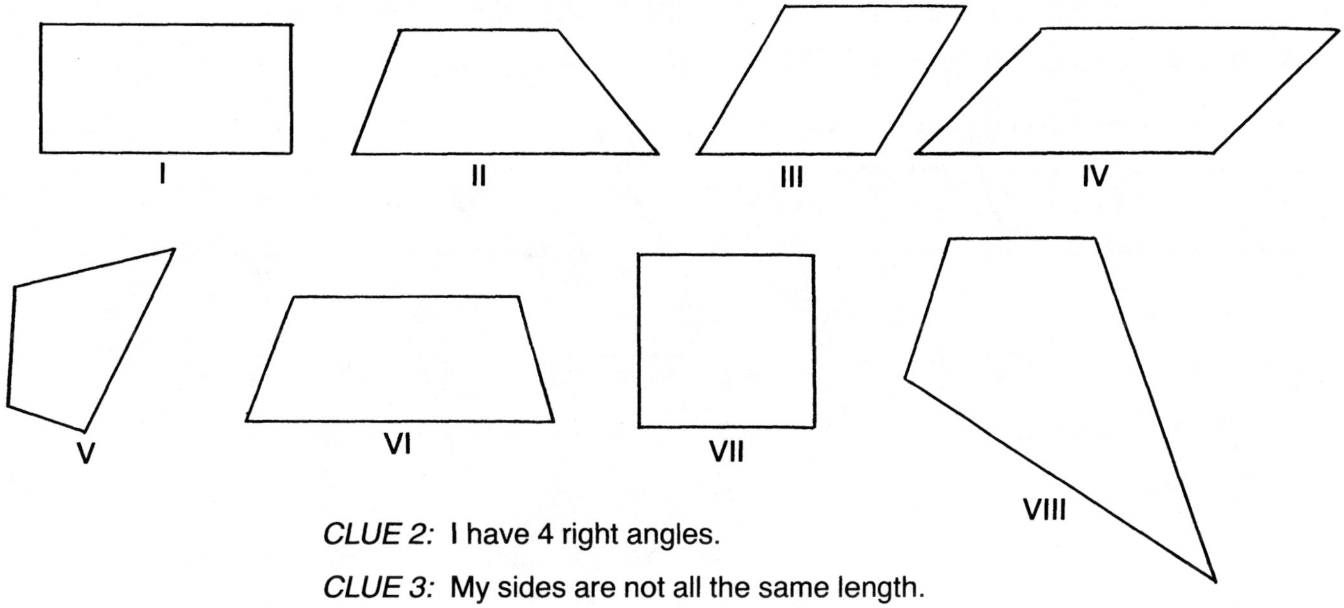

CLUE 2: I have 4 right angles.

CLUE 3: My sides are not all the same length.

Which quadrilateral am I? ______

Case G-65

CLUE 1: I am one of the quadrilaterals of Case G-64: I, II, III, IV, V, VI, VII, or VIII.

CLUE 2: All my sides are the same length.

CLUE 3: I don't have any right angles.

Which quadrilateral am I? ______

Case G-66

CLUE 1: I am one of the quadrilaterals pictured below: I, II, III, IV, V, VI, VII, or VIII.

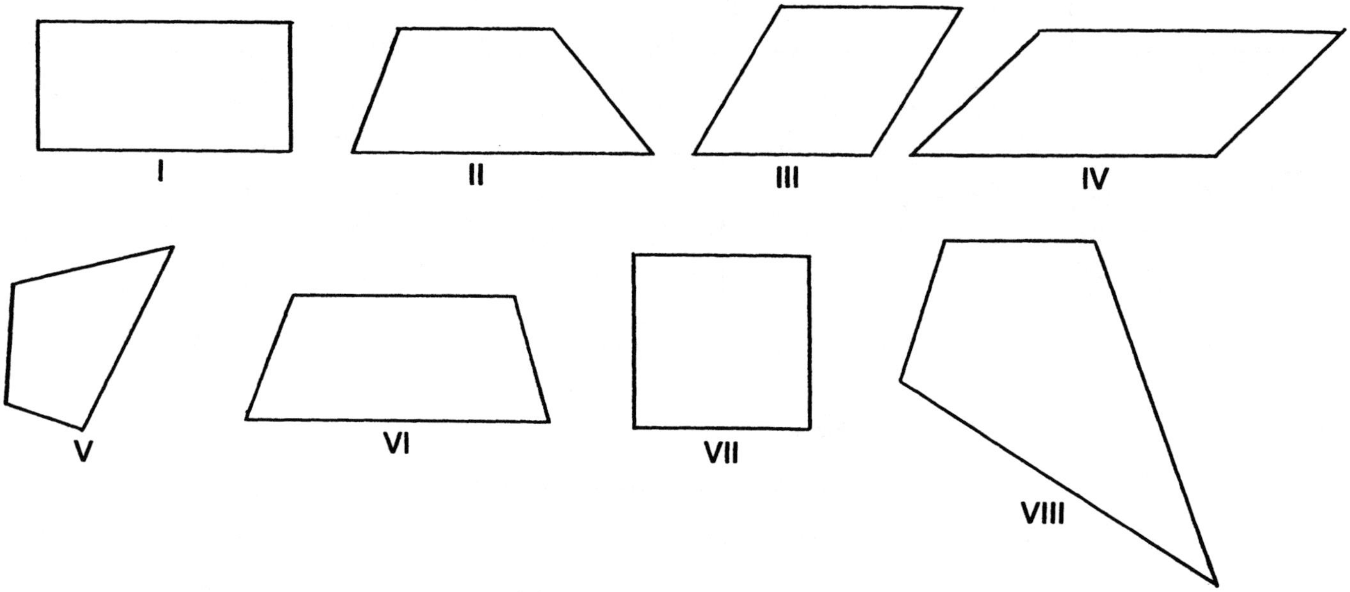

CLUE 2: I am a **parallelogram***.

CLUE 3: My sides are not all congruent.

CLUE 4: I have no right angles.

Which quadrilateral am I? ______

---

*A **PARALLELOGRAM** is a **quadrilateral** with **two pairs** of **parallel sides.**

The symbol "m∠A" is used to name the **degree measure** of ∠A. In the next three cases, you will be finding the degree measures of angles of triangles. To do this, you will need to remember that the sum of the (degree) measures of the angles of any triangle is 180°.

Case G-67

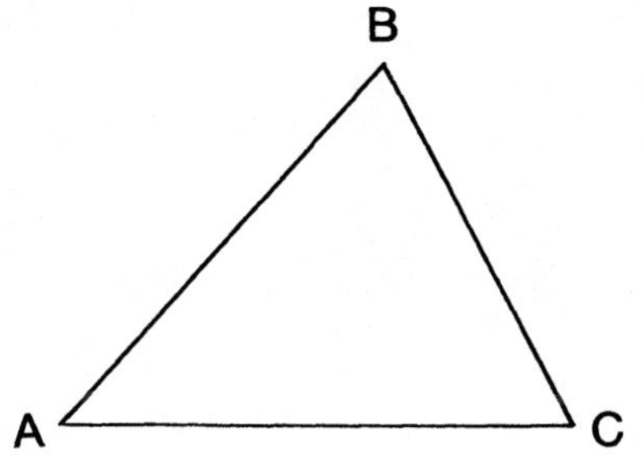

CLUE 1: m∠A = 49.

CLUE 2: m∠C = 61.

Then m∠B = ______.

Case G-68

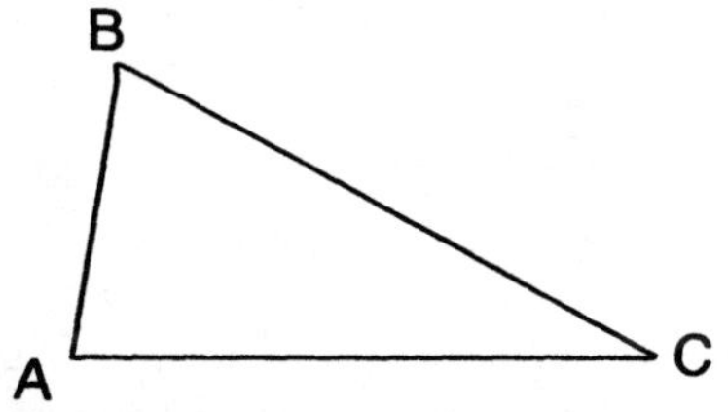

CLUE 1: m∠B = 68.

CLUE 2: m∠A = 83.

Then m∠C = ______.

Case G-69

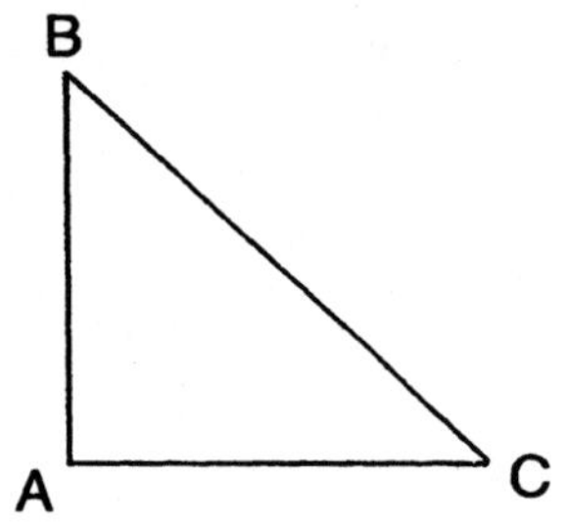

CLUE 1: m∠B = 47.

CLUE 2: △ABC is a right triangle.

Then m∠C = ______.

In several previous cases ∠A was used to name the angle with vertex at A. However, it is also common to use **three points** to **name an angle.** In particular, in the picture below, ∠BAC is a name that is used.

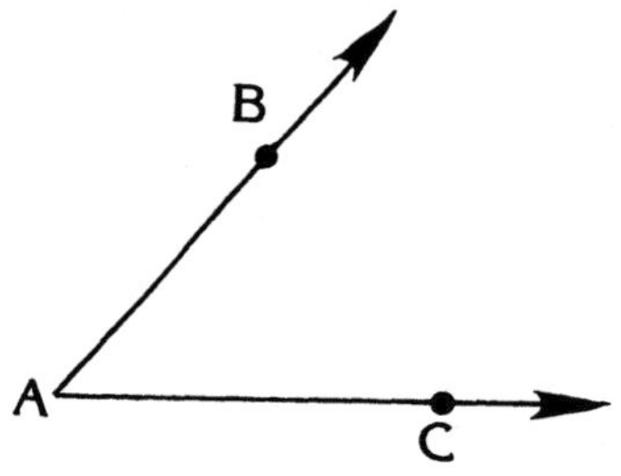

Notice that the **middle letter** is used to indicate the **vertex** while the first and third letters are points on the sides of the angle. The use of three letters is necessary when there is **more than one** angle with the **same** vertex, which is what happens in the next four cases. As is to be expected, m∠BAC is used to mean the degree measure of the angle, and in each of these cases you are to find the degree measure of an angle.

Case G-70

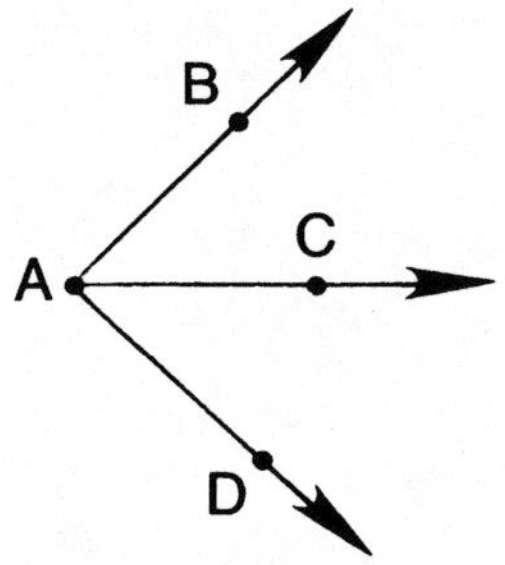

CLUE 1: m∠BAC = 43.

CLUE 2: m∠CAD = 41.

Then m∠BAD = ______.

Case G-71

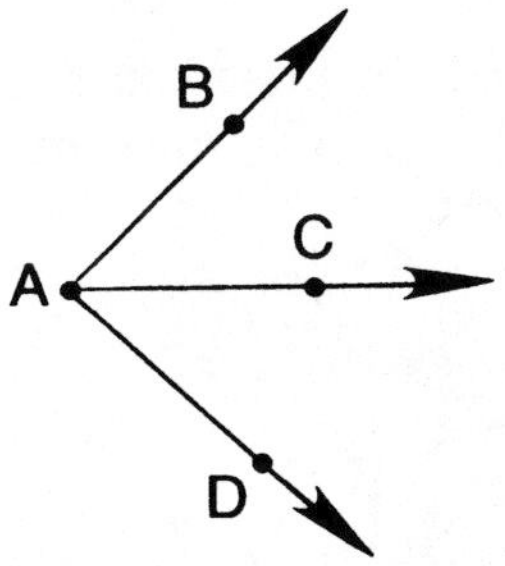

CLUE 1: m∠BAC = 49.

CLUE 2: m∠BAD = 83.

Then m∠CAD = ______.

Case G-72

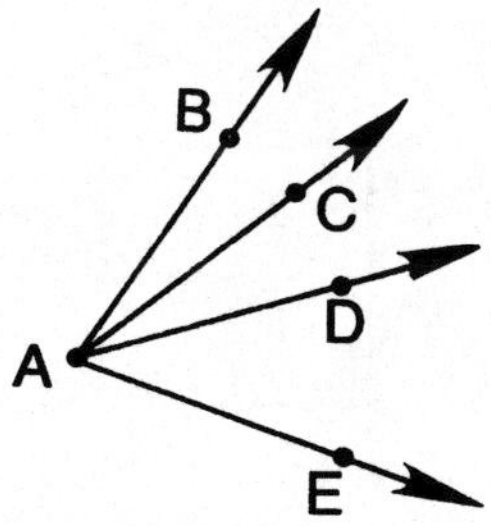

CLUE 1: m∠BAC = 17.

CLUE 2: m∠CAD = 21.

CLUE 3: m∠DAE = 35.

Then m∠BAE = ______.

Case G-73

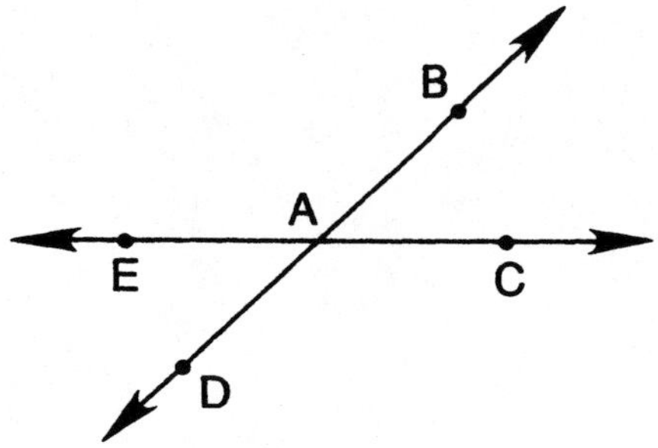

CLUE 1: m∠BAC = 43.

Then m∠BAE = ______.

The **AREA** of a closed curve is the **number of square units** it takes to "cover" it, and the **PERIMETER** is the **distance around** it. For instance, the area of the quadrilateral below is 10 square units and its perimeter is 14 units.

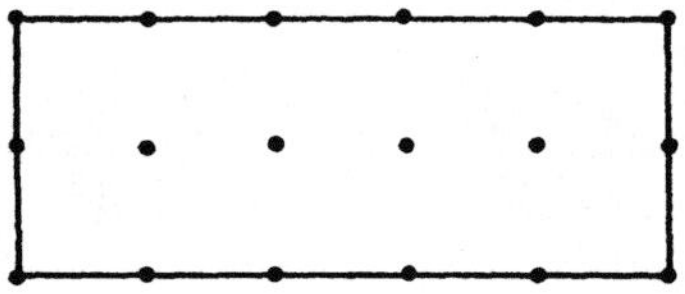

Case G-74

CLUE 1: I am one of the figures below: I, II, III, IV or V.

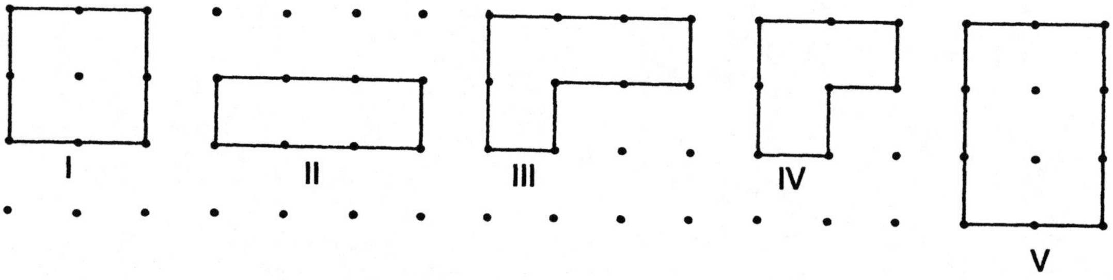

CLUE 2: I have a perimeter of 10 units.

CLUE 3: I have an area greater than 5 square units.

Which figure am I? ______

Case G-75

CLUE 1: I am one of the figures below: I, II, III, IV, or V.

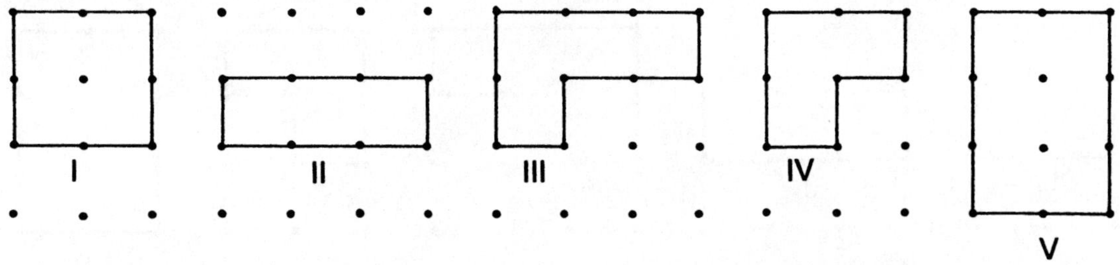

CLUE 2: I have a perimeter of 8 units.

CLUE 3: I have an area of 3 square units.

CLUE 4: I have 4 vertices (corners).

Which figure am I? ______

Case G-76

CLUE 1: I am one of the figures of Case G-75: I, II, III, IV, or V.

CLUE 2: I have a perimeter of 10 units.

CLUE 3: I have an area less than 5 square units.

Which figure am I? ______

Case G-77

CLUE 1: I am one of the figures of G-75: I, II, III, IV, or V.

CLUE 2: I have a perimeter of 8 units.

CLUE 3: I have an area of 4 square units.

Which figure am I? ______

Case G-78

CLUE 1: I am one of the figures below: I, II, III, IV, or V.

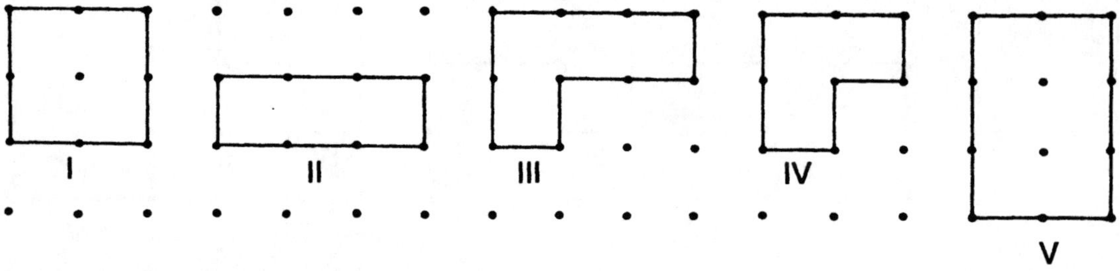

CLUE 2: I have a perimeter of 8 units.

CLUE 3: I have an area of 3 square units.

CASE 4: I am not a quadrilateral.

Which figure am I? ______

Case G-79

CLUE 1: I am one of the figures below: I, II, III, IV, or V.

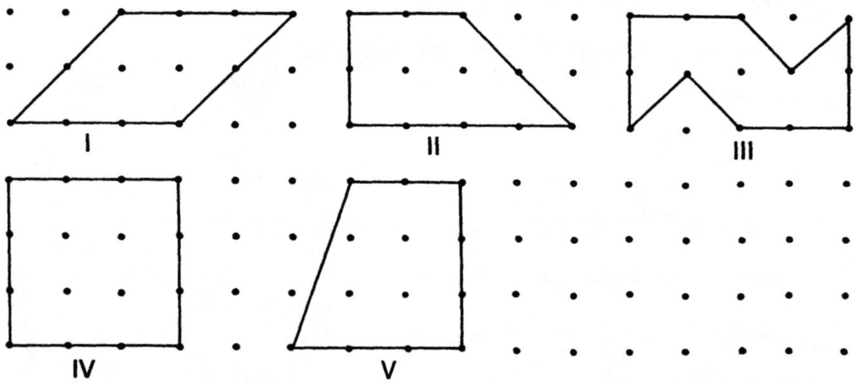

CLUE 2: My area is 6 square units.

CLUE 3: I have 4 sides.

CLUE 4: I am not a trapezoid.

Which figure am I? ______

Case G-80

CLUE 1: I am one of the figures below: I, II, III, IV, or V.

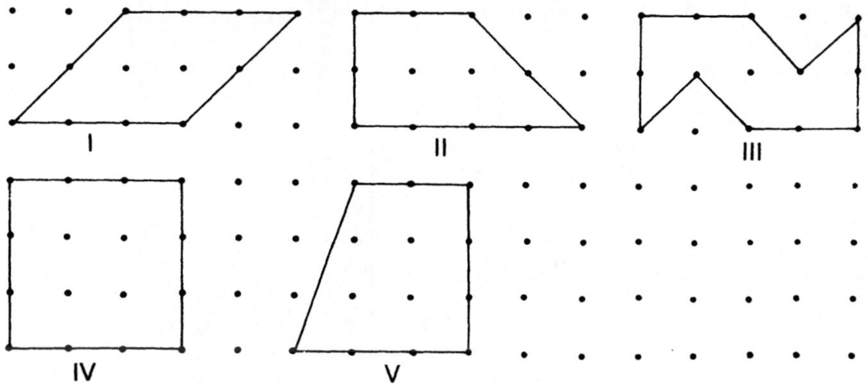

CLUE 2: I have 4 sides.

CLUE 3: I have an area greater than 6 square units.

CLUE 4: I am not the largest figure (in area).

Which figure am I? ______

Case G-81

CLUE 1: I am one of the figures of Case G-80: I, II, III, IV, or V.

CLUE 2: I have at least one right angle.

CLUE 3: My area is less than 7 square units.

CLUE 4: I am not a trapezoid.

Which figure am I? ______

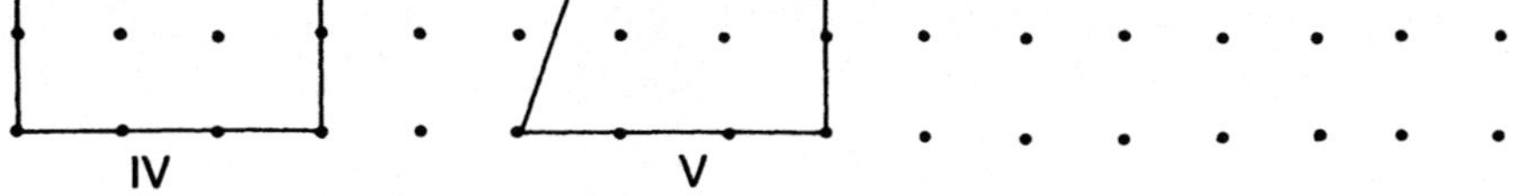

The next five detective stories all involve the **SUMS OF THE MEASURES OF THE ANGLES** of certain figures. For instance, the sum of the measures of the angles of a triangle is 180°. Consider the quadrilateral below. Note that the **diagonal** (dotted segment) forms two triangles and so the sum of the measures of the angles of the quadrilateral is 180° + 180° = 360°.

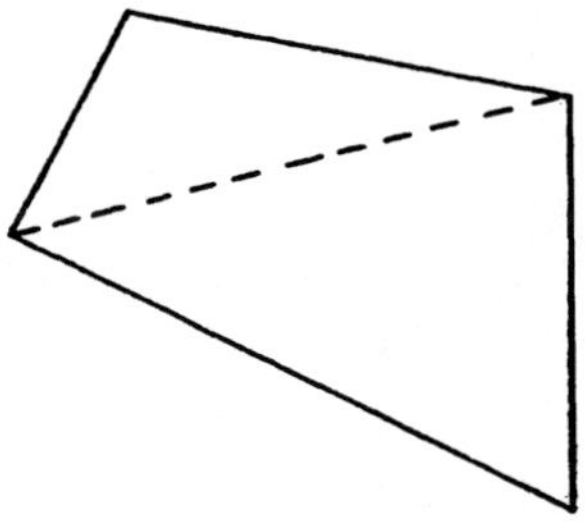

For the pentagon below, the two diagonals form three triangles and hence the sum of the measures of the angles of the pentagon is 180° + 180° + 180° = 540°.

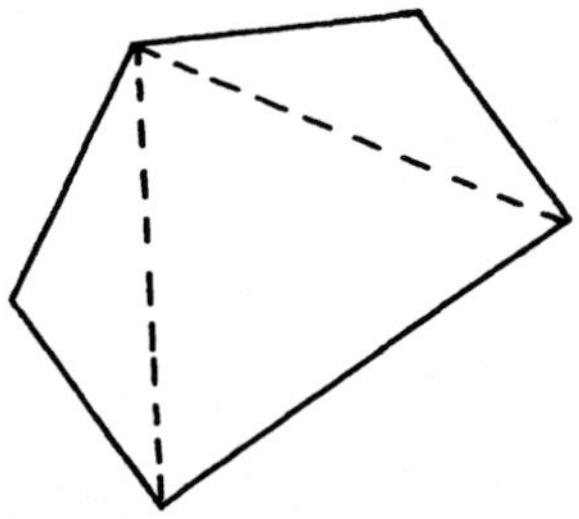

The sum of the measures of the angles of a hexagon can be found in a similar manner.

Case G-82

CLUE 1: I am one of the figures below: I, II, III, IV, V, or VI.

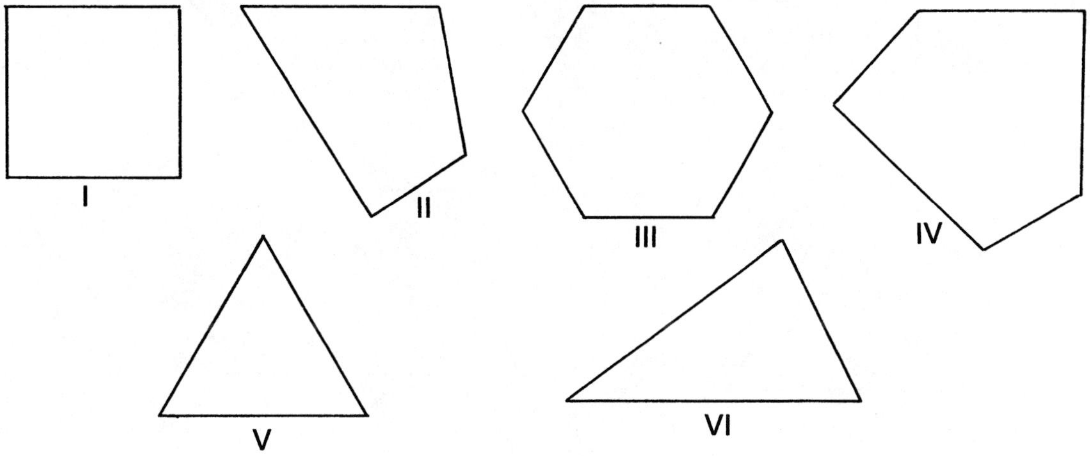

CLUE 2: The sum of the measures of my angles is 360°.

CLUE 3: I don't have any right angles.

Which figure am I? ______

Case G-83

CLUE 1: I am one of the figures of Case G-82: I, II, III, IV, V, or VI.

CLUE 2: The sum of the measures of my angles is 180°.

CLUE 3: My angles are all the same size.

Which figure am I? ______

Case G-84

CLUE 1: I am one of the figures below: I, II, III, IV, V, or VI.

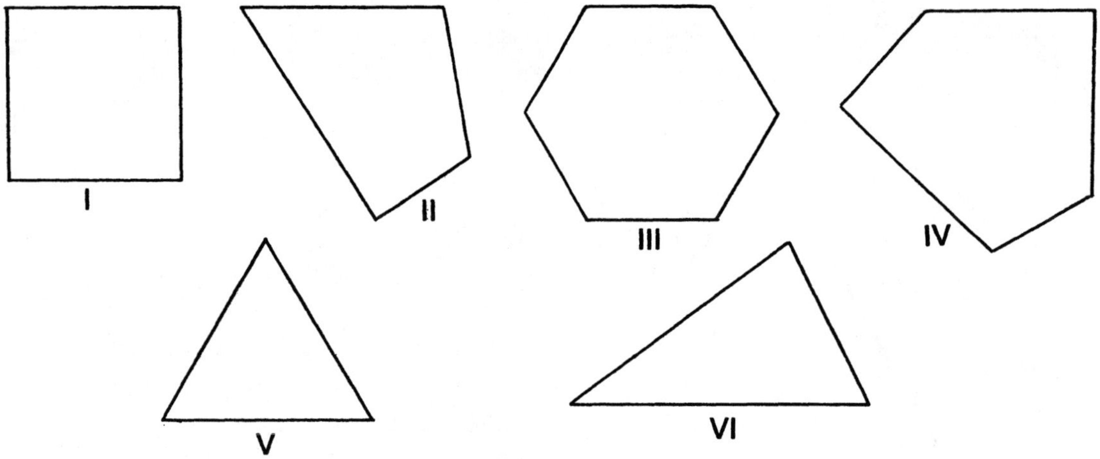

CLUE 2: The sum of the measures of my angles is greater than 360°.

CLUE 3: My sides are not all the same length.

Which figure am I? ______

Case G-85

CLUE 1: I am one of the figures of Case G-84: I, II, III, IV, V, or VI.

CLUE 2: All my sides are congruent.

CLUE 3: The sum of the measures of my angles is greater than 360°.

Which figure am I? ______

Case G-86

CLUE 1: I am one of the figures of Case G-84: I, II, III, IV, V, or VI.

CLUE 2: My angles are all **congruent***.

CLUE 3: I am a quadrilateral.

Which figure am I? ______

---

*ANGLES are CONGRUENT if they have the **same degree measure.**

The next six detective stories all involve quadrilaterals and their diagonals. In the following quadrilateral, notice that the diagonals, $\overline{AC}$ and $\overline{BD}$ are not perpendicular to each other since no right angles are formed. When a segment is **BISECTED**, it is separated into **two parts** which are the **same size**. Notice that $\overline{AC}$ does not bisect $\overline{BD}$ and $\overline{BD}$ does not bisect $\overline{AC}$.

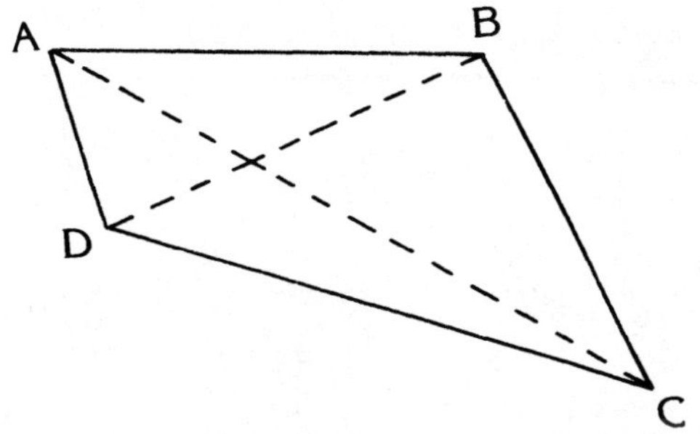

On the other hand, the diagonals of the quadrilateral below are perpendicular to each other, since right angles are formed, and they bisect each other, since **I** is the **midpoint** of $\overline{EG}$ and **I** is the midpoint of $\overline{FH}$.

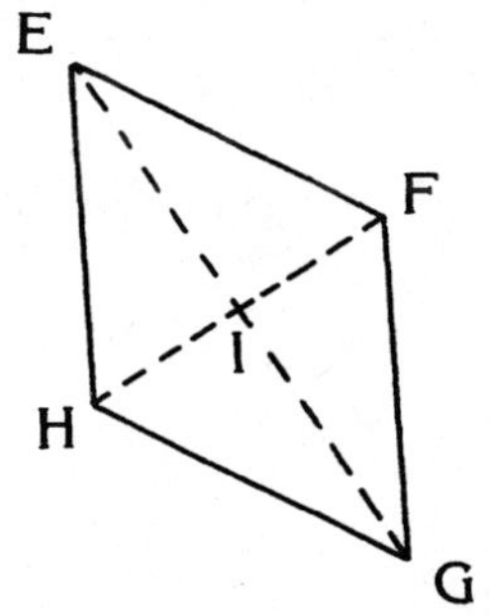

To solve these cases you will need to draw in the diagonals and examine them.

Case G-87

CLUE 1: I am one of the quadrilaterals below: I, II, III, IV, V, or VI.

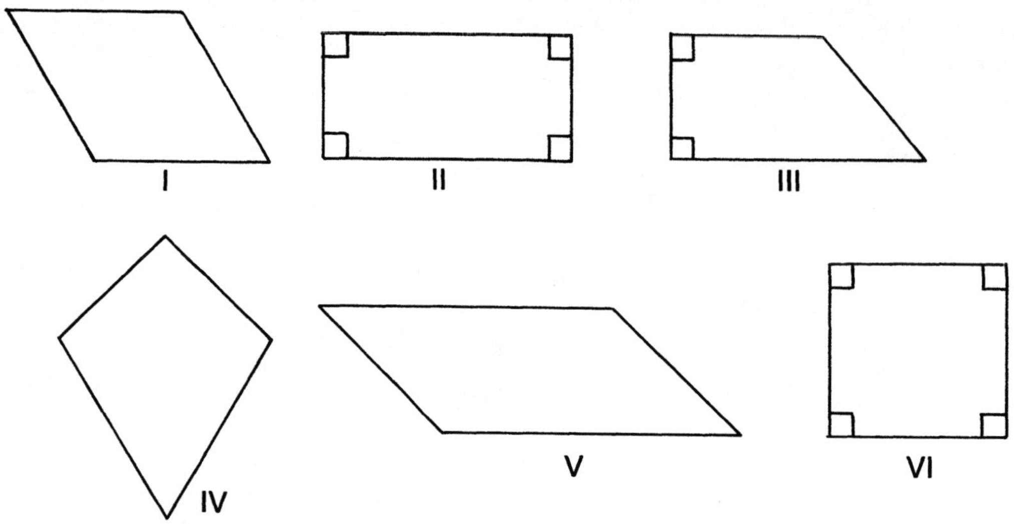

CLUE 2: My diagonals are perpendicular to each other.

CLUE 3: My diagonals are not congruent.

CLUE 4: My diagonals do not bisect each other.

Which quadrilateral am I? ______

Case G-88

CLUE 1: I am one of the quadrilaterals of Case G-87: I, II, III, IV, V, or VI.

CLUE 2: My diagonals are not perpendicular.

CLUE 3: My diagonals are not congruent.

CLUE 4: My diagonals do not bisect each other.

Which quadrilateral am I? ______

Case G-89

CLUE 1: I am one of the quadrilaterals below: I, II, III, IV, V, or VI.

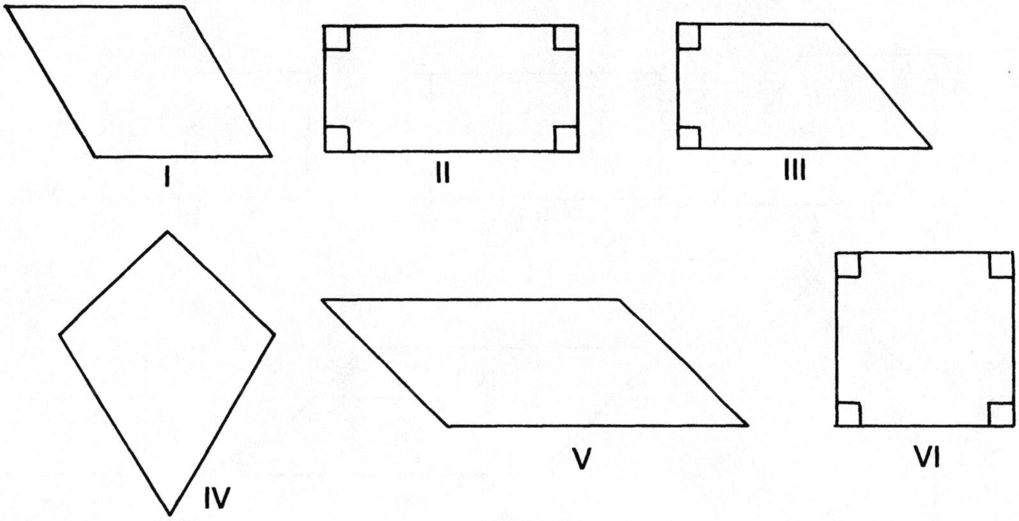

CLUE 2: My diagonals are perpendicular.

CLUE 3: My diagonals are not congruent.

CLUE 4: My diagonals bisect each other.

Which quadrilateral am I? ______

Case G-90

CLUE 1: I am one of the quadrilaterals of Case G-89: I, II, III, IV, V, or VI.

CLUE 2: My diagonals are not perpendicular.

CLUE 3: My diagonals bisect each other.

CLUE 4: My diagonals are not congruent.

Which quadrilateral am I? ______

Case G-91

CLUE 1: I am one of the quadrilaterals below: I, II, III, IV, V, or VI.

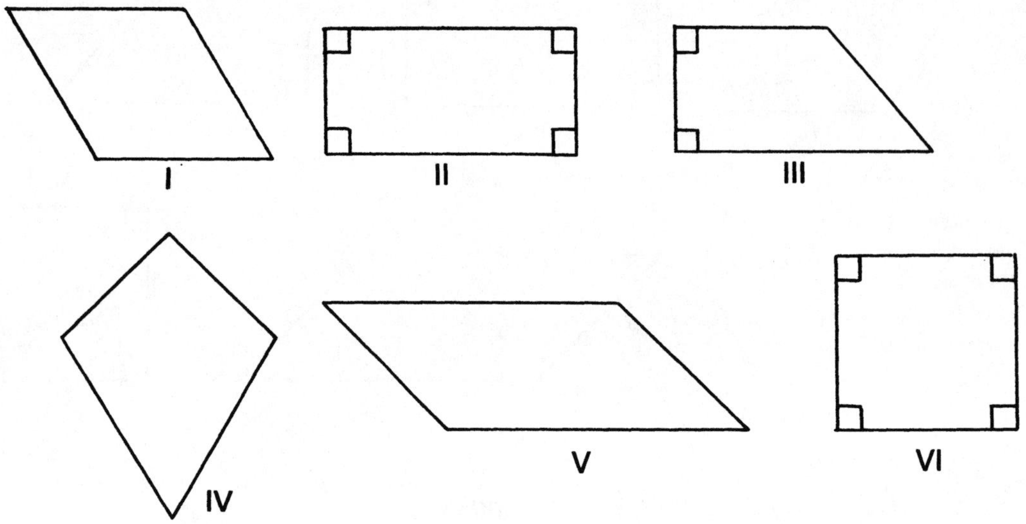

CLUE 2: My diagonals are not perpendicular.

CLUE 3: My diagonals are congruent.

Which quadrilateral am I? ______

Case G-92

CLUE 1: I am one of the quadrilaterals of Case G-91: I, II, III, IV, V, or VI.

CLUE 2: My diagonals are perpendicular.

CLUE 3: My diagonals are congruent.

Which quadrilateral am I? ______

The next four cases concern the area and circumference of circles. (The **CIRCUMFERENCE** of a circle is the distance around it. Circumference is another name for perimeter.) The formula for the **AREA OF A CIRCLE** is $A = \pi r^2$ and the formula for the **CIRCUMFERENCE** $C = 2\pi r$. Remember $\pi \approx 3.14$. You will need to measure the radius of each circle in the next case so that you find the area and circumference.

Case G-93

CLUE 1: I am one of the circles below I II, III, or IV.

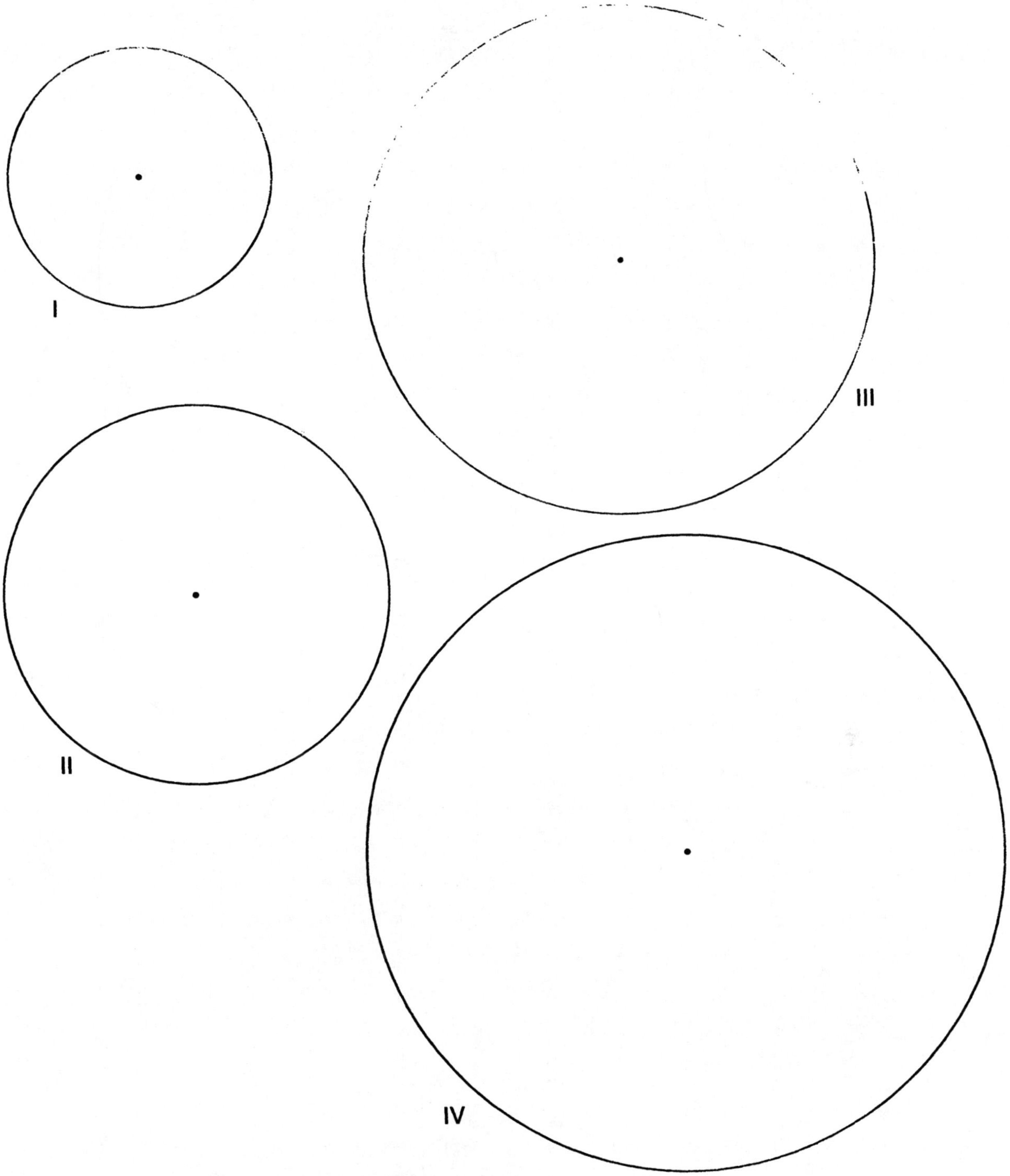

CLUE 2: My area is greater than 27 square centimeters.

CLUE 3: My circumference is less than 20 centimeters.

Which circle am I? ______

Case G-94

CLUE 1: I am one of the circles below: I, II, III, or IV.

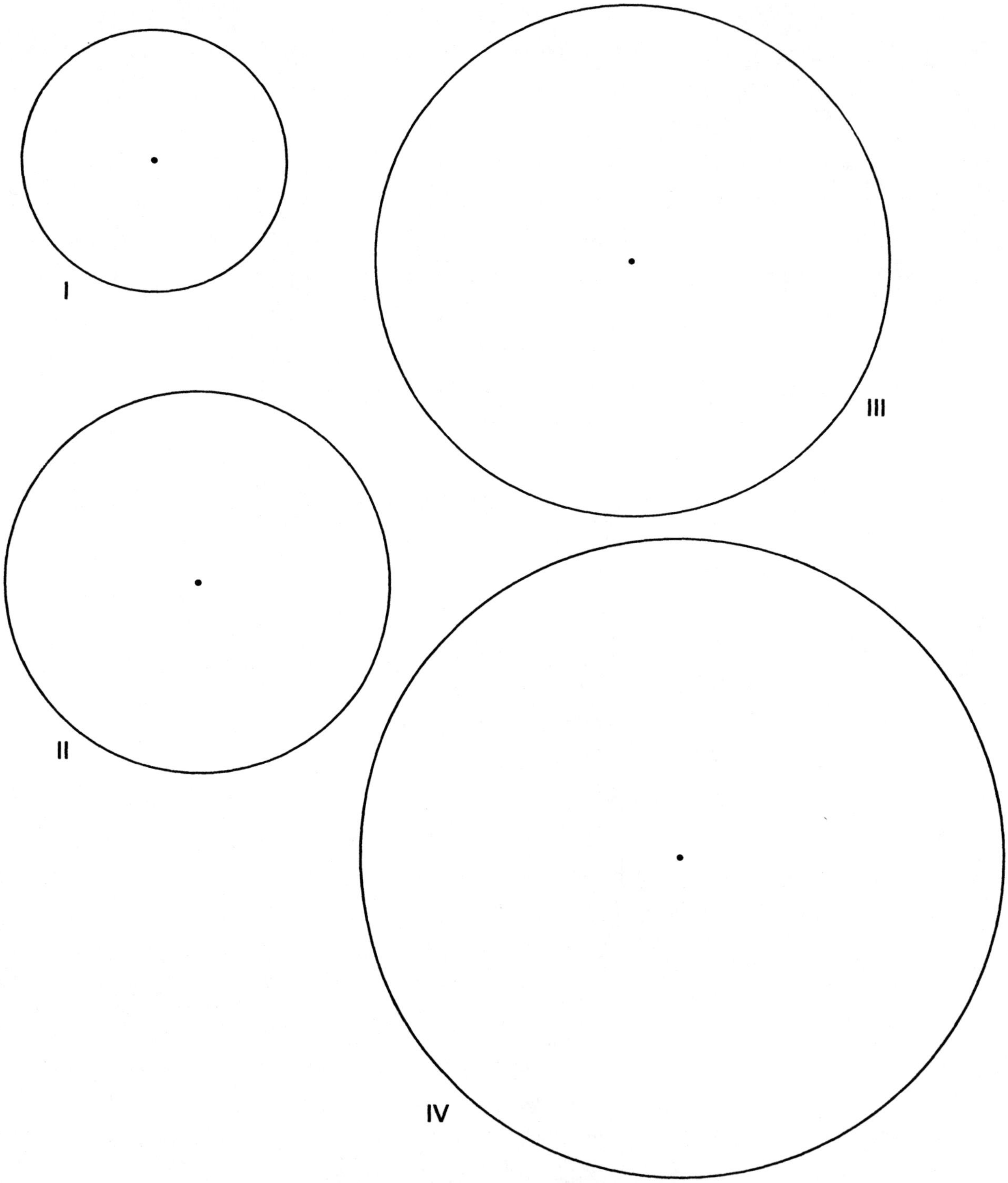

CLUE 2: My circumference is less than 30 centimeters.

CLUE 3: My area is greater than 48 square centimeters.

Which circle am I? ______

Case G-95

CLUE 1 I am one of the circles below: I, II, III, or IV

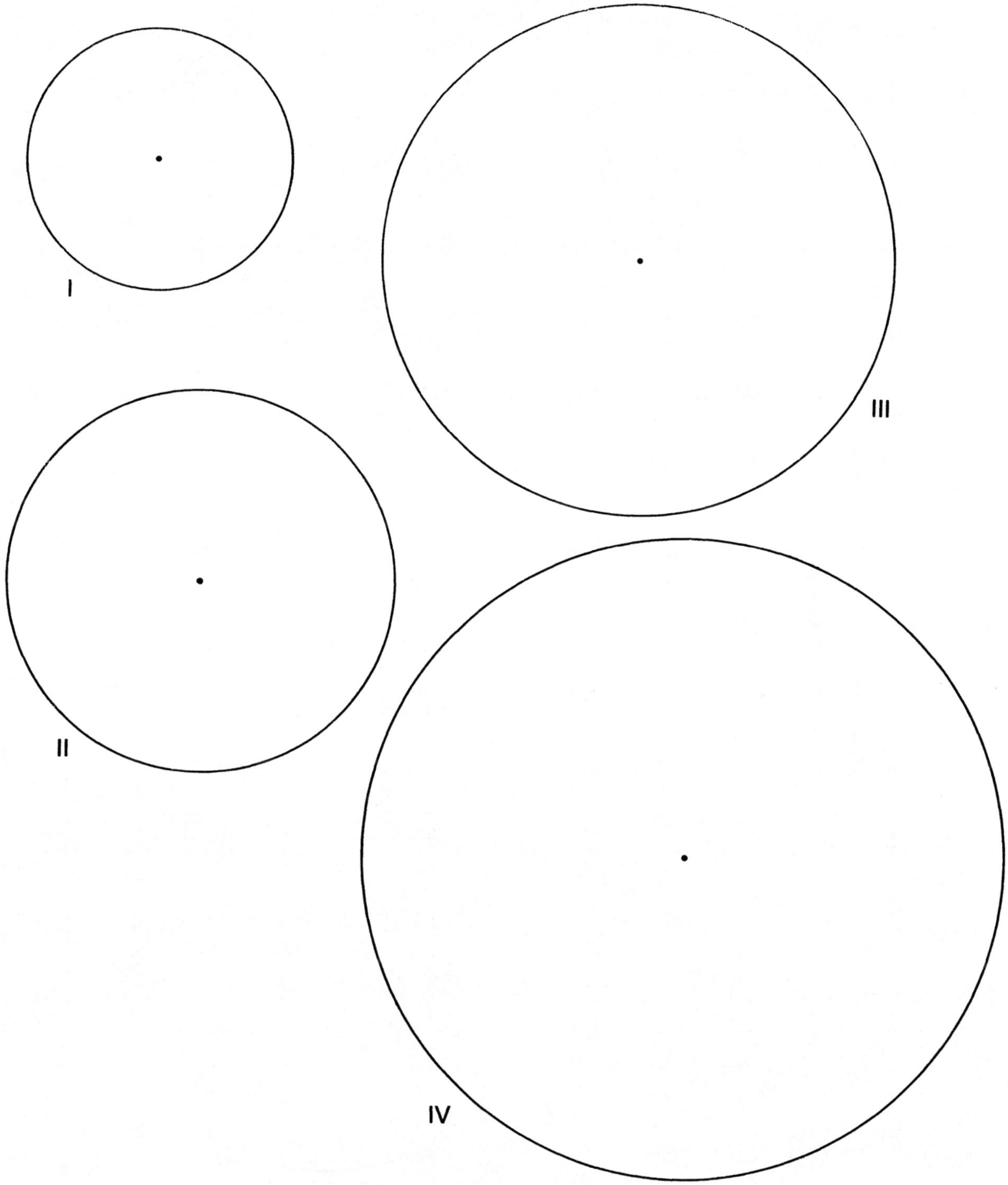

CLUE 2: My area (in square centimeters) is equal to my circumference (in centimeters).

Which circle am I? ______

Case G-96

CLUE 1: I am one of the circles below: I, II, III, or IV.

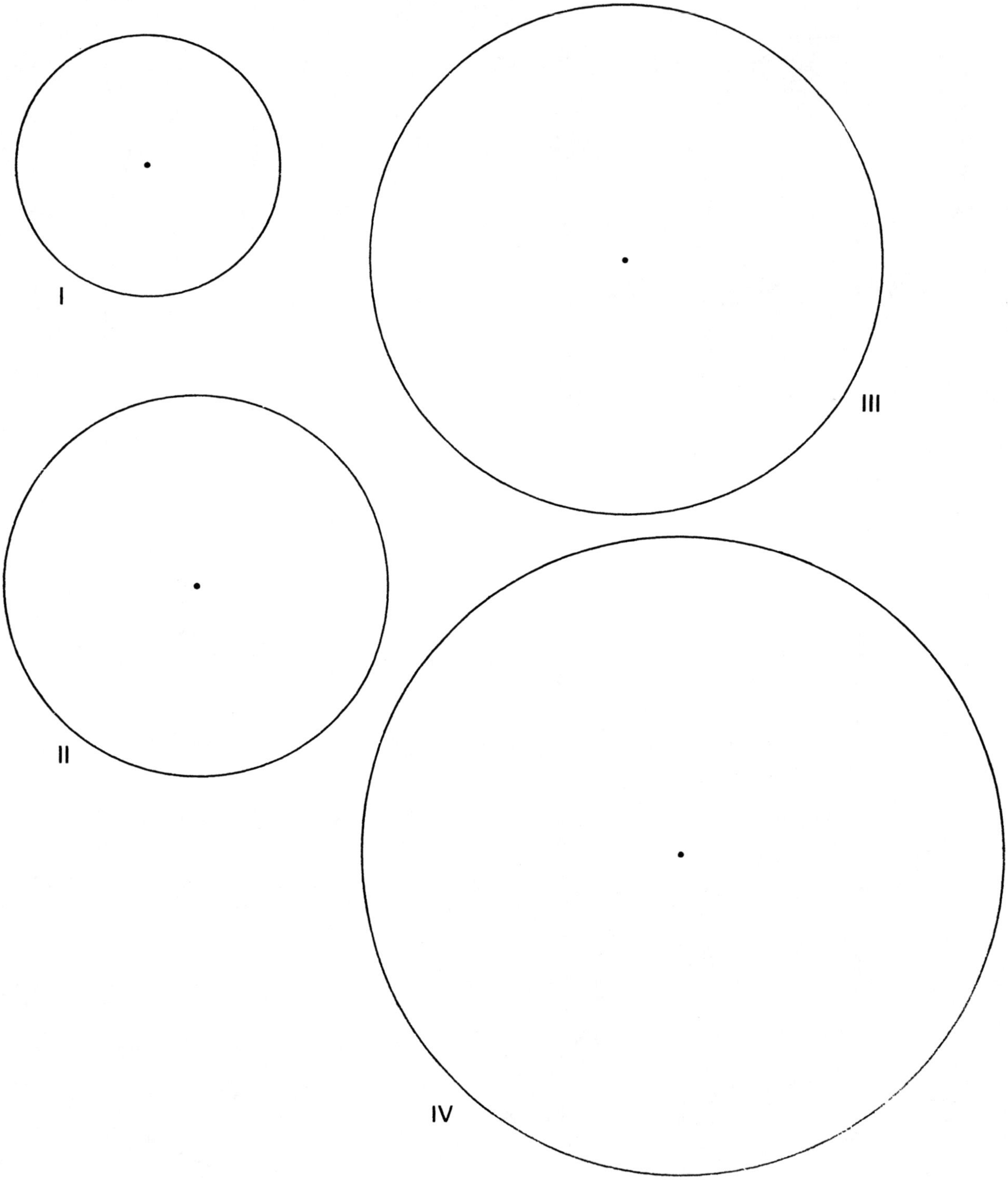

CLUE 2 My area (in square centimeters) is 2 ½ times my circumference (in centimeters)

Which circle am I?

As you work the next seven detective stories, you will need to determine the **VOLUME** of geometric solids. In these cases you will be able to do this by **counting** the small **cubes** pictured.

Case G-97

CLUE 1: I am one of the solids below: I, II, III, IV, or V.

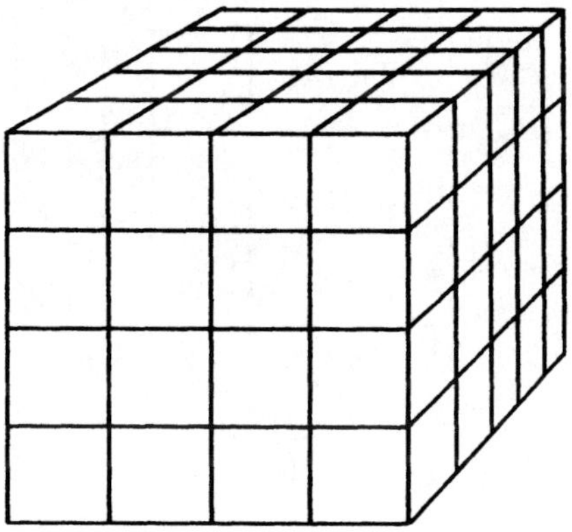

I

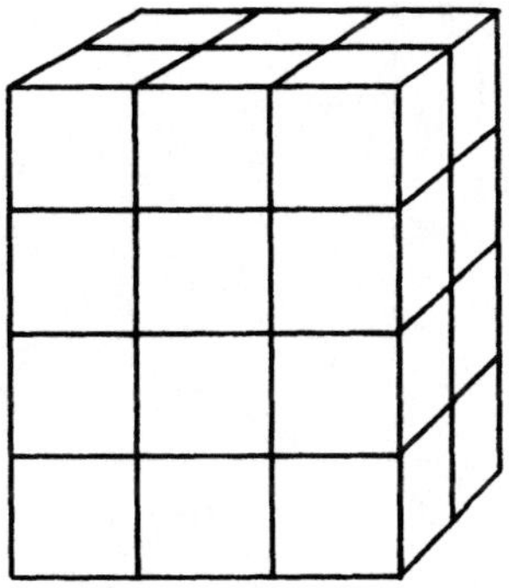

II

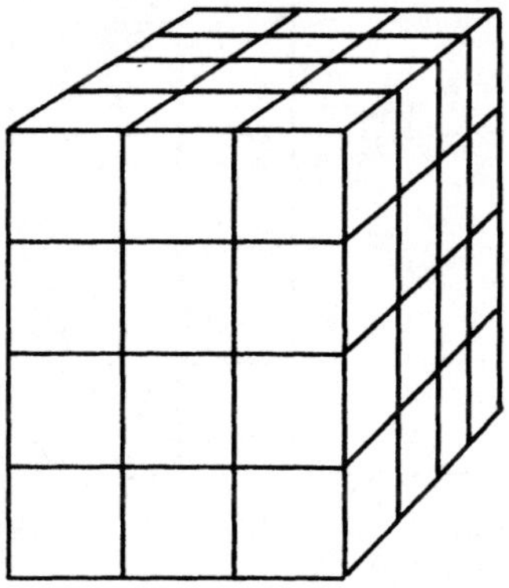

III

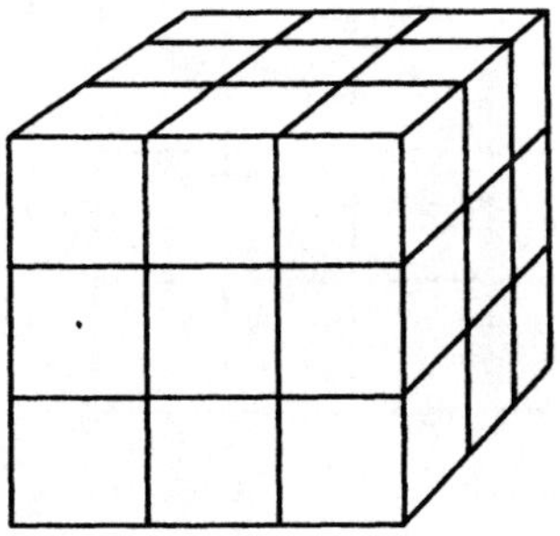

IV

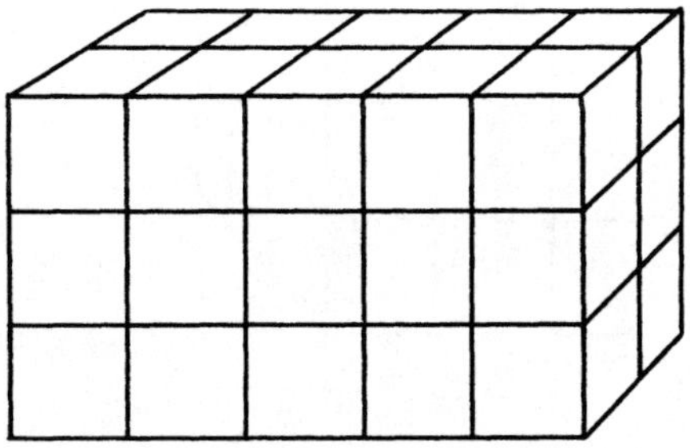

V

CLUE 2: I have the greatest volume of all these solids.

Which solid am I? ______

CLUE 1: I am one of the solids below: I, II, III, IV, or V.

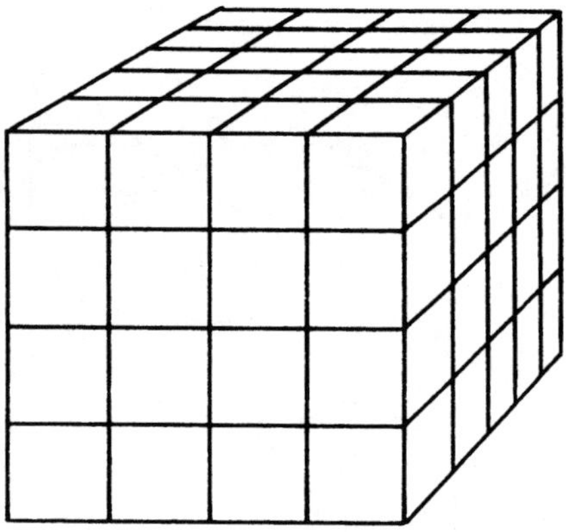

I

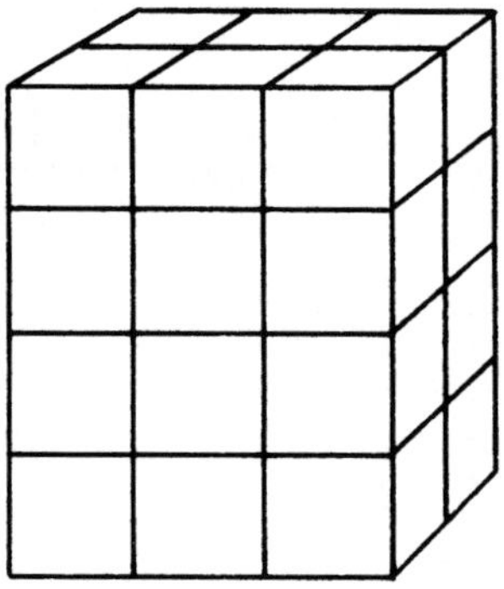

II

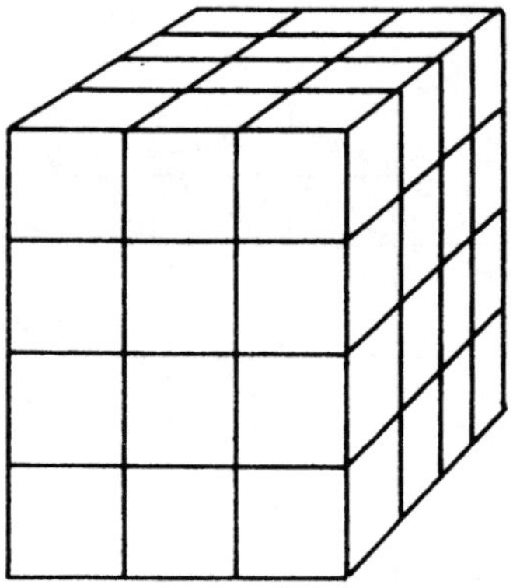

III

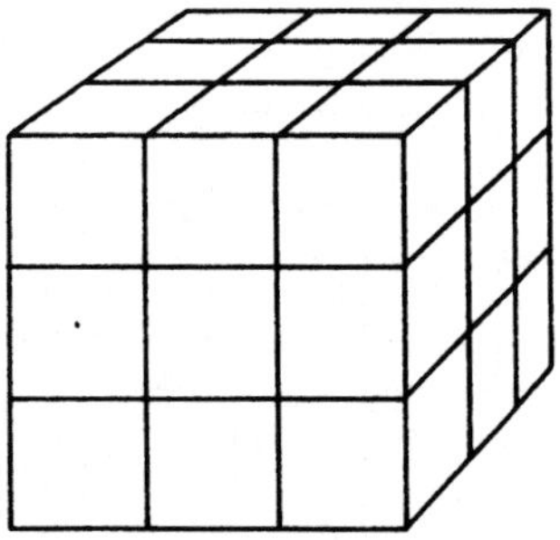

IV

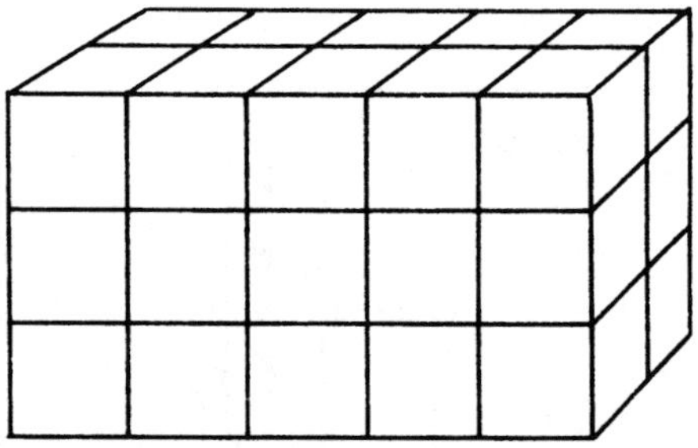

V

CLUE 2: My volume is less than 50 cubic units.

CLUE 3: My volume is greater than 30 cubic units.

Which solid am I? ______

Case G-99

CLUE 1: I am one of the solids below: I, II, III, IV, or V.

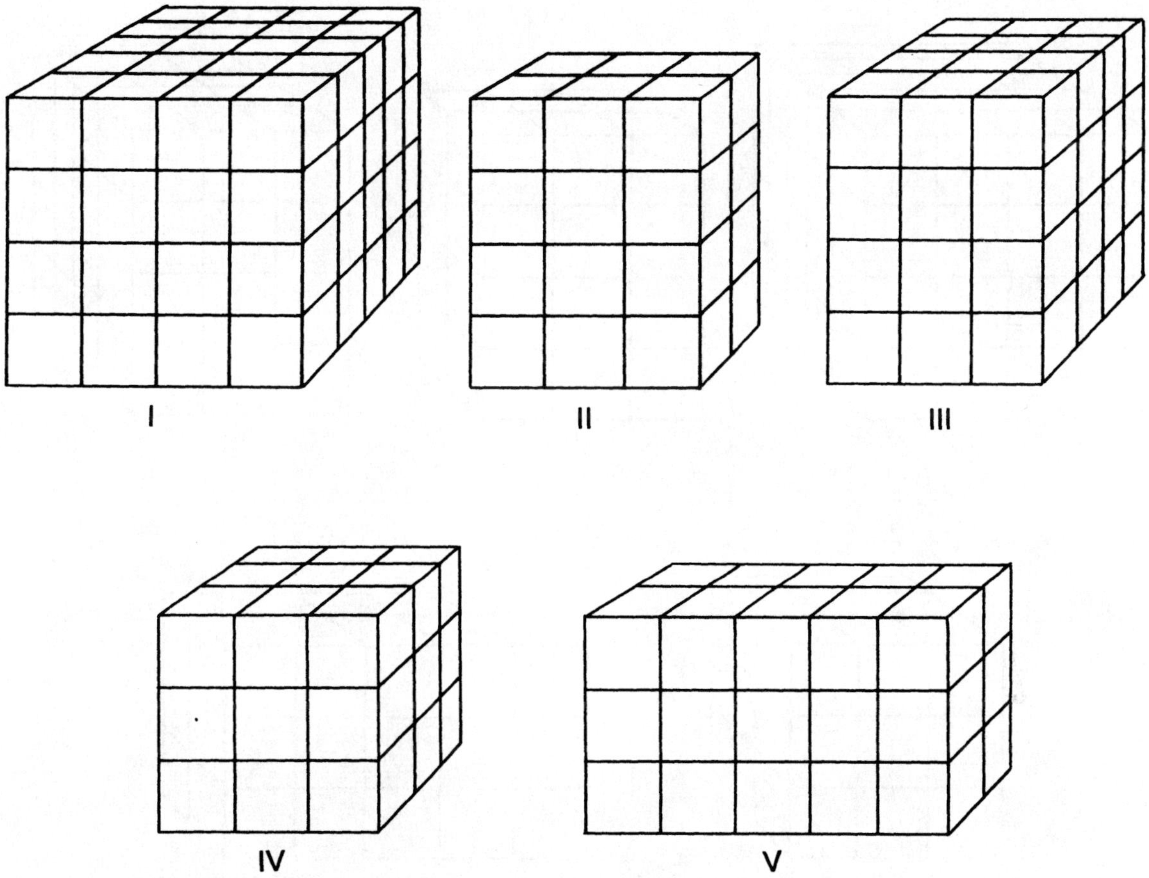

CLUE 2: My volume is greater than 25 cubic units.

CLUE 3: My volume is less than 30 cubic units.

Which solid am I? ______

Case G-100

CLUE 1: I am one of the solids below: I, II, III, IV, or V.

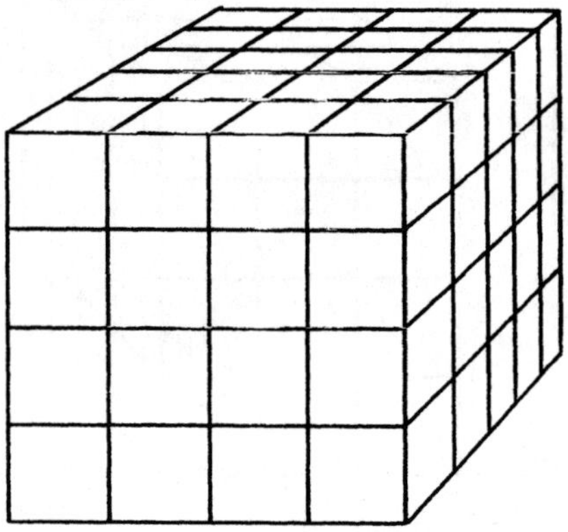

I

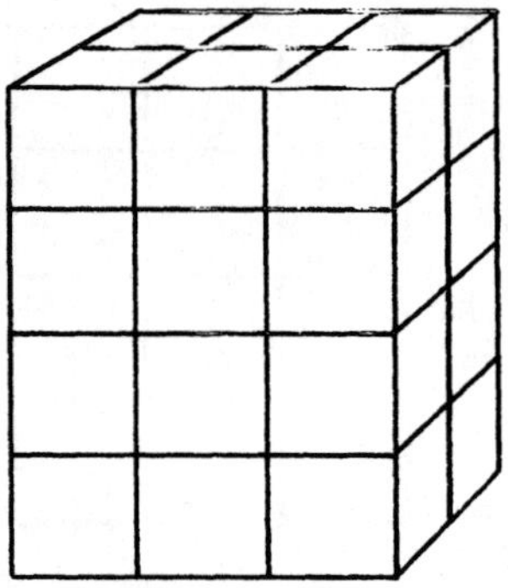

II

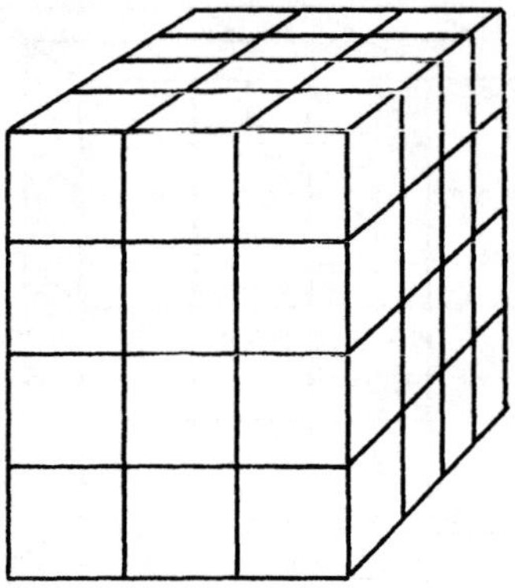

III

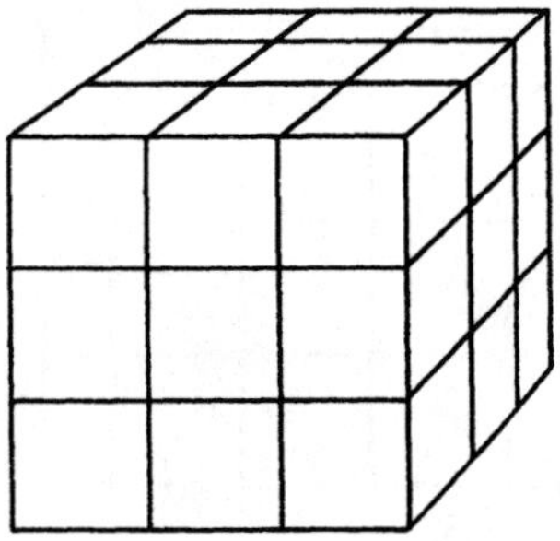

IV

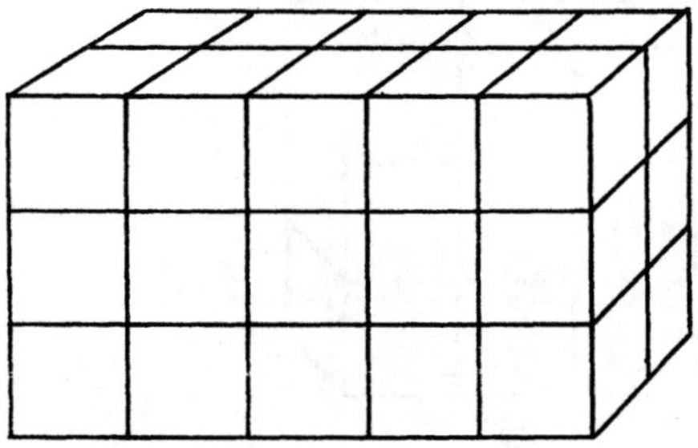

V

CLUE 2: My volume is less than 40 cubic units.

CLUE 3: My volume is greater than 28 cubic units.

Which solid am I? ______

Case G-101

CLUE 1: I am one of the solids below: I, II, III, IV, or V.

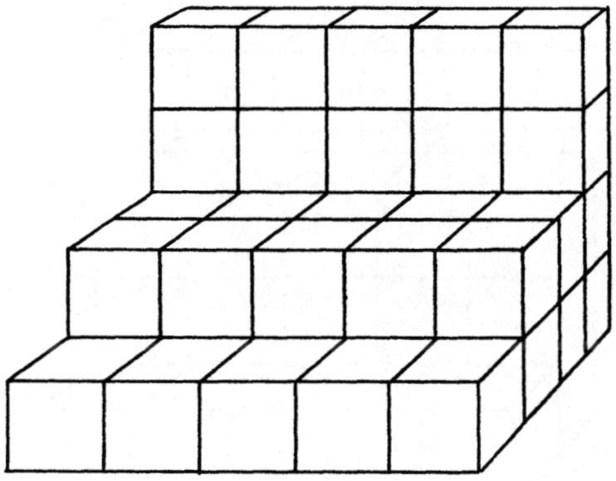

I

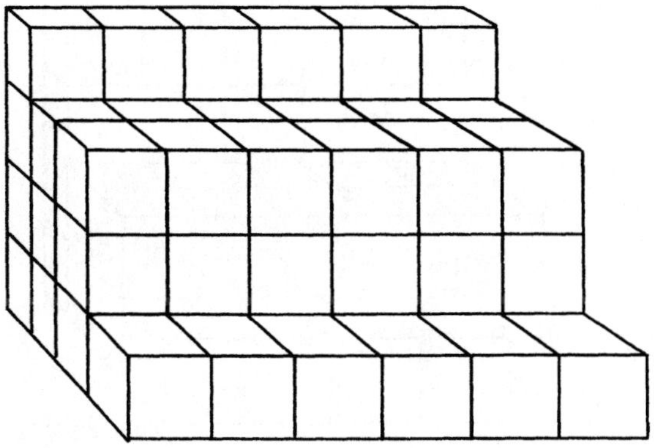

II

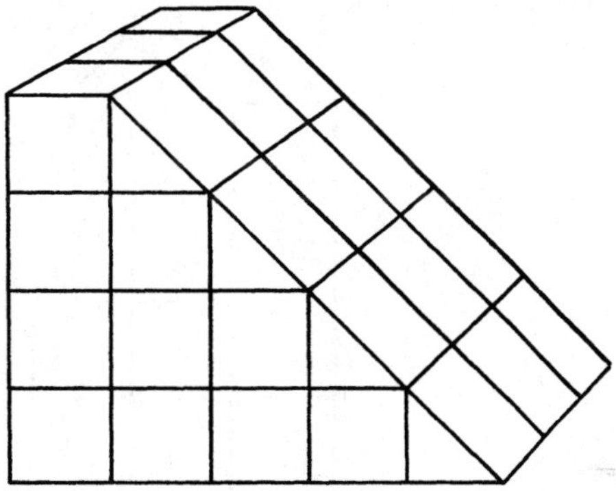

III

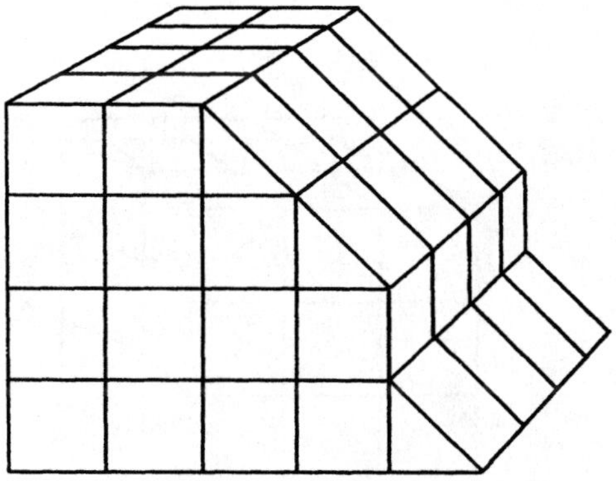

IV

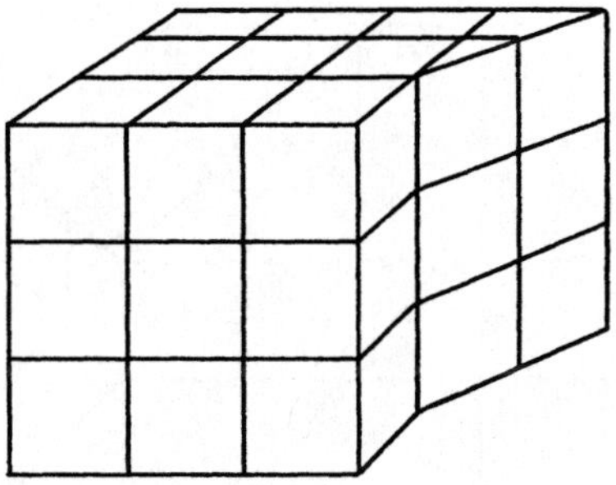

V

CLUE 2: I am the smallest of these solids.

Which solid am I? ______

Case G-102

CLUE 1: I am one of the solids below: I, II, III, IV, or V.

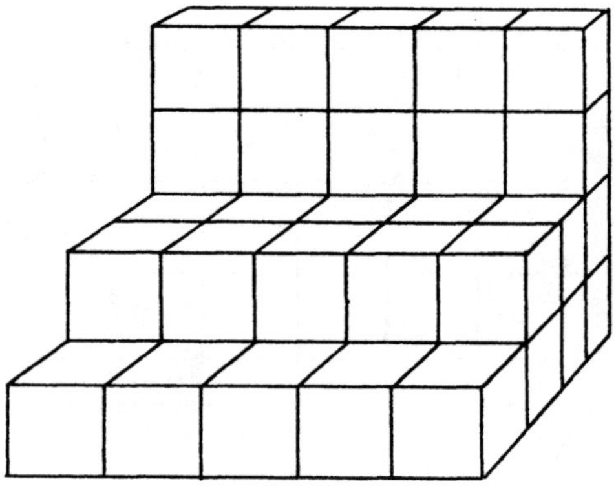

I

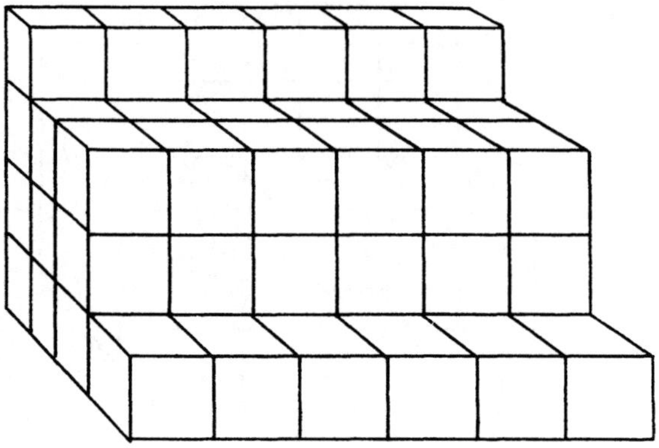

II

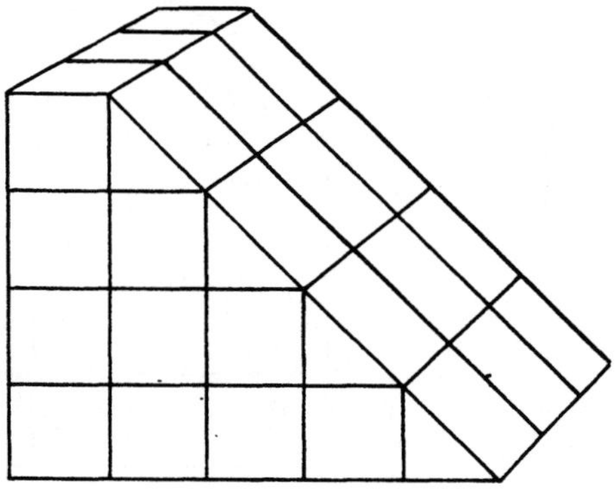

III

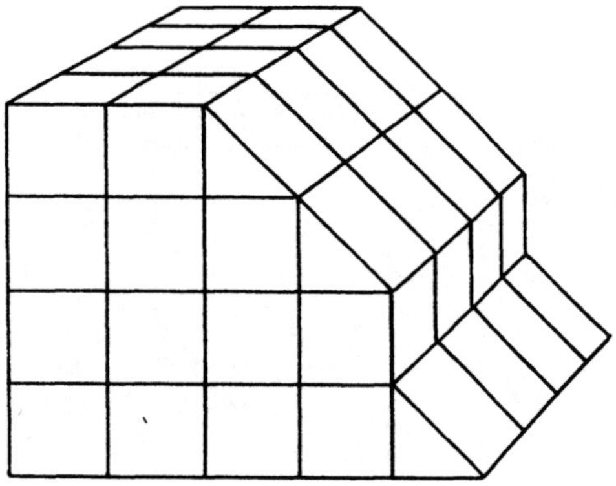

IV

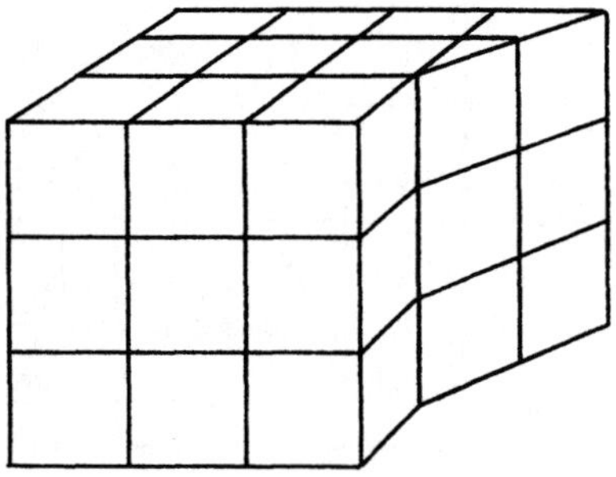

V

CLUE 2: My volume is less than 60 cubic units.

CLUE 3: My volume is more than 50 cubic units.

Which solid am I? ______

Case G-103

CLUE 1: I am the one of the solids below: I, II, III, IV, or V.

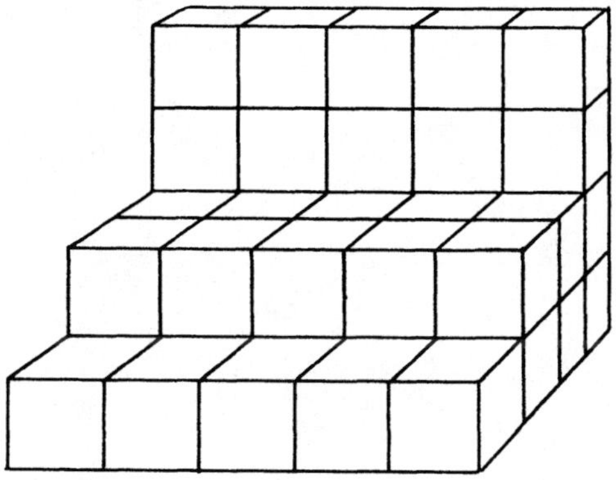

I

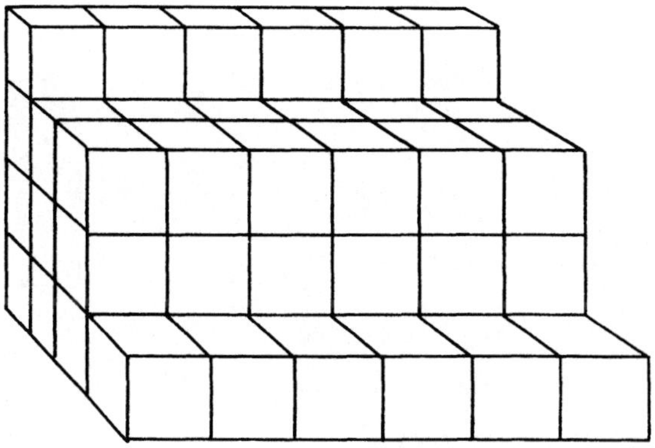

II

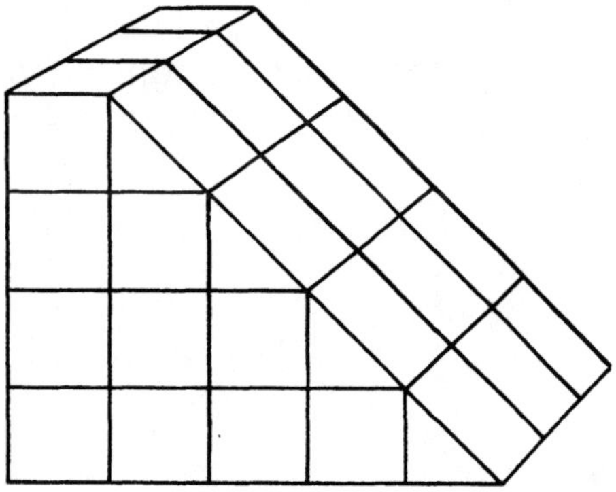

III

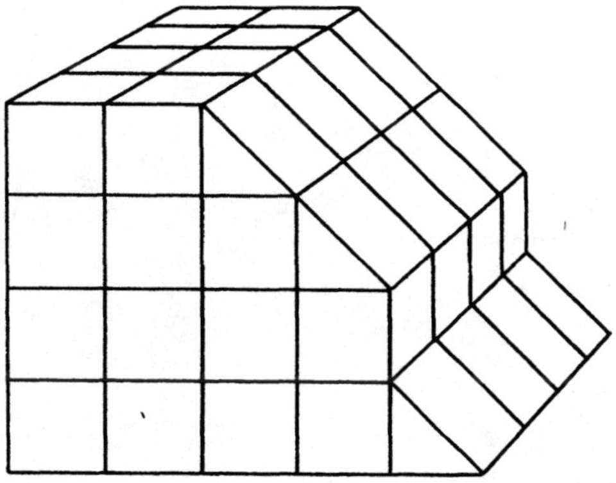

IV

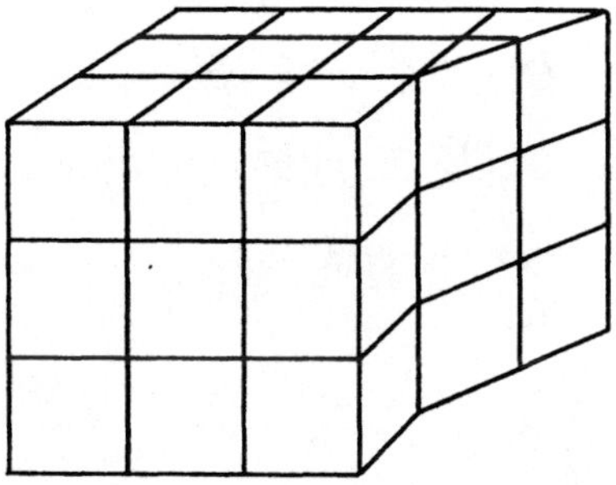

V

CLUE 2: My volume is less than 50 cubic units.

CLUE 3: My volume is greater than 40 cubic units.

Which solid am I? ______

The next three cases involve right triangles, and to be successful solving them, you must be able to apply the Pythagorean theorem. In a right triangle, the **side opposite the right angle** (the longest side) is called the **HYPOTENUSE** and the **other two sides** are called the **LEGS**. The **PYTHAGOREAN THEOREM states that the square of the length of the hypotenuse is equal to the sum of the squares of the lengths of the other two sides.** For instance, in the triangle below, the length of the hypotenuse is c and the length of the legs are a and b, and $c^2 = a^2 + b^2$.

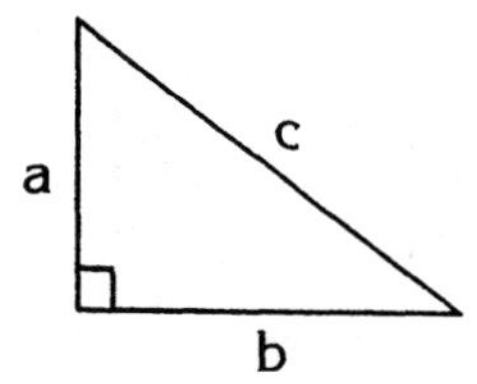

Case G-104

CLUE 1: I am the shortest leg in the right triangle below.

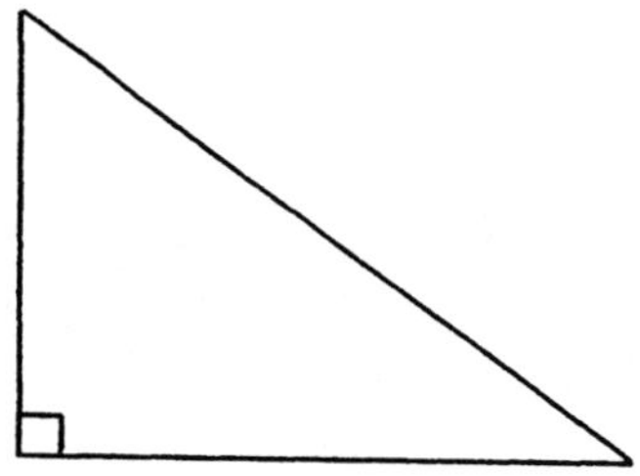

CLUE 2: The longest leg is 4 units long.

CLUE 3: The hypotenuse in this triangle is 5 units long.

How long am I? ______

Case G-105

CLUE 1: I am the hypotenuse in the right triangle below.

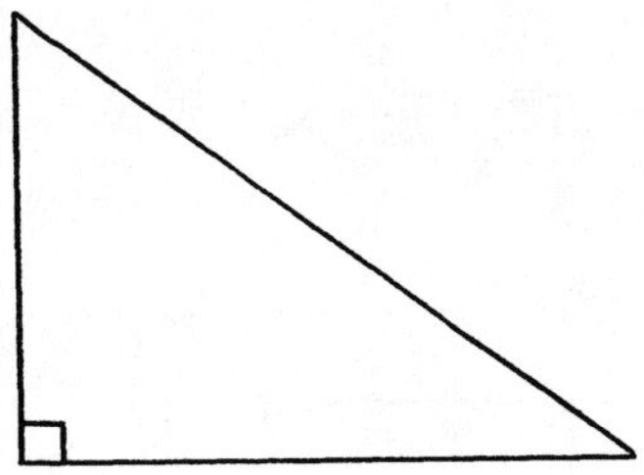

CLUE 2: The shortest leg in this triangle is 6 units long.

CLUE 3: The longest leg in this triangle is 8 units long.

How long am I? ______

Case G-106

CLUE 1: I am the longest leg in the right triangle below.

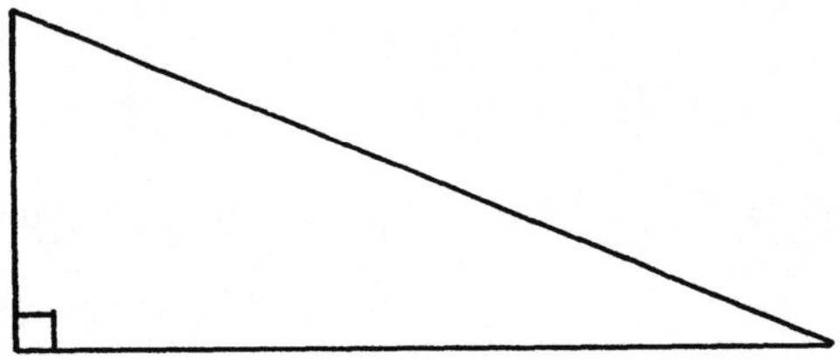

CLUE 2: The shortest leg in this triangle is 5 units long.

CLUE 3: The hypotenuse in this triangle is 13 units long.

How long am I? ______

The last three cases in this chapter concern faces and vertices of solids. A **FACE** is a **flat surface** and a **VERTEX** is a **corner.** You will need to count the faces and vertices of the solids to solve these cases.

Case G-107

CLUE 1: I am one of the figures below: I, II, III, or IV.

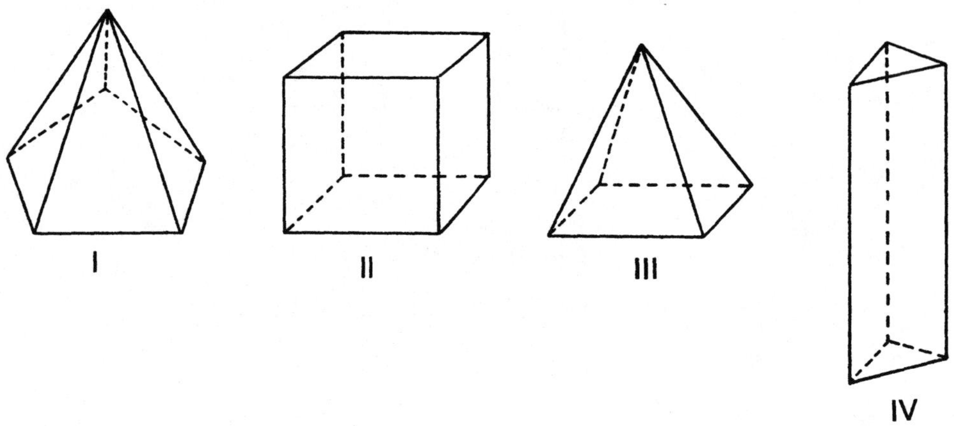

CLUE 2: I have 5 faces.

CLUE 3: I have 6 vertices.

Which figure am I? ______

Case G-108

CLUE 1: I am one of the figures below: I, II, III, or IV.

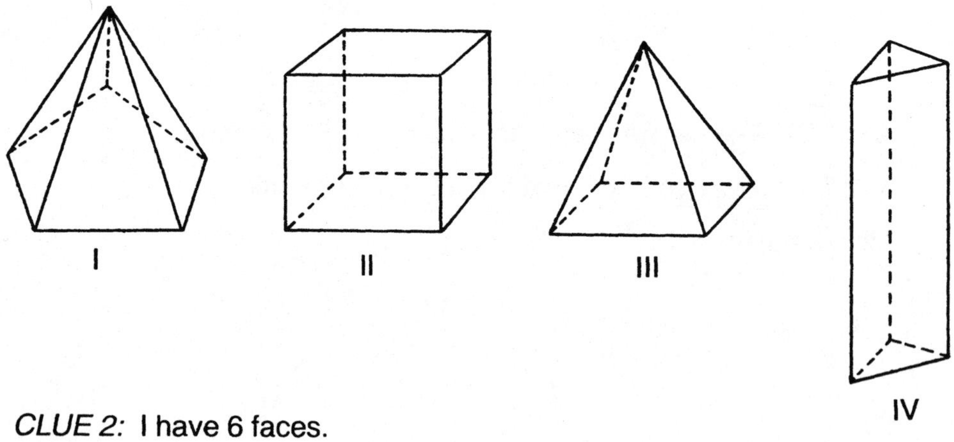

CLUE 2: I have 6 faces.

CLUE 3: I have 6 vertices.

Which figure am I? ______

Case G-109

CLUE 1: I am one of the figures below: I, II, III, or IV.

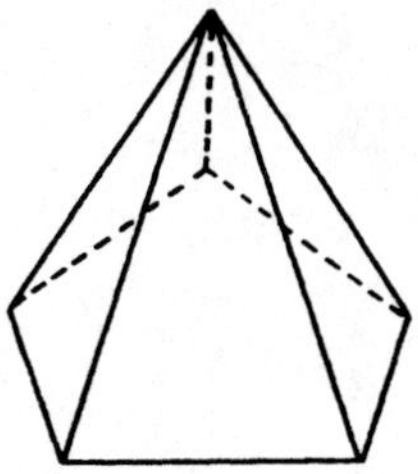
I

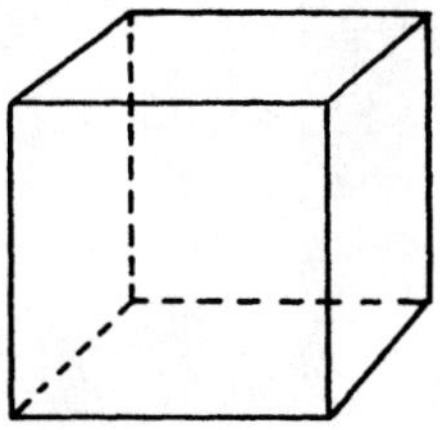
II

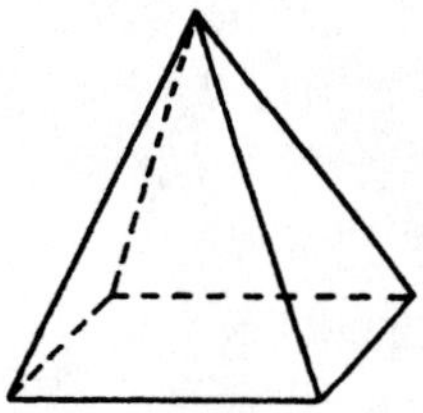
III

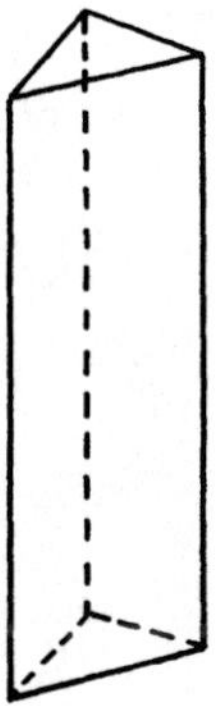
IV

CLUE 2: I have 5 faces.

CLUE 3: I have 5 vertices.

Which figure am I? ______

Case G-110

CLUE 1: I am one of the figures below: I, II, III, or IV.

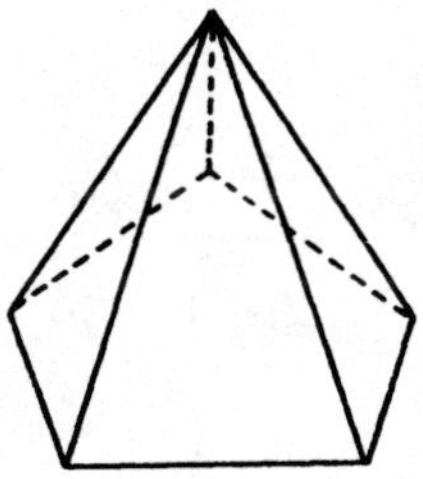
I

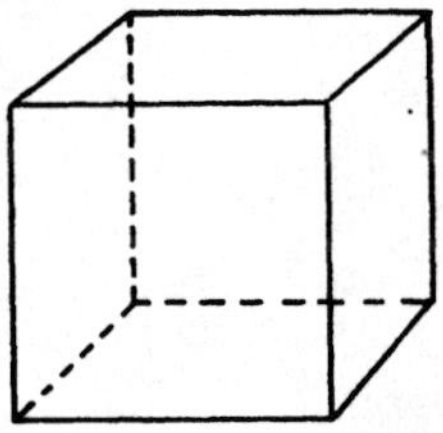
II

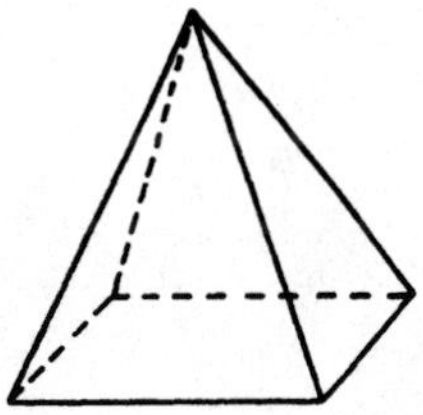
III

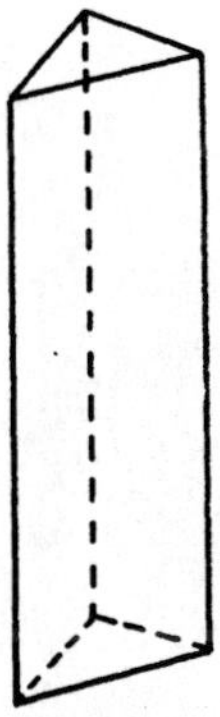
IV

CLUE 2: I have 6 faces.

CLUE 3: I do not have 6 vertices.

Which figure am I? ______

CHAPTER VI

MISCELLANEOUS TOPICS

This chapter is similar to the others in that it is a chapter of detective stories. You are to solve the cases by using clues to eliminate the suspects just as you have before. However, in this chapter the cases are about such things as graphs, calendars, time zones, telephone calls, and money.

The first three cases refer to the **GRAPH** below.

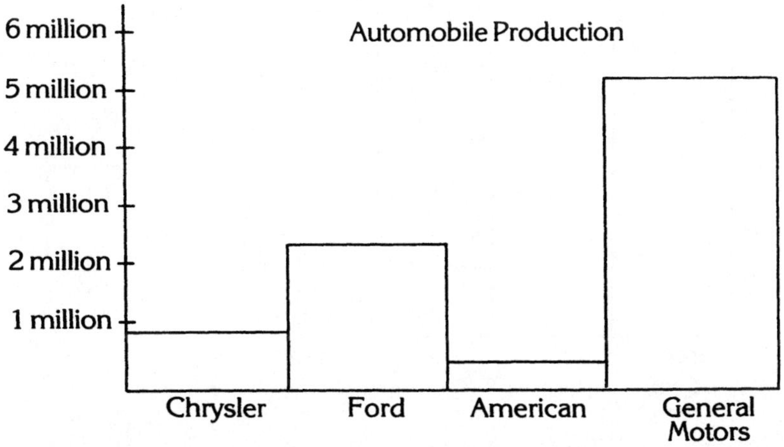

Case M-1

CLUE 1: I am the car company which produced the most cars.

Which car company am I? ______

Case M-2

CLUE 1: I am a car company which produced fewer than 1,000,000 cars.

CLUE 2: I am a car company which produced more than 500,000 cars.

Which car company am I? ______

Case M-3

CLUE 1: I am a car company which produced more than 2,000,000 cars.

CLUE 2: I am a car company which produced fewer than 3,000,000 cars.

Which car company am I? ______

The next three cases refer to the graph below.

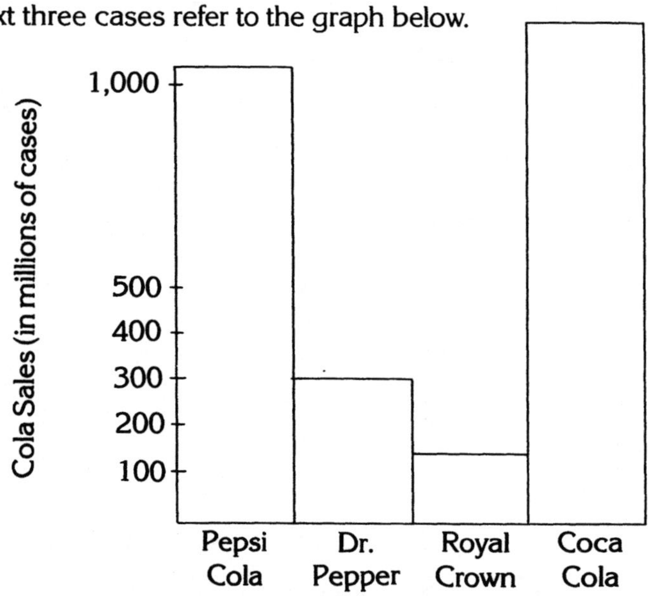

Case M-4

CLUE 1: I am the most popular cola.

Which cola am I? ______

Case M-5

CLUE 1: People bought about 300 million cases of me.

Which cola am I? ______

Case M-6

CLUE 1: People bought more than 1,000,000,000 cases of me.

CLUE 2: People bought less than 1,200,000,000 cases of me.

Which cola am I? ______

In the earlier chapters, you used arrow pictures to find number suspects. Now, in the next four cases, you **IDENTIFY** what the **ARROWS** could be for the given numbers.

Case M-7

CLUE 1: I am one of the following labels for an arrow in an arrow picture.

A	B	C	D	E
3x	I am less than you.	2x	4x	+3

CLUE 2: I could be used in the arrow picture below.

CLUE 3: I could be used in the arrow picture below.

CLUE 4: I could be used in the arrow picture below.

Which label am I? ______

Case M-8

CLUE 1: I am one of the following labels for an arrow in an arrow picture.

A I am greater than you.	B +5	C 2x
D −6	E ÷3	F I am less than you.

CLUE 2: I could be used in the arrow picture below.

CLUE 3: I could be used in the arrow picture below.

CLUE 4: I could not be used in the arrow picture below.

Which label am I? ______

Case M-9

CLUE 1: I am one of the following labels for an arrow in an arrow picture.

A I am less than you.	B +4	C I am greater than you.
D ÷5	E −3	F 2x

CLUE 2: I could not be used in the arrow picture below.

CLUE 3: I could not be used in the arrow picture below.

Which label am I? ______

Case M-10

CLUE 1: I am one of the following labels for an arrow in an arrow picture.

A +6	B −6	C 3x
D ÷2	E I am less than you.	F I am greater than you.

CLUE 2: I could not be used in the arrow picture below.

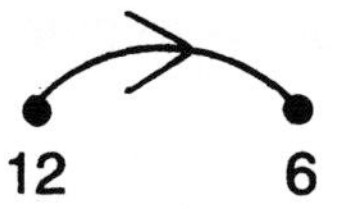

CLUE 3: I could not be used in the arrow picture below.

Which label am I? ______

In the next three cases you are to identify towns on the map below. using clues about time and **TIME ZONES.**

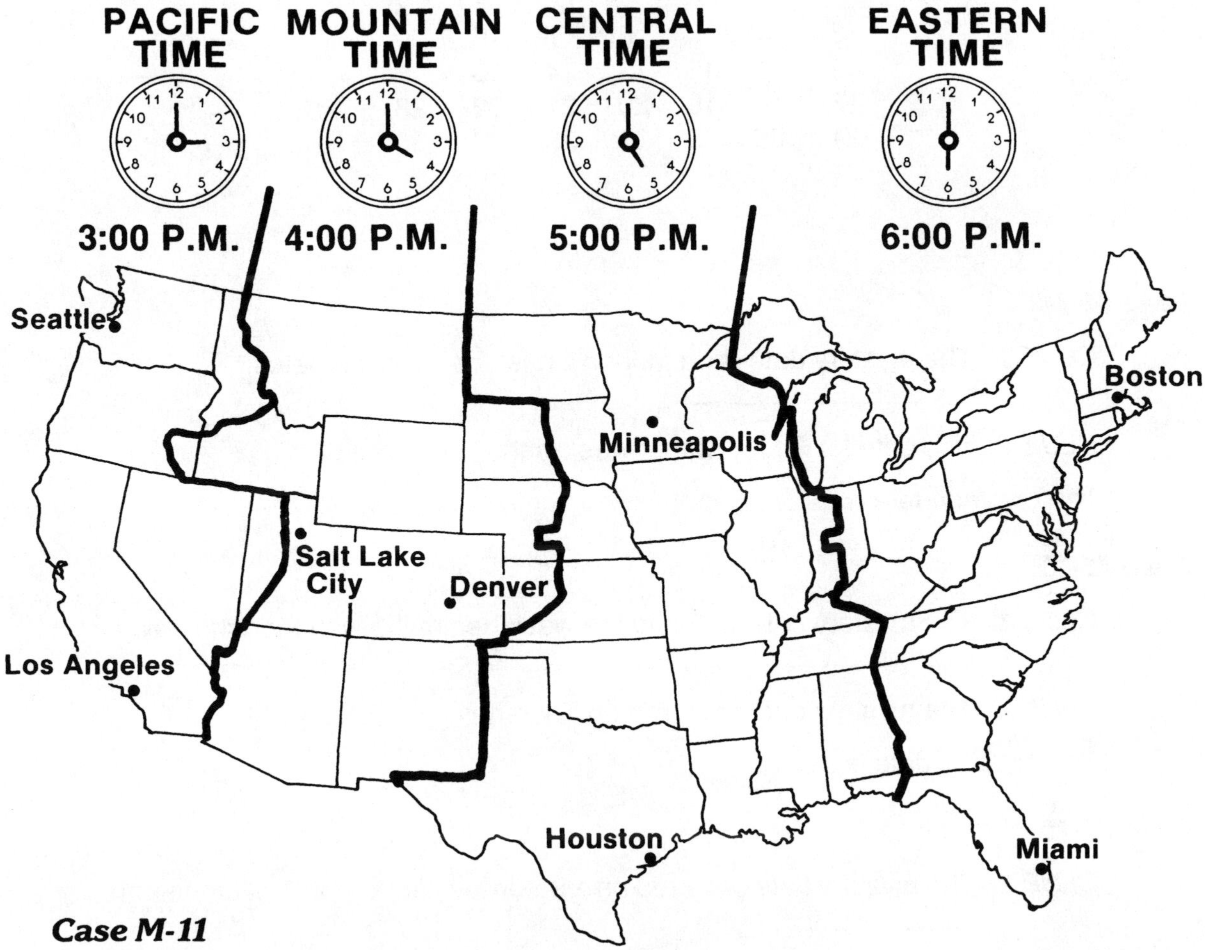

Case M-11

CLUE 1: I am in the Mountain Time zone.

CLUE 2: I am on the western edge of this time zone.

Which town am I? ______

Case M-12

CLUE 1: When it is 2:00 A.M. in Seattle, it is 5:00 A.M. in my time zone.

CLUE 2: I am in the northern part of this time zone.

Which town am I? ______

Case M-13

CLUE 1: When it is 8:00 A.M. in Boston, it is 7:00 A.M. in my time zone.

CLUE 2: I am in the southern part of this time zone.

Which town am I? ______

The following four cases refer to the **CALENDAR** below, and all the mystery dates are in this month.

JANUARY 1982

S	M	Tu	W	Th	F	S
					1	2
3	4	5	6	7	8	9
10	11	12	13	14	15	16
17	18	19	20	21	22	23
24	25	26	27	28	29	30
31						

Case M-14

CLUE 1: The mystery date is on Monday. (List the possible dates.)

____, ____, ____, ____

CLUE 2: The date for Friday of that week is the 15th.

The mystery date is ______.

Case M-15

CLUE 1: The mystery date is during the week beginning with the 24th day.

____, ____, ____, ____, ____, ____, ____

CLUE 2: The mystery date occurred on Thursday.

The mystery date is ______.

Case M-16

CLUE 1: The mystery date occurred on a Saturday after the 15th of the month.

____, ____, ____

CLUE 2: The mystery date did not occur on the last Saturday of the month.

CLUE 3: The mystery date did not occur on the third Saturday of the month.

The mystery date is ______.

Case M-17

CLUE 1: The mystery date occurred on a Tuesday.

____, ____, ____, ____

CLUE 2: The mystery date did not occur on the first Tuesday of the month.

CLUE 3: The mystery date did not occur on the week which began on the 24th.

CLUE 4: The mystery date did not occur in the week which ended on the 16th.

The mystery date is ______.

The following table is a summary of **DIRECT-DIAL RATES** from Clarksville, Tennessee, to various cities throughout the United States.

If, for example, you were to call from Clarksville to Atlanta on a weekday and if the call were for 3 minutes, then the first minute would cost $.48, the next two minutes would cost a total of $.68, so your entire bill for that call would be $1.16.

	Weekday		Evening		Night and Weekend	
	First Minute	Each Additional Minute	First Minute	Each Additional Minute	First Minute	Each Additional Minute
Atlanta, GA	.48	.34	.31	.23	.19	.14
Chicago, IL	.50	.36	.32	.24	.20	.25
Los Angeles, CA	.55	.38	.35	.25	.22	.16
Seattle, WA	.57	.40	.37	.26	.22	.16
Washington, D.C.	.53	.36	.34	.24	.21	.15

In the next six cases you will be given information about a call from Clarksville and you will be required to name the city to which the call was placed. In each case, the suspects are the towns in the table above.

Case M-18

CLUE 1: The call was placed on the weekend.

CLUE 2: The call lasted 2 minutes.

CLUE 3: The cost of the call was $.45.

The call was placed to ________.

Case M-19

CLUE 1: The call was placed during the evening.

CLUE 2: The call lasted 4 minutes.

CLUE 3: The cost of the call was $1.00.

The call was placed to ________.

Case M-20

CLUE 1: The call was placed on a weekday.

CLUE 2: The call lasted 4 minutes.

CLUE 3: The cost of the call was $1.69.

The call was placed to ________.

	Weekday		Evening		Night and Weekend	
	First Minute	Each Additional Minute	First Minute.	Each Additional Minute	First Minute	Each Additional Minute
Atlanta, GA	.48	.34	.31	.23	.19	.14
Chicago, IL	.50	.36	.32	.24	.20	.25
Los Angeles, CA	.55	.38	.35	.25	.22	.16
Seattle, WA	.57	.40	.37	.26	.22	.16
Washington, D.C.	.53	.36	.34	.24	.21	.15

Case M-21

CLUE 1: The call was placed during the evening.

CLUE 2: The call lasted 5 minutes.

CLUE 3: The cost of the call was $1.23.

The call was placed to ________.

Case M-22

CLUE 1: The call was placed at night.

CLUE 2: The call lasted 11 minutes.

CLUE 3: The cost of the call was $1.71.

The call was placed to ________.

Case M-23

CLUE 1: The call was placed on a weekday.

CLUE 2: The call lasted 6 minutes.

CLUE 3: The cost of the call was $2.57.

The call was placed to ________.

The next two cases concern **HORSE RACES.** In the first of these cases, you are to use the clues to find the order of finish of the horses, while in the second case you are to find the first place horse.

Case M-24

CLUE 1: The horses were numbered 3, 4, 6, 7, and 8.

CLUE 2: Horse 8 came in last.

CLUE 3: Horse 7 came in first.

CLUE 4: Horse 6 came in directly behind horse 4.

CLUE 5: Horse 3 came in directly in front of horse 4.

The order of finish is

First	Second	Third	Fourth	Fifth

Case M-25

CLUE 1: The horses were numbered 2, 3, 4, 5, and 6.

CLUE 2: The sum of the numbers of the horses that came in first and second equals the sum of the numbers of the other horses.

CLUE 3: Of the horses that came in first and second, the horse that came in first had the smaller number.

Which horse won the race? ______

The following six detective stories refer to the pages of a book which has exactly 300 pages. In each case you are to find a **PAGE NUMBER** using the clues you are given.

Case M-26

CLUE 1: The sum of me and the page which comes after me is 63.

Which page am I? ______

Case M-27

CLUE 1: The sum of me and the page that comes before me is 375.

Which page am I? ______

Case M-28

CLUE 1: The product of me and the page which comes after me is 20.

Which page am I? ______

Case M-29

CLUE 1: The product of me and the page that comes before me is 930.

Which page am I? ______

Case M-30

CLUE 1: The sum of me and the page that comes 100 pages beyond me is 266.

Which page am I? ______

Case M-31

CLUE 1: The product of me and the page that comes before me is 15,500.

Which page am I? ______

For people who are paid for working by the hour, it is common to receive a fixed hourly wage for the first 8 hours of a day and then to receive "time and a half" for those hours beyond 8 hours on any day. For instance, if a man's regular hourly wage is $5, he will receive $7.50 (1½ × $5) for all hours beyond 8 hours on a given day. If he works 11 hours on a given day, his wages for that day will be

$$(8 \times \$5) + (3 \times \$7.50) = \$62.50.$$

The next five detective stories all involve hourly wage with the "time and a half" option. In the first three of these cases, you are to find the **DAILY WAGE**, while in the last two, you are to find the **HOURLY WAGE.**

Case M-32

CLUE 1: I started work at 8:00 A.M.

CLUE 2: I finished work at 7:00 P.M.

CLUE 3: I had one hour off for lunch and I am not paid for my lunch hour.

CLUE 4: My standard hourly wage is $5.00.

How much did I earn? ______

Case M-33

CLUE 1: I started work at 6:00 A.M.

CLUE 2: I finished work at 6:30 P.M.

CLUE 3: I had one-half hour off for lunch.

CLUE 4: My standard hourly wage is $6.00.

How much did I earn? ______

Case M-34

CLUE 1: I started work at 7:05 A.M.

CLUE 2: I finished work at 7:35 P.M.

CLUE 3: I had one-half hour off for lunch.

CLUE 4: My standard hourly wage is $5.50.

How much did I earn? ______

Case M-35

CLUE 1: I started work at 8:25 A.M.

CLUE 2: I finished work at 7:25 P.M.

CLUE 3: I had one hour off for lunch.

CLUE 4: I earned $66 for that day.

What is my standard hourly wage? ______

Case M-36

CLUE 1: I started work at 8:10 A.M.

CLUE 2: I finished work at 5:40 P.M.

CLUE 3: I had one-half hour off for lunch.

CLUE 4: I earned $95 for that day.

What is my standard hourly wage? ______

The next several detective stories involve money. When **COINS** are mentioned, this will mean fifty-cent pieces, quarters, dimes, nickels and pennies (not silver dollars or ten-dollar gold pieces).

Case M-37

CLUE 1: I have two coins, neither of which is a fifty-cent piece. (Blanks are left for possible amounts of money.)

______, ______, ______, ______, ______, ______, ______, ______, ______, ______

CLUE 2: This amount of money could not be made with dimes only. (For example, this clue would eliminate 30¢ because 30¢ can be made with 3 dimes. It also would eliminate 10¢, since 10¢ can be made with 1 dime.)

CLUE 3: The value of the coins is greater than 25¢.

CLUE 4: Neither of the coins is a dime.

What are the coins? ______

Case M-38

CLUE 1: I have two coins, neither of which is a penny.

______, ______, ______, ______, ______, ______, ______, ______, ______, ______

CLUE 2: This amount of money could not be made with quarters only.

CLUE 3: This amount of money could be made with dimes only.

CLUE 4: The value of the coins is greater than 40¢.

What are the coins?______

Case M-39

CLUE 1: I have 3 coins where the possible coins are pennies, dimes, and nickels. (Complete the table below.)

Dimes	3	2								
Nickels		1								
Pennies										
Value										

CLUE 2: This amount of money could not be made with nickels only.

CLUE 3: I have fewer than 2 pennies.

CLUE 4: I have less than 15¢.

What are the coins? ______

Case M-40

CLUE 1: I have 6 coins. Some of the coins are dimes and the rest are nickels.

Nickels	5				
Dimes	1				
Value	35¢				

CLUE 2: The total value of the coins is 50¢.

How many nickels do I have? ______ How many dimes do I have? ______

Case M-41

CLUE 1: I have 7 coins. They are quarters and nickels (at least one of each).

Nickels						
Quarters						
Value						

CLUE 2: The total value of the coins is 95¢.

How many nickels do I have? ______ How many quarters do I have? ______

Case M-42

CLUE 1: I have 6 coins. They are quarters and dimes (at least one of each).

Quarters					
Dimes					
Value					

CLUE 2: The total value of the coins is 75¢.

How many quarters do I have? ______ How many dimes do I have? ______

Case M-43

CLUE 1: I have several coins. All these coins are dimes and nickels (at least one of each).

CLUE 2: The total value of the coins is 45¢.

Nickels				
Dimes				
Value	45¢	45¢	45¢	45¢

CLUE 3: I have more dimes than nickels.

How many nickels do I have? ______ How many dimes do I have? ______

The following three cases involve **PAPER MONEY** where two-dollar bills are not allowed.

Case M-44

CLUE 1: I have two bills where the possible individual bills have value less than $50. (List possible amounts.)

_____, _____, _____, _____, _____, _____, _____, _____, _____, _____

CLUE 2: This amount of money could not be made with only five-dollar bills.

CLUE 3: The value of the bills is greater than $20.

Which bills do I have? ______

Case M-45

CLUE 1: I have several bills. All the bills are ten-dollar bills and twenty-dollar bills (at least one of each).

CLUE 2: The total value of the bills is $90.

Tens				
Twenties				
Value	$90	$90	$90	$90

CLUE 3: I have more ten-dollar bills than twenty-dollar bills.

CLUE 4: I have more than one twenty-dollar bill.

How many ten-dollar bills do I have? ______

How many twenty-dollar bills do I have? ______

The next five cases involve **SALES TAX.** A portion of a sales-tax table for the State of Tennessee is given. To solve these cases you will need to use the table. Notice, for instance, that if the amount of the sale is $19.36, then the sales tax is $1.31. On the other hand, if the sales tax is $1.31, then the amount of the sale is in the range of $19.34 to $19.48. It is quite easy to find the tax, given the amount of sale, but if you are given only the sales tax you will not know exactly what the amount of the sale is. In these cases you are to find the amount of the sale from the clues concerning the sales tax.

Amount of Sale			Tax	Amount of Sale			Tax
18.60	through	18.74	1.26	19.93	through	20.07	1.35
18.75	through	18.88	1.27	20.08	through	20.22	1.36
18.89	through	19.03	1.28	20.23	through	20.37	1.37
19.04	through	19.18	1.29	20.38	through	20.51	1.38
19.19	through	19.33	1.30	20.52	through	20.66	1.39
19.34	through	19.48	1.31	20.67	through	20.81	1.40
19.49	through	19.62	1.32	20.82	through	20.96	1.41
19.63	through	19.77	1.33	20.97	through	21.11	1.42
19.78	through	19.92	1.34	21.12	through	21.25	1.43

Case M-46

CLUE 1: The sales tax is $1.36. (List the possible amounts of the sale.)

______, ______, ______, ______, ______, ______, ______, ______, ______, ______, ______,

______, ______, ______, ______

CLUE 2: If the amount of the sale were 3¢ less, the tax would be $1.35.

CLUE 3: If the amount of the sale were 13¢ more, the tax would be $1.37.

What is the amount of the sale? ______

Amount of Sale			Tax	Amount of Sale			Tax
18.60	through	18.74	1.26	19.93	through	20.07	1.35
18.75	through	18.88	1.27	20.08	through	20.22	1.36
18.89	through	19.03	1.28	20.23	through	20.37	1.37
19.04	through	19.18	1.29	20.38	through	20.51	1.38
19.19	through	19.33	1.30	20.52	through	20.66	1.39
19.34	through	19.48	1.31	20.67	through	20.81	1.40
19.49	through	19.62	1.32	20.82	through	20.96	1.41
19.63	through	19.77	1.33	20.97	through	21.11	1.42
19.78	through	19.92	1.34	21.12	through	21.25	1.43

Case M-47

CLUE 1: The sales tax is $1.38.

____, ____, ____, ____, ____, ____, ____, ____, ____, ____, ____,
____, ____, ____, ____

CLUE 2: If the amount of the sale were 7¢ less, the tax would still be $1.38.

CLUE 3: If the amount of the sale were 6¢ more, the tax would still be $1.38.

What is the amount of the sale? ______

Case M-48

CLUE 1: The sales tax is $1.41.

____, ____, ____, ____, ____, ____, ____, ____, ____, ____, ____,
____, ____, ____, ____

CLUE 2: If the amount of the sale were 12¢ more, the tax would be $1.42.

CLUE 3: If the amount of the sale were 4¢ less, the tax would be $1.40.

What is the amount of the sale? ______

Case M-49

CLUE 1: The sales tax is $1.30.

____, ____, ____, ____, ____, ____, ____, ____, ____, ____, ____,
____, ____, ____, ____

CLUE 2: If the amount of the sale were 10¢ less, the tax would be $1.29.

CLUE 3: If the amount of the sale were 6¢ more, the tax would be $1.31.

What is the amount of the sale? ______

Case M-50

CLUE 1: The sales tax is $1.35.

____, ____, ____, ____, ____, ____, ____, ____, ____, ____, ____,
____, ____, ____, ____

CLUE 2: If the amount of the sale were 7¢ more, the tax would still be $1.35.

CLUE 3: If the amount of the sale were 7¢ less, the tax would still be $1.35.

What is the amount of the sale? ______

The next five detective stories all involve a game called **NICK, NACK, NO**. One player selects a secret two-digit number and the second player tries to guess it. When the second player guesses, the first player must respond Nick, Nack, or No, where

Nick means **at least one** digit is **correct** but in the **wrong place,**

Nack means **exactly one** digit is **correct** and is in the **correct place,** and

No means that **both** digits are **incorrect.**

The idea of the game is for the second person to correctly select the secret number with as few guesses as possible. For example, here are some responses to guesses when the secret number is 34.

Guess	Response
57	No
42	Nick
24	Nack

The following cases involve some games that have been played. You are to use these clues to enable you to find the secret number.

Case M-51

CLUE 1: 72 No

CLUE 2: 84 Nack

CLUE 3: 21 Nick

What is the secret number? __________

Case M-52

CLUE 1: 37 No

CLUE 2: 45 Nack

CLUE 3: 32 No

CLUE 4: 68 Nick

CLUE 5: 96 Nack

What is the secret number? __________

Case M-53

CLUE 1: 80 No

CLUE 2: 21 No

CLUE 3: 43 Nick

CLUE 4: 67 Nick

CLUE 5: 34 Nack

CLUE 6: 96 No

What is the secret number? ________

Case M-54

CLUE 1: 43 No

CLUE 2: 72 No

CLUE 3: 25 Nick

CLUE 4: 51 Nack

CLUE 5: 80 Nack

What is the secret number? ________

Case M-55

CLUE 1: 72 No

CLUE 2: 54 No

CLUE 3: 83 Nick

CLUE 4: 37 No

CLUE 5: 10 No

CLUE 6: 96 Nack

What is the secret number? ________

The next three cases are about the **FACES** of a **CUBE.** The following are three pictures of the **same** cube.

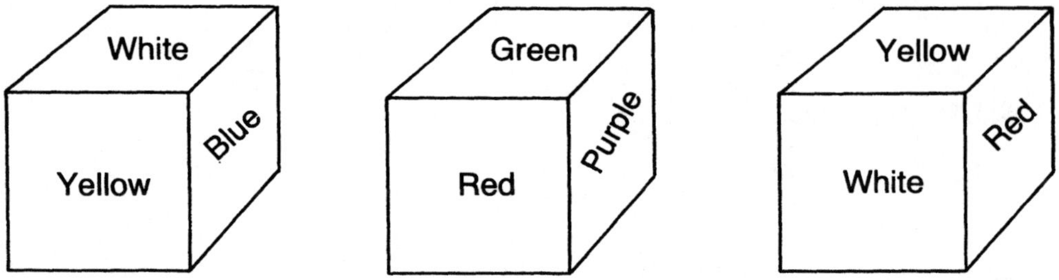

Case M-56

CLUE 1: I am the face opposite the red face.

Which face am I (color)? __________

Case M-57

CLUE 1: I am the face opposite the yellow face.

Which face am I? __________

Case M-58

CLUE 1: I am the face opposite the green face.

Which face am I? __________

Case M-59

CLUE 1: Harry never tells the truth.

CLUE 2: Tom always tells the truth.

CLUE 3: Dick sometimes tells the truth.

Who is the guy in the middle? __________

Mathematicians sometimes use a **DIAGRAM** to illustrate **SETS.** They also have a way of indicating the **number of elements** in a set. For example, in the illustration which follows, the rectangle represents the set of girls in the ninth grade in a particular school, the circle on the left represents the set of all girls who play basketball, and the circle on the right represents the set of all girls who play softball.

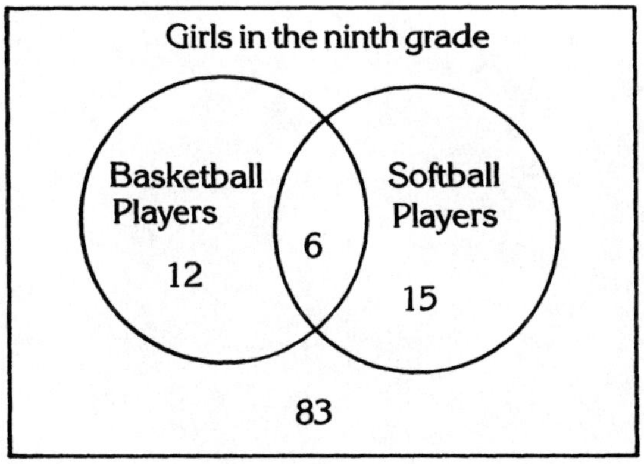

The "6" written in the region that is common to both circles means that there are 6 girls who play **both** sports, the "12" means that there are 12 girls who play basketball but **not** softball, the "15" means that there are 15 girls who play softball but **not** basketball, while the "83" means that there are 83 girls who don't play either sport. Note that there are exactly 18 basketball players (12 + 6), exactly 21 softball players (6 + 15), and exactly 116 girls all together in the class (12 + 6 + 15 + 83).

In the detective stories that follow, you are to write numbers in the appropriate regions as a result of the clues. Then you should be able to solve the cases from the illustration.

Case M-60

CLUE 1: In the eighth grade in a particular school, there are 7 boys who play both football and basketball.

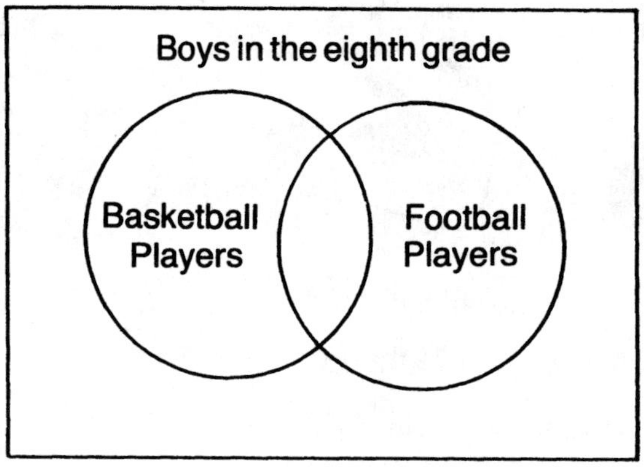

CLUE 2: There are 8 boys who play basketball but not football.

CLUE 3: There are 26 boys who play football but not basketball.

CLUE 4: There are 56 boys who don't play either sport.

How many boys are there all together in the class? __________

Case M-61

CLUE 1: In a survey conducted recently, 6 people said they used both Super Sudsy Soap (SSS) and Big Blue Bleach (BBB).

CLUE 2: Of the people interviewed, 21 said they used Super Sudsy Soap.*

CLUE 3: Of those interviewed, 15 said they used Big Blue Bleach.

CLUE 4: There were 143 people interviewed.

How many people who were interviewed didn't use either Super Sudsy Soap or Big Blue Bleach? ________

*This total includes those who used both products and also those who used only Super Sudsy Soap.

Case M-62

CLUE 1: Of the 275 students in the seventh grade in McGillicutty's Middle School, 55 are in the band.

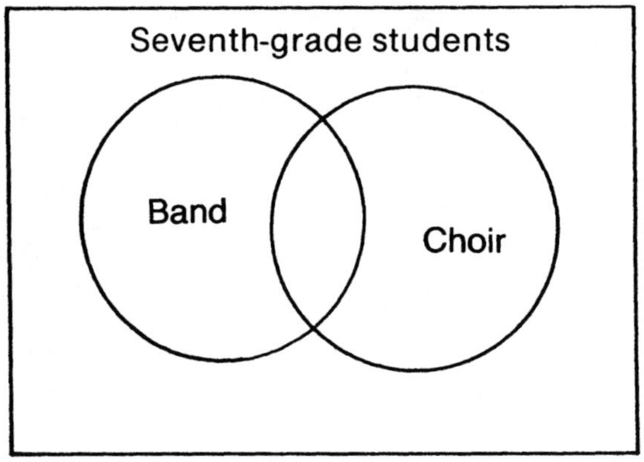

CLUE 2: There are 125 students in the choir.

CLUE 3: There are 125 students who aren't in either the band or the choir.

How many students are in both the band and the choir? __________

The next six cases involve sets and set language.The symbol "$\subset$" is used to mean "**is a subset of.**" If A and B are sets **A$\subset$ B** means **every element of A is an element of B.** For instance,

$$\{a, b, c\} \subset \{a, b, c, d\}$$

is a true sentence. Also **A $\cup$ B** is read **"the union of A and B"** and means the set of all elements that are **in at least one** of the two sets, while **"A $\cap$ B"** is read **"the INTERSECTION of A and B"** and means the set of all elements which are **in both** sets. The following two sentences are both true.

$$\{a, b, c\} \cup \{c, d, e\} = \{a, b, c, d, e\}$$
$$\{a, b, c\} \cap \{c, d, e\} = \{c\}$$

A set that contains no elements is called the empty set and is written: Ø. The following three statements are all true.

$$\varnothing \subset \text{all sets}$$
$$\varnothing \cup \{a, b, c\} = \{a, b, c\}$$
$$\varnothing \cap \{a, b, c\} = \phi$$

The empty set is a subset of every set.

In the cases that follow you are to identify the set described by the clues.

Case M-63

CLUE 1: I am a subset of $\{a, b, c, d, e\}$.

CLUE 2: $\{a, b, c\} \subset$ me.

CLUE 3: I have 4 elements.

CLUE 4: e is not an element of me.

What set am I? __________

Case M-64

CLUE 1: I am a subset of $\{a, b, c, d, e\}$.

CLUE 2: I am a subset of $\{x, y, z\}$.

What set am I? __________

Case M-65

CLUE 1: I am a subset of $\{a, b, c, d, e\}$.

CLUE 2: $\{a, b, c\} \cap \text{Me} = \{b\}$

CLUE 3: $\{d, e\} \cap \text{Me} = \{d\}$

What set am I? __________

Case M-66

CLUE 1: I am a subset of $\{1, 2, 3, 4\}$.

CLUE 2: I have two elements.

CLUE 3: $\{2, 3, 4\} \cap \text{Me} = \{3\}$

What set am I? __________

Case M-67

CLUE 1: $\text{Me} \cup \{2, 3, 4\} = \{1, 2, 3, 4, 6\}$

CLUE 2: $\text{Me} \cap \{2, 3, 4\} = \{3\}$

What set am I? __________

Case M-68

CLUE 1: I have 3 elements.

CLUE 2: $\{3, 4, 5\} \cap \text{Me} = \{4, 5\}$

CLUE 3: $\{1, 2, 3\} \cap \text{Me} = \{1\}$

What set am I? __________

The last three detective stories all involve **PROBABILITY.** You must be able to determine the probabilities of various sums when a pair of dice is thrown.

Case M-69

CLUE 1: I am one of the possible outcomes (sum) from tossing a pair of dice.

____, ____, ____, ____, ____, ____, ____, ____, ____, ____, ____

CLUE 2: I am between 2 and 7.

CLUE 3: The probability that I will occur is $1/18$.

Which outcome am I? ______

Case M-70

CLUE 1: I am one of the possible outcomes from tossing a pair of dice.

____, ____, ____, ____, ____, ____, ____, ____, ____, ____, ____

CLUE 2: The probability that I will occur is $5/36$.

CLUE 3: I am less than 7.

Which outcome am I? __________

Case M-71

CLUE 1: I am one of the possible outcomes from tossing a pair of dice.

____, ____, ____, ____, ____, ____, ____, ____, ____, ____, ____

CLUE 2: The probability that I will occur is $1/12$.

CLUE 3: If a 6 comes up on one die, I cannot be made.

Which outcome am I? __________

A Glossary of Mathematical Terms

ACUTE ANGLE	an angle that is smaller than a right angle.
ACUTE TRIANGLE	a triangle that contains three acute angles.
ADDITIVE INVERSE	the opposite of a number. **Example:** the additive inverse of -3 is +3.
AREA	the number of square units it takes to "cover" a surface.
BISECTED	separated into two parts that are the same size.
CHORD	a segment that has its endpoints on a circle.
CIRCUMFERENCE	the distance around a circle. The formula is $C = 2\pi r$.
CLOSED CURVES	curves that can be traced **starting and ending at the same point** without lifting the pencil or retracing a path.
CONGRUENT	1. angles that have the same degree measure; 2. figures that are the same size and shape; 3. segments that are the same length.
CURVE	a figure that can be traced without lifting the pencil from the paper or retracing a path.
DENOMINATOR	the term below the line in a fraction. **Example:** in the fraction $3/4$ the denominator is 4.
DIAGONAL	a line segment which joins any two nonadjacent corners.
DIAMETER	a chord that passes through the center of the circle.
DIVISORS	the numbers that **evenly** divide a given number. To divide a number evenly means to divide it without any remainders left over. **Example:** the divisors of 6 are 1, 2, 3, and 6. **Important reminder:** the **divisors** and the **factors** of counting numbers are the same.
EQUILATERAL TRIANGLE	a triangle in which all three sides are equal.
EVEN NUMBERS	numbers that have no remainder when divided by 2.

EXTERIOR	outside a geometric shape.
FACE	a flat surface of a solid shape.
FACTORS	any of the numbers that form a given product when they are multiplied together. **Example:** the number 6 has two pairs of factors, (1 and 6) and (2 and 3). **Important reminder:** the **factors** and **divisors** of counting numbers are the **same.**
GREATEST COMMON DIVISOR	the largest number which is a common divisor of two or more other numbers. **Example:** the greatest common divisor of 30 and 42 is 6.
HEXAGON	a six-sided shape.
HUNDRED'S DIGIT	**Example:** 4 is the hundred's digit in the number 427.
HYPOTENUSE	in a right triangle, the side opposite the right angle (the longest side).
IDENTITY NUMBER	1. the identity number for addition is 0. 2. the identity number for multiplication is 1.
INFINITE NUMBER	when referring to number suspects, it indicates an endless number of possible suspects. Expressed in a problem by a number of blanks followed by three dots. **Important reminder:** you must eventually eliminate numbers which come after the last number in the blanks.
INTERIOR	inside a geometric shape.
INTERSECTION	the set of all elements which are in both sets. Indicated by the symbol: $\cap$.
ISOSCELES TRIANGLE	a triangle in which two sides are equal.
LEAST COMMON MULTIPLE	the smallest number which is a common multiple of two or more other numbers. Can also be thought of as the smallest number that is exactly divisible by each of the given numbers. **Example:** the least common multiple of 2, 3, 4, and 6 is 12.
LEGS	in a right triangle, either one of the sides next to the right angle.
MIDPOINT	the point that divides a line segment into two equal parts.
MULTIPLE(S)	a number that is the product of some specified number and another number. **Examples:** 12 is a multiple of 3; the multiples of 5 are 5, 10, 15, 20, ...
NONTERMINATING	in decimals, having an endless number of digits following the decimal point. **Example:** .3333 . . . is nonterminating.
NUMERATOR	the term above the line in a fraction. **Example:** in the fraction $\frac{3}{4}$ the numerator is 3.
OBTUSE ANGLE	an angle that is larger than a right angle.
OBTUSE TRIANGLE	a triangle that contains one obtuse angle.

ODD NUMBERS numbers that have a remainder when divided by 2.

PARALLEL LINES lines that are on the same surface and that do not intersect (meet).

PARALLELOGRAM a quadrilateral with two pairs of parallel sides.

PENTAGON a five-sided shape.

PERFECT SQUARE(S) in arithmetic, the product you get when you multiply a number by itself. **Example:** 4 is a perfect square since $4 = 2 \times 2$.

PERIMETER the total distance around a figure.

PERPENDICULAR LINES lines that intersect (meet) to form square corners.

PRIME NUMBER a number greater than 1, with exactly two divisors, itself and 1. **Example:** 13 is prime since its only divisors are 1 and 13. 17 is prime since its only divisors are 1 and 17. Note that 10 is not prime because it has 4 divisors (1, 2, 5, and 10). **Important reminder:** 1 is not prime.

PYTHAGOREAN THEOREM states that the square of the length of the hypotenuse is equal to the sum of the squares of the other two sides. **Formula:** $a^2 + b^2 = c^2$.

QUADRILATERAL a four-sided figure.

RADIUS a segment with one endpoint at the center of a circle and the other endpoint on the circle.

RECIPROCAL 1. of a fraction: the fraction formed by interchanging the numerator and the denominator in a given fraction. **Example:** the reciprocal of $\frac{3}{7}$ is $\frac{7}{3}$.
2. of a whole number: the fraction formed by putting 1 over the number. **Example:** $\frac{1}{2}$ is the reciprocal of 2.

REPEATING BLOCK the part of a decimal in which all the digits (after a certain one) consist of a set of one or more digits repeated indefinitely. **Example:** the nonterminating decimal .858585 . . . has **two** digits in the repeating block since 85 is repeated over and over again, while .777 . . . has **one** digit in the repeating block.

RIGHT ANGLE the angle formed by a square corner.

RIGHT TRIANGLE a triangle that contains one right angle.

SCALENE TRIANGLE a triangle in which all sides are different lengths.

SEGMENT the shortest possible path connecting two points.

SIMILAR two or more figures that have the same shape. **Important reminder:** similar figures do not have to have the same size.

SIMPLE CURVES curves that do not intersect themselves.

SIMPLEST FORM — a fraction in which the only common divisor that its numerator and denominator have is 1. **Example:** 9/12 is not in simplest form since 3 is a divisor of both 9 and 12. However, 9/12 = 3/4 and 3/4 **is** in simplest form.

SQUARE — in arithmetic, to square a number you multiply that number by itself. **Example:** the square of 5 is 25 because $5 \times 5 = 25$.

SUBSET — If A and B are sets, A is a subset of B if every element of A is also an element of B. **Example:** (a, b, c) is a subset of (a, b, c, d). The symbol for subset is $\subset$.

SYMBOLS

1. $\subset$ means subset;
2. $\cup$ means union;
3. $\cap$ means intersection;
4. $\neq$ means not equal to;
5. m∠a means the measure of angle A in degrees.
6. . . . means continued on endlessly;
7. $\emptyset$ means the empty set;
8. 10^{-1} means 1/10;
9. 10^0 is defined as being equal to 1.

TEN'S DIGIT — **Example:** 2 is the ten's digit in the number 427.

TERMINATES — ends. (See **nonterminating.**) **Example:** .25 is a terminating decimal.

TRAPEZOID — a quadrilateral with exactly one pair of parallel sides.

UNION — the set of all elements that are in at least one of the two sets. Indicated by the symbol $\cup$.

UNIT'S DIGIT — **Example:** 7 is the unit's digit in the number 427.

VERTEX — 1. the corner point of an angle; 2. one of the corner points of a solid shape.

VOLUME — the amount of space occupied by a solid. Measured by the number of unit cubes it contains.